A Genealogical Analysis of Nietzschean Drive Theory

Brian Lightbody

A Genealogical Analysis of Nietzschean Drive Theory

palgrave
macmillan

Brian Lightbody
Department of Philosophy
Brock University
St. Catharines, ON, Canada

ISBN 978-3-031-27147-2   ISBN 978-3-031-27148-9 (eBook)
https://doi.org/10.1007/978-3-031-27148-9

This Palgrave Macmillan imprint is published by the registered company Springer Nature Switzerland AG.
The registered company address is: Gewerbestrasse 11, 6330 Cham, Switzerland

Portions of this work have been presented at conferences and to dozens of undergraduate and graduate students at Brock University over several years. In particular, I would like to thank the students in my most recent fourth-year course on Nietzsche (4V24 Philosophical Methodologies), for their engagement with the material and their overall philosophical acumen.

Most importantly, I would like to thank my wife, Kelly, and my four amazing children: Sadie, Bram, Jackson, and Ruby, for putting up with me during the final preparatory stages of writing this work.
Sine caritate, nihil sum.

Contents

List of Abbreviations

Primary Sources (Nietzsche)

(KGW) Nietzsche, Friedrich. *Werke: Kritische Gesamtausgabe*. 22 vols. ed(s)., Giorgio Colli and Mazzino Montinari. Berlin: Walter de Gruyter, 1967–84.

(KSW) Nietzsche, Friedrich. *Kritische Studienausgabe*. ed(s)., Giorgio Colli and Mazzino Montinari. Berlin: Walter de Gruyter, 1967–88.

(NF) *Nachgelassene Fragmente*. In eKGWB

Translations of Nietzsche's Published Works

(BGE) *Beyond Good and Evil in Basic Writings of Nietzsche*. Trans. Walter Kaufmann. Intro. Peter Gay. New York: Random House, 2000.

(D) *Daybreak*, trans. R.J. Hollingdale. Cambridge University Press, 1982

(EH) *Ecce Homo*, Trans. Walter Kaufmann Basic Writings of Nietzsche, 2000.

(GM) *On the Genealogy of Morals: A Polemic*. Trans. Walter Kaufmann and R.J. Hollingdale. New York: Vintage Books, 1989.
On the Genealogy of Morals in Basic Writings of Nietzsche. Trans. Walter Kaufmann. Intro Peter Gay New York: Random House, 2000

(GM1) *On The Genealogy of Morals: A Polemic*. Trans. Maudemarie Clark and Alan Swensen. Intro. Maudemarie Clark. Indianapolis, IN: Hackett Publishing, 1998.

(GS) *The Gay Science*. Trans. Walter Kaufmann. New York: Vintage Books, 1974.

(HH) *Human all too Human*. Trans. R.J. Hollingdale. Intro. Richard Schact. Cambridge University Press: 1996.

(NR) *A Nietzsche Reader*, selected and translated with an introduction by R.J. Hollingdale, London: Penguin Books 1977.

(TI), (A) *Twilight of the Idols*/The Anti-Christ. Trans. R.J. Hollingdale. Harmondsworth, Middlesex: Penguin, 1972.

(WTP) "The Will to Power." In *The Will to Power*, trans. Walter Kaufmann and R. J. Hollingdale, with an introduction by Walter Kaufmann. New York: Vintage, 1968.

(Z) *Thus Spoke Zarathustra*. Trans. by R.J. Hollingdale. Harmondsworth, Middlesex: Penguin, 1975.

1

Introduction

Nietzsche's "drive theory," as it is referred to in the secondary literature, is a rich, unique, and fascinating articulation of the human condition. According to the standard reading in the scholarship, Nietzsche contends that all human psychology is either directly reducible to primal, animal drives (e.g. sex, aggression) or indirectly explicable to the historical transformations thereof (e.g. *ressentiment*).

Moreover, drive theory, as expressed in many of Nietzsche's works (See *Human and all Too Human*, I. 32, *Daybreak* 119, GM III: 24) is well-complemented with a rich, mature, and profound articulation of the theory in the secondary literature. While it would be beyond the scope of this book to define all of the positions on Nietzsche's view of drives in the scholarship, still one can say, minimally, that drives motivate behaviors and thus are the bedrock for Nietzsche's system of values and psychology.[1] Nietzsche intends his drive theory not only to explain our initial evaluations as to why some objects should be pursued or avoided but

[1] I write "minimally" because there are more controversial, robust views of drives in the literature. One such view is the "homunculi" drive position which stipulates that drives are like proto-agents. See Maudemarie Clark and David Dudrick's *The Soul of Nietzsche's Beyond Good and Evil*, (Cambridge, Cambridge University Press), 2012.

B. Lightbody, *A Genealogical Analysis of Nietzschean Drive Theory*,
https://doi.org/10.1007/978-3-031-27148-9_1

indeed to explain the reflective value judgments we come to have on said evaluations.[2] As Paul Katsafanas summarizes its role, the drive is, "Nietzsche's principle explanatory token within psychology."[3] The statement accurately describes the role drives play in the secondary literature.

Yet, there remains a glaring lacuna for all the discussion of drive theory in the scholarship. The secondary literature fails to justify how these drives became digested within their present container, namely the psyche.[4] As I demonstrate, there is a gap in the research surrounding the formulation and genesis of what, on the surface, seems to be an encapsulation or psychical digestion of animal drives. The account provided by Nietzsche to explain how these drives became inhibited from their natural expression is referred to as the Internalization Hypothesis (I.H.) and is advanced in Nietzsche's celebrated work, *On The Genealogy of Morals*.

In GM II 16, Nietzsche argues that violent and aggressive drives that do not find outward expression turn inward, creating new targets for the drives' successful manifestations. The primal drives to which Nietzsche is referring are the animal-like instincts of pre-humans, or so it would appear. The standard reading of this passage in the scholarship suggests that when proto-humans were prevented from acting on these natural predispositions, it caused the origin of the "entire inner world," the birth of subjectivity. As Nietzsche explains, the 'self' "expanded and extended itself, acquired depth, breadth and height in the same measure outward discharge was inhibited." (GM II 16). The blockage of primal instincts transformed our ancestors from what Nietzsche calls "semi-animals" to the rational agents we (erroneously) believe ourselves to be today. (GM II 16). The expression of these drives carves out our character, indeed, our very identity and, as such, may lead to life denying and self-lacerating feelings like ressentiment—along with its corresponding ethics, the

[2] Paul Katsafanas, *The Nietzschean Self: Moral Psychology, Agency and the Unconscious*, (New York: Oxford University Press, 2016), 11.

[3] Paul Katsafanas, *The Nietzschean Self: Moral Psychology, Agency and the Unconscious*, 74.

[4] The description of the psyche as an encapsulation of drives may seem peculiar but here, I am simply providing a literal reading of Nietzsche's Internalization Hypothesis where Nietzsche posits that subjectivity is simply the container for competing drives and where these drives have an animal base.

ascetic ideal–or, if harnessed correctly, could "become the womb of all ideal and imaginative phenomena." (GM II 18).

The Internalization Hypothesis is a crucial component in explaining drive theory. Yet, given the apparent importance of drives to Nietzsche's ethics and psychology, it is perplexing to note that scholars have not focused on challenging the very historical foundation for the idea itself, which is, of course, I.H as articulated in GM II 16. In order to fully capture Nietzsche's theory of drives, it is critical to examine the role I.H. plays within the confines of *The Genealogy*, as a whole, in this regard.

Minimally the I.H. performs two functions in Nietzsche's theory of mind. First, it explains how human beings acquired a bad conscience and later a more fully developed sense of agency and moral being. The explanation for the creation of self was an enfolding, as it were, of instinctual, animal drives. The I.H., therefore, plays a grounding role in terms of naturalizing the process of transformation from that of our animal ancestors to the contemporary, rational, and free agents we assume ourselves to be today. When we situate GM II 16 with sections like GM II 1–3, then Nietzsche's explanation for this process of internalization is biological or, indeed, zoological in that it purports to show how we were transformed into a different species than we once were.

My argument is that because scholars in the secondary literature usually pass over this connection, they do not fully appreciate the complexifying, problematic ramifications that result.[5] Moreover, on the rare occasions when they note the importance of I.H. in relation to other critical passages in *The Genealogy* which clarify its functionality and scope, they do not fully express just how difficult the position is to hold when it sits side by side with Nietzsche's drive theory *per se*.

However, I.H. also plays a further psychological role in that it attempts to explain the behavior of agents as well as the reasons subjects use to describe/rationalize their actions. For example, it underpins Nietzsche's development of slave vs. noble values, as explained in the *Genealogy*'s first

[5] The hypothesis is appallingly undertheorized in the secondary literature a point well-established in William Beals's relatively recent and significant article, William Beals, "Internationalization and Its Consequences" *Journal of Nietzsche Studies*, Vol 44. No. 3 Autumn, 2013, 435–445, 435.

essay. In addition, it plays a significant explanatory role in Nietzsche's account of what he diagnosed as the substantial sickness in the current age, nihilism.[6] In this latter role, the Internalization Hypothesis, at least on the surface, attempts to reduce topics that would fall under the category of *quid juris* to a mere *quid facti* or etiological approach.[7] Whatever way one reads it, the Internalization Hypothesis, I submit, is the lynchpin connecting Nietzsche's reductionist biological naturalism with his philosophy of psychology.

I seek to examine the connection between the Internalization Hypothesis and Nietzsche's drive theory in the following book. I argue that a straightforward, traditional reading of GM II 16 poses significant epistemic problems for Nietzsche's naturalized account of humanity's "breeding up" in the *Genealogy*, if, that is, what Nietzsche intends to do.[8] My argument is that the only way to see ourselves out of the many problems that a standard reading of the Internalization Hypothesis engenders for drive theory is to read both within the larger context of *The Genealogy* itself. I propose that the Internalization Hypothesis is simply a way to operationalize one of the standard methodological principles of genealogy *qua* genealogy, the Separation Thesis (see GM II 12–13). The Separation Thesis holds that one must keep the means of some phenomenon (e.g. punishment) distinct from its utility or supposed purpose. Once one reads I.H. in light of this framework, the various epistemic, psychological, and philological issues pertaining to Nietzsche's

[6] Nietzsche, GM: III: 28.

[7] Immanuel Kant, *The Critique of Pure Reason*, Trans. Norman Kemp Smith, (London: Palgrave Macmillan), 2007, A 84, B116.

[8] In brief, the standard reading of GM II 16 holds that Nietzsche is describing our collective, proto-human pre-history. Brian Leiter, in his *Nietzsche on Morality*, explains this idea well: "What bears emphasizing here is that we are discussing a phenomenon of *pre-history*: we are discussing what the *animal man* had to be like before regular civilized intercourse with his fellows (the advantages of society) would even be possible. That means, of course, that the phenomenon we are discussing—the development of conscience and, in particular, bad conscience—predates the events discussed in the First Essay of the Genealogy". (My bolding, Leiter, 229). I call this interpretation of GM II 16 the standard reading as Conway, Hatab, Janaway, Owen, and many others hold something like it. This reading, which on the surface, seems the most natural–especially when situated with GM II 1–5 and GM II 17–is, nonetheless, deeply problematic when one thinks through its implications. I explore this reading in much more detail in Chap. 4.

drive theory are dissolved.[9] Moreover, Nietzsche's actual (and coherent) psychological position snaps into place. The touchstone for my reading is to view both the Internalization Hypothesis and drives as examples of the Separation Thesis. My position is worked out in five chapters.

Chapter 2: What is Genealogy? A Defense of Implexic Genealogy

I do not read the Internalization Hypothesis as a substantive thesis that accurately tracks how proto-humans developed the bad conscience and the capacities that underpin our "moral seriousness," such as memory. Instead, I understand the Hypothesis as an exemplification of a methodological principle. This principle appears in the passages immediately preceding GM II 16. Before outlining what, I call "implexic genealogy," I examine several interpretations of genealogy (e.g. documentary, pragmatic and ironic) advanced in the secondary literature and the problems each of these models generate. I then offer my novel reinterpretation of Nietzsche's *Genealogy of Morals* which places GM II 12 as the touchstone of genealogy *qua* method.

[9] Will to power is one of Nietzsche's core ideas and, as expected, there is a plethora of interpretations of the concept in the secondary literature. I explore my own position on will to power, in full, in Chap. 2. Having said that, my approach chimes with the upshot of James I. Porter's article: "Nietzsche's Theory of the Will to Power," (*A Companion to Nietzsche*, Ed. Keith Ansell Pearson. UK: Blackwell Publishers, 2006, 548–565). Although it is tempting to think, that, with will to power Nietzsche is offering a new metaphysics, this interpretation is mistaken. Will to power is an allegory of sorts according to Porter. Nietzsche uses it to remind his readers of an all too human need to totalize the world. The moral lesson of will to power, then, is this: don't totalize. Do not engage in metaphysical thinking full stop. In my view, Paul Loeb develops a similar and more thoroughly explored notion of this idea. In his judgment, will to power is not advancing a panpsychism (as is often contended in the secondary literature) but rather denotes a thought-experiment that aims at disabusing us of thinking that any truths may be discovered through metaphysical thinking. He notes, "BGE [36] does indeed outline a panpsychist conception of will to power, but only as a heuristic and counterfactual thought experiment that grants us a purely explanatory and analogical perspective on the radically de-anthropomorphic features of cosmological will to power." 84 Paul Loeb, "Will to Power and Panpsychism: A New exegesis of Beyond Good and Evil 36". *Nietzsche on Mind and Nature* (Ed(s) Manuel Dries and P.J.E. Kail Oxford University Press, 2015), 57–88. For different readings of will to power in the literature, see my book: Brian Lightbody *Nietzsche's Will to Power Naturalized: Translating the Human into Nature and Nature into the Human*. (Lanham, MD: Lexington Books, 2017).

In GM II 12 Nietzsche discusses his much debated and perplexing idea of will to power. What is unique here, in this passage, is that he advances will to power as a heuristic principle (much as he does in BGE 36) that promotes a critical ethos which urges philosophers (and especially genealogists) to challenge philosophical, historical or scientific ideas that claim some value, or object has some inherent function. In other words, will to power serves as a reminder, methodologically speaking, that any attempt to grasp the fundamental well-springs of nature (or if genealogically construed, true origin of some historical phenomenon) is doomed to fail. This skeptical attitude, however, is supported by a darker thesis: Life itself promotes its own gain of function strategy; it continues to find new ways to break free from its many different forms of crystallization in order to accumulate more power. Understood in this way, will to power, or so I submit, is then operationalized according to three procedures: the Separation Thesis (GM II 13), the Internalization Hypothesis (GM II 16), and the Rule of Conceptual Transformation (GM I 3). I explain each of these methods in detail.

Before proceeding, I need to say something more about "implexic genealogy." I examine what I refer to as implexic genealogy in detail in Chap. 2. But briefly stated here, implexic genealogy claims that the overall project of philosophical genealogy–which is to trace the threads that allowed a new concept, practice, value, or feeling to emerge—is best conducted by thinking about the threads that comprise this tracing as an intersection of vertical lines on the one hand and horizontal lines on the other. The vertical lines are those of descent and are analogous to the lines that move from the oldest member of a family tree to the youngest. For example, I am connected to my grandfather because he is my ancestor. There are biological conditions that ensure that I would not exist had my grandfather been killed in World War 1 or had never been born. My grandfather's DNA is a necessary component underwriting my personal identity. By analogy the philosophical genealogist, when viewing a phenomenon in terms of its vertical lines, traces an idea, value or emotion by looking at how the changing material conditions of bodies (which include forms of torture) within a historical era led to new social and political realities.

In contrast, dashed lines of a family tree represent the union (marriage) of two lines of inheritance. When the two lines combine, they form a new node of the family tree, which then produces a new vertical line. Typically, when one informs someone else about their family pedigree, the characteristics of each person forming the new union (and perhaps new lines of descent, i.e. children) are discussed (e.g. profession, temperament, cause of death), how the two met and what their marriage was like.

Analogously, implexic genealogy provides a narrative explaining how two lines of descent from a previous epoch fused to form a new phenomenon. While each vertical line is grounded on ample historical, anthropological, biological, or other evidence, as the case maybe, to confirm its existence, the narrative (horizontal connections) one constructs to explain the emergence of the new phenomenon from these lines is perspectival being predicated, as all investigations are, on some predetermined slant or agenda (GM III 12). In this manner, implexic genealogy affirms the reductive like features of the standard approach to genealogy in the secondary literature (i.e. the documentary model) and yet it is not, in the words, of Bernard Williams, advocating a "brute naturalism" for infused into the very methodological features of the model is an acknowledgment of will to power, which, as noted, is construed negatively as the refutation of function.

Thus, I call my model implexic genealogy because implex may be defined as "enfolding." I use the term in its zoological context as "the point where muscles are attached to the integument of an arthropod." A genealogy is the juncture where the strands of descent meet with, but are not reducible to, the narrative one provides to explain the emergence that results from the intersection of these vertical lines. I will say more about this in Chap. 2.

Chapter 3: Drives in the Secondary Literature

This chapter explains the main features of drive theory as advanced in the secondary literature. I use Mattia Riccardi's article, "Virtuous Homunculi: Nietzsche on the Order of Drives" and its five-fold account of drives as a model unfolding each component of this framework in greater detail.[10] In examining these five aspects of drive theory, I explore each feature's principal problems. For this last component, the critical part, I utilize Tom Stern's incisive article, "Against Nietzsche's Theory of Drives" which analyzes the problematic philosophical and philological features of Nietzsche's drive theory.[11] In combining Stern's insights with my own, I demonstrate that applying the Separation Thesis to drive theory itself marks the way forward. To this end, I conceive of drives as implexes: they are the symbolic intersection between cognitive and affective components.[12] I then argue that the task of genealogy is to trace how earlier, more ancient threads of these systems come to form new practices, discourses, and, principally, subjects. Finally, with this drive model now worked out schematically, I turn my attention to explaining drives in light of the Internalization Hypothesis in Chap. 4.

Another critical issue raised in this chapter is the homunculi problem. Of the five-fold features of drives explained in this chapter, one aspect stands out as the most challenging: drives evaluate. The idea that drives can evaluate some object of action as 'good' leads to the Homunculi problem where drives are like little agents. Riccardi attempts to solve this problem by relying on Dennett's intentional theoretic stance model. I demonstrate that Riccardi is an insincere intentionalist and that his solution conjures up more difficulties than it solves.

Chapter 4: The Internalization Hypothesis: A New Reading

Chapter 4 connects the project of Chap. 3, namely the attempt to trace drives to less complex "adders and subtractors" a la Dennett to the Internalization Hypothesis. In Chap. 4, I begin by reconstructing the customary view of GM II 16 along with the passages that support the

[10] Mattia Riccardi, "Virtuous Homunculi: Nietzsche on the Order of Drives", *Inquiry*, 61:1, 21–41, 2018.

[11] Tom Stern, "Against Nietzsche's Theory of Drives," *Journal of the American Philosophical Association* Vol 1. Issue 1 Spring (2015) 121–140.

[12] In Chap. 4, I explain how these components may be thought of as "strands" or "threads" which, over a relatively short period of time, become interwoven.

standard model (most notably GM II 1, 3, and 17.) According to the Received View, there is evidence suggesting that Nietzsche accepts a false scientific theory, namely, Lamarck's Inheritability Thesis, to account for the growth of a new human "organ"—morality. I demonstrate that the passages interpreted by some scholars to prove that Nietzsche is a Lamarckian can be reinterpreted along Darwinian lines. I show that Nietzsche hits upon the correct drivers of phenotypical change in humans, namely, torture and enclosures (e.g., walls of early states), but misinterprets their actual impact. Nietzsche believes that these technologies are responsible for producing what I call "culture-serving memory" and the bad conscience by causing emotions that once were expressed outwardly to turn inward, triggering the "psychological digestion" of the human animal. In reality, however, these mechanisms are conducive to culling a specific type of undesirable individual, at least according to those individuals (whom Nietzsche calls warrior-artists), namely those who are ultra-aggressive and instead breeding another class of individuals (*Die Herde*) who are docile. Early states accomplish this goal by introducing artificial and unconscious selective pressures into the environment of humans.

The second task of the chapter involves solving another mystery introduced by a recent paper by Iain Morrison.[13] Morrison argues that the standard reading of GM II 16 is wrong: the events described in GM II 19–20 occur, chronologically speaking, before GM II 16, assuming, of course, Nietzsche's intent in GM II is to provide an accurate portrayal of how the human species came to be. If that's correct, then it behooves Nietzsche's readers to understand who is being tortured in GM II 16 (when read in light of GM II 3) and who these "blond beasts of prey" (GM II 17) are doing the torturing. If Morrison is right, and I think he is, then Nietzsche's use of the term "semi-animals" to denote those who were domesticated by the forces of civilization must be hyperbole. I reveal that the semi-animals Nietzsche is referring to are tribal peoples who were captured and enslaved in political states. I put historical flesh on my interpretation in the subsequent chapter.

[13] Iain P. Morrisson, "Nietzsche, the Anthropologists, and the Genealogy of Trauma" *Genealogy* 1–16, 1, 2021.

Chapter 5: A Closer Look at the Internalization of Drives as Implexes: The Cognitive and Affective Strands[14]

Now that the mystery surrounding the semi-animals and warrior-artists Nietzsche refers to in GM II 16 and GM II 17 is solved, I begin tracing the individual skeins, in this case, cognitive and affective threads, that become entwined to create the kind of agency Nietzsche claims emerges in GM II 16. My argument suggests that the internalization of drives is too symbolic and therefore cannot perform any real explanatory work. In keeping with implexic genealogy, I investigate the stable and fluid or perspectival dimensions that account for the emergence of new phenomena in history. A more likely account for the formation of a new form of subjectivization, borrowing that term from Foucault, namely Christian subjectivity, is the novel environment enslaved people found themselves after being captured and sold in state marketplaces like Rome. This strange, hostile world must have seemed to such peoples much like "The situation that faced sea animals when they were compelled to become land animals or perish" (GM II 16). When Nietzsche further suggests that such semi-animals could no longer rely on their infallible drives and instead were reduced to "thinking, inferring, reckoning" and so on (GM II 16), I take this to mean that political states augmented the need for tribal people–now as slaves and therefore finding themselves, to paraphrase Orlando Patterson, stripped of their identity and social standing–to utilize their dormant capacities of instrumental reason in order to survive. The counterstroke to this enhancement, however, was that it dampened the particular cognitive virtues which well-served these same individuals when they occupied a particular rank and place in their respective tribes.

On the affective side, religious narratives within states like Rome, allowed enslaved people to release the pent-up trauma they experienced

[14] I was inspired to use the term "implex" after reading Rajiv Kaushik's, "Literature, Ontology, and Implex in Merleau-Ponty: Writing and Finding the Concrete Limit of Phenomena", *Humanities* 2021, 10(4) 2021,1–12. However, in contrast to Kaushik, I use the term in accordance with its zoological definition.

at the hands of their master, the *Paterfamilias*, into socially accepted ways. I use Christopher Fowles's helpful article: "The Heart of the Flesh," to explain Nietzsche's theory of emotions to help concretize my thesis. I demonstrate that an Impure Somatic model of emotion justifies Nietzsche's genealogical account for the rise, and advancement of Christian morality in history.

Chapter 6: A Test Case Comparing Augustinian to Tertullian Christian Subjectivity

My implexic account of drives and the context that informs them, which I have labeled "implexic genealogy," is tested against two forms of Christian subjectivity. The first I call the internalized Augustinian model. The second I refer to is Tertullian's externalist paradigm. First, I demonstrate how my theory of affects, which has both somatic and cognitive elements, explains a new phenomenon in history: conversion experiences exemplified in Augustine's *Confessions*. I then demonstrate how we can better understand Augustine's unique internalized Christian form of subjectivity by contrasting it with that of Tertullian's externalized type. Toward the end of GM I, Nietzsche quotes extensively from Tertullian's *De Spectaculus* ostensibly to justify the claim that the actual engine of Christian sentiments is the very hostile drives Nietzsche discusses in GM II 16. I don't doubt that Nietzsche's quoting of the pen-ultimate passage of the *Spectacles* is meant to justify this claim. However, I contend there is perhaps another reason why Nietzsche invokes Tertullian in the final section of GM I. The logic of Christianity, whether this includes the Incarnation, the Day of Judgment, or *causa sui* freewill, are conceptual developments meant to decipher and utilize (albeit unknowingly) ancient, affective neural pathways. Such concepts are not *sui generis* but emerge, genealogically speaking, due to prior existing material conditions and social practices. The movement from the internal to the external, the symbolic to the literal, is in keeping with the fundamental process of genealogy, which is discovering the lines of descent that made a new phenomenon possible. Finally, I show how the evolution of one naïve kind of Christian subjectivization to a more sophisticated version took place.

Conclusion

This book is an attempt to work through the difficulties posed by a natural reading of the Internalization Hypothesis as advanced in GM II 16 *and* Nietzsche's theory of drives *per se*. One would think that since I.H. contextualizes Nietzsche's drive theory, the philosophical problems each of these components creates separately ramifies when the two are brought together. But this is not the case. I argue that if the Internalization Hypothesis is simply a way to operationalize a genealogical construal of will to power (i.e. as the refutation of inherent function) and, that if the purpose of the Hypothesis is to explain the process for the transformation of animal instincts to human drives, then drives fall within the scope of will to power. If that's right, then drives represent the symbolic intersection of two more ancient threads: cognitive abilities on the one hand and affective dispositions on the other. By understanding the origin of each these threads, genealogically speaking, we go a long way to naturalizing and, therefore, understanding both the Internalization Hypothesis and, therefore, drive theory.

References Used in this Chapter

Beals, William. "Internationalization and Its Consequences" *Journal of Nietzsche Studies,* Vol 44. No. 3 Autumn, 2013, 435–445

Clark, Maudemarie and Dudrick, David. *The Soul of Nietzsche's Beyond Good and Evil,* (Cambridge, Cambridge University Press), 2012

Fowles, Christopher. "The Heart of the Flesh: Nietzsche on Affects and the Interpretation of the Body", *Journal of the History of Philosophy*, Volume 58, Number 1, January 2020, pp. 113–139

Kant, Immanuel. *The Critique of Pure Reason*, Trans. Norman Kemp Smith, (London: Palgrave Macmillan), 2007

Katsafanas, Paul. *The Nietzschean Self: Moral Psychology, Agency and the Unconscious*, (New York: Oxford University Press, 2016

Kaushik, Rajiv. "Literature, Ontology, and Implex in Merleau-Ponty: Writing and Finding the Concrete Limit of Phenomena", *Humanities* 2021, 10(4) 2021,1–12.

Leiter, Brian. *Nietzsche on Morality*. New York: Routledge, 2002.

Lightbody, Brian. *Nietzsche's Will to Power Naturalized: Translating the Human into Nature and Nature into the Human.* Lanham, MD. Lexington Books, 2017.

Loeb, Paul. "Will to Power and Panpsychism: A New exegesis of Beyond Good and Evil 36". *Nietzsche on Mind and Nature* (Ed(s) Manuel Dries and P.J.E. Kail Oxford University Press, 2015), 57–88.

Morrisson, Iain, P. "Nietzsche, the Anthropologists, and the Genealogy of Trauma" *Genealogy* 1–16, 1, 2021.

Porter, James, I. "Nietzsche's Theory of the Will to Power," *A Companion to Nietzsche*. Ed. Keith Ansell Pearson. UK: Blackwell Publishers, 2006, 548–565

Riccardi, Mattia. "Virtuous Homunculi: Nietzsche on the Order of Drives", *Inquiry*, 61:1, 21–41, 2018.

Stern, Tom. "Against Nietzsche's Theory of Drives", *Journal of the American Philosophical Association* Vol 1. Issue 1 Spring (2015) 121–140

2

What Is Genealogy? A Defense of Implexic Genealogy

Section I: What Is Genealogy?

Before articulating what I am referring to as "implexic genealogy," it is crucial, I think, to canvass some of the other interpretations of philosophical genealogy in the recent secondary literature. There are three principal ways of conceiving the method. The first model is the substantive or documentary interpretation. This template provides, at least ideally, close, rigorous documentation of the events and circumstances surrounding the historical emergence of some idea, moral code, observance, or practice. More importantly, it tracks how and why the initial notion, desire, value, or practice changed. This approach is naturalistic, broadly construed, in that it sticks closely, as Nietzsche put it, "to what is documented what can actually be confirmed and has actually existed in short the entire long hieroglyphic record so hard to decipher of the moral past of mankind!" (GM Preface 7) Foucault reaffirms and amplifies this maxim. Genealogy, he evinces, "consequently requires patience and a

B. Lightbody, *A Genealogical Analysis of Nietzschean Drive Theory*,
https://doi.org/10.1007/978-3-031-27148-9_2

knowledge of details and it depends on a vast accumulation of source material. In short, genealogy requires constant erudition."[1]

The second, I call the ironic model. This model is similar to the above paradigm, the documentary model, but with a twist: it argues that since all claims are shot through with perspectives, including the genealogist's own, tracing the history of some idea to discover the true purpose of its value or origin is incoherent. The point of this approach, according to some accounts, is to demonstrate the belief that a purely objective, historical investigation of, for example, the origin of emotions, rational thinking, morality, and so on, devoid of prejudice and bereft of sentiment, is silly. Thus, the reader should approach *The Genealogy* or *Discipline and Punish* as performative works, the true philosophical import of which does not lie in the accuracy of the so-called claims made in each separate piece but in the ability of these texts, in particular, to erode the reader's quest for objective knowledge.[2] The result demonstrates that embracing a post-modern celebration of perspectives on illocutionary grounds is the best we can hope for in understanding our history.[3]

Following Mathieu Queloz, I shall call the third method the pragmatic approach.[4] Pragmatic styles of genealogy are a kind of conceptual reverse engineering; they seek to demonstrate how a complex idea like truth emerged from a social need. Queloz sums up this view succinctly when he writes, "My concern, by contrast, is with the practical origins of ideas: with

[1] Michel Foucault, "Nietzsche, Genealogy, History" In *Language, Counter-Memory, Practice Selected Essays and Interviews by Michel Foucault* Ed. Donald F. Bourchard (Ithaca: Cornell University Press) 1977, sec. 1 76–77.

[2] See Jean Granier's, *Le probleme de la Verite dans la Philosophie de Nietzsche* (Paris: Seuil, 1966) and Sarah Koffman's, *Nietzsche et la Metaphor* (Paris: Payot) 1972. John Rajchman argues much the same for Foucault's genealogies. See his "The Story of Foucault's History" in *Michel Foucault: Critical Assessments*. (Hereafter known as MCFA). Ed. Barry Smart. Volume II. New York: Routledge, 1994, 389–411.

[3] C.G. Prado writes: "Essentially Foucault offers his genealogies as opportunities for us to think differently because they enabled him to think differently and so to become a different subject." (C.G. Prado, *Searle and Foucault on Truth* (Cambridge University Press: 2006), 135.

[4] For a succinct introduction to pragmatic genealogy see Mathieu Queloz, "Tracing Concepts to Needs", *The Philosopher*, 109, (3) 34–39, 2021.

the ways in which the ideas we live by can be shown to be rooted in practical needs and concerns generated by facts about us and our situation."[5]

Two paradigmatic and relatively recent genealogies in this vein are Edward Craig's work: *Knowledge and The State of Nature*, and Bernard William's book, *Truth and Truthfulness: An Essay in Genealogy*.[6] However, if the criteria "practical need" is broadly construed, then Hobbes's functional account for the origin of society in *Leviathan* and Hume's story regarding the emergence of justice in *A Treatise on Human Nature* belong to this category.[7] Indeed as Queloz argues, Nietzsche's account of truth as given in "Truth in a Non-moral Sense" is a species of this genus as well. Queloz evinces, "Nietzsche's early genealogy of truthfulness answers this question by showing that truthfulness has practical origins in the exigencies of social life."[8] Given that a large number of works fall into this class, I cannot entertain all of the respective formulations in the category. Instead, I will outline Williams's picture of genealogy as a representative work in this group.

Implexic genealogy cleaves more tightly to the substantive approach than the two others. Still, as will become apparent, there are inflections of the pragmatic and rhetorical models within this model too. I will say much more about this below.

My goals in examining these different interpretations of genealogy are twofold: First, I wish to clarify the advantages and disadvantages of each position. Secondly, but of paramount importance, I demonstrate that the implexic genealogical approach shares features with the other methods. Thus, the techniques of each approach that I will examine in full below

---

[5] Matthieu Queloz, *The Practical Origin of Ideas: Genealogy as Conceptual Reverse-Engineering* (Oxford University Press, 2020), 2.

[6] Edward Craig, *Knowledge and the State of Nature* (Oxford University Press: 1990). Bernard *Williams Truth and Truthfulness: An Essay on Genealogy* (Princeton: Princeton University Press), 2002. Thomas Hobbes, *Leviathan,* Edited by Michael Oakeshott, (New York: Collier), 1966. David Hume, *A Treatise of Human Nature*, edited by L. A. Selby-Bigge, 2nd ed. revised by P. H. Nidditch, Oxford: Clarendon Press, 1975.

[7] Brian Lightbody, "The Passive Body and States of Nature: An Examination of the Methodological Role State of Nature Theory Plays in Williams and Nietzsche" in the Special Issue *Philosophical Genealogy from Nietzsche to Williams Genealogy* MPDI (5) 2, 38, 2021 1–15, 6–7.

[8] Queloz, *The Practical Origin of Ideas*, 116.

are not mutually exclusive. It is more accurate to say that they are different only in what each type of genealogy accentuates. The methodology I adopt, which is heavily influenced by Foucault's inspired interpretation of *On the Genealogy of Morals*—articulated in his "Nietzsche, Genealogy History,"——offers a cohesive and capacious model. It can accommodate other viewpoints because it places significance on some methods rather than others, but it is not opposed to other techniques *per se.*

Before discussing each template in greater detail, I wish to examine a common medical analogy in the secondary literature when describing genealogy. This analogy will help sharpen the salient features of each model and is one that Nietzsche often utilizes. The metaphor posits that the genealogist is a physician of culture.[9] Genealogists diagnose the ills (or in rare cases), strengths of modern society, and to borrow the parlance of Williams, if the genealogy is condemnatory, they prescribe the appropriate antidote. In sporadic instances in which the account is vindicatory, which is more commonly the case for pragmatic genealogists, the readers better understand why particular values in a society should be appreciated.

There are at least three passages in *the Genealogy* where Nietzsche draws on this analogy. The first is the infamous note at the bottom of GM I. Nietzsche there writes:

> Indeed, every table of values every thou shalt known to history or ethnology requires first a physiological investigation and interpretation rather than a psychological one and every one of them needs a critique on the part of medical science the question what is the value of this or that table of

[9] I am of course only referring to the term physiology and related cognates. A wide variety of other related medical and physiological terms can also be found in Nietzsche's work. For a look at several important secondary works which emphasize the biological and physiological aspects of Nietzsche's philosophy, see Gregory Moore *Nietzsche, Biology, Metaphor,* (Cambridge University Press, 2002). Daniel Ahern's *Nietzsche as Cultural Physician,* (Pennsylvania State University Press, 1995). Richard S.G. Brown's two articles, "Nihilism: "Thus Speaks Physiology" in *Nietzsche and the Rhetoric of Nihilism: Essays on Interpretation, Language and Politics* edited by Tom Darby, Bela Egyed and Ben Jones (Ottawa: Carleton University Press, 1989), 133–144. "Nietzsche: That Profound Physiologist." *Nietzsche and Science* Eds Gregory Moore and Thomas Brobjer, (Aldershot: Ashgate Press, 2004). Wayne Klein's *Nietzsche and the Promise of Philosophy* (Albany, NY: State University of New York Press, 1997). For semiological interpretations of Nietzsche's biologism, see Eric Blondel *Nietzsche: The Body and Culture. Philosophy as a Philological Genealogy*, trans. Sean Hand (Stanford University Press, 1991) Blondel argues that genealogy's true purpose is to allow space for *Verfuhrer zum Leben* (to live life dangerously).

> values and morals should be viewed from the most divers perspectives for the problem value for what cannot be examined too subtly. (GM I 17 Note)

The second can be found in section 5 of the preface:

> One has taken the value of these values as given as factual as beyond all question when is hitherto never doubted or hesitated in the slightest degree in supposing the good man to be of greater value than the evil man of greater value in the sense of furthering the advancement and prosperity of men in general the future of man included but what if the reverse were true what if a *symptom* of regression were inherent in the good likewise a danger a seduction a *poison* a *narcotic* through which the present was possibly living at the expense of the future perhaps more comfortably less dangerously but at the same time in a meaner style more basely. (GM Preface 5)

The above passages underscore the diagnostic aspects of genealogy. But Nietzsche, a true physician of culture, offers his patients, namely us, his readers, a cure: cheerfulness. "For cheerfulness–or in my own language gay science–is the reward of a long brave industrious and subterranean seriousness of which to be sure not everyone is capable." (GM Preface sec. 7) The long brave industrious seriousness Nietzsche is discussing in this passage is the attitude one must take up when embarking on a genealogy of values. Such a task requires courage and erudition. Erudition because genealogy uses a plethora of empirical data drawn from diverse fields (e.g. etymology, psychology, biology) when investigating the source of moral values and practices. Furthermore, it requires courage because there will likely be an upturning of our traditional values and the emotional infrastructure that supports them. This affective upturning leads to a transvaluation of values.

Many scholars in the secondary literature hold this idea, namely that values are ingrained and subtended by powerful emotions. Christopher Janaway in his incredibly insightful and helpful early work, "Genealogy and Naturalism" and, later, in *Beyond Selflessness: Reading Nietzsche's Genealogy*, clarifies the relationship between these two. As he informs us, "It seems clear that the revaluation of values Nietzsche seeks is not just a change in judgments but a revision at the level of the affects too. After we have learned not to make judgments using "good", "evil", "right" and "wrong", we finally may come, says Nietzsche, *to feel differently*. And it is plausible that the therapeutic or educative aim of bringing about revised affective habits has the arousal of affects as a prequisite."[10]

All the models below are consistent with the medical analogy: each has a diagnostic and curative component. These elements, however, will come to mean different things depending on the model invoked.

Section: II Three Models of Genealogy: Model 1—The Ironic

In discussing the traditional way of thinking about genealogy (at least in Continental circles) and Nietzsche's *Genealogy* in particular, the first interpretation is predicated upon a specific reading of the *Genealogy of Morals* that places pride of place on power. To be more precise, this reading, the one I call ironic, suggests that the work's central thesis is to persuade its readers that *all tools* for rational thinking are constructions of power. This reading elevates Nietzsche's famous passage on perspectivism in GM III: 12 to a universal. "There is only a perspective seeing, only a perspective 'knowing;' and the more affects we allow to speak about one thing, the more eyes, different eyes, we can use to observe one thing, the more complete will our 'concept' of this thing, our 'objectivity,' be." (GM III 12). To be clear, all assertions, whether historical, philosophical or otherwise, including those in the *Genealogy* are informed and colored, reflexively, by this passage.

It is vital to amplify the idea's implications to clarify what the method entails. The position holds: (1) That all statements reflect one's historical

[10] Christopher Janaway, "Naturalism and Genealogy", In *Blackwell's Companions to Philosophy: A Companion to Nietzsche.* Edited By Keith Ansell Pearson. (London: Blackwell Publishers, 2006), 337–353, 347 See also Kathleen Marie Higgins' "On the Genealogy of Morals—Nietzsche's Gift" *On the Genealogy of Morals" in Nietzsche, Genealogy Morality*: *Essays on Nietzsche's Genealogy of Morals.* Ed. Richard Schacht (Berkeley California: University of California Press, 1994), 49–63. Higgins writes, "Laughter is the ultimate cathartic that can alleviate our overly poisoned systems. Having himself, contributed to our excessively poisoned state, Nietzsche leaves us to laugh it out." 61. One can now also see the irony of Higgins title. Gift in German, means poison, to poison, *vergiften*. So Higgins', title, we might say, is Nietzsche's gift that poisons.

and yet contingent enculturation; (2) That said enculturation is inescapable; (3) Values are construed as essential components of a culture; and (4) That cultures are manifestations of power formations. If we accept all four theses, there cannot be distinctions between descriptive and evaluative assertions. The results of an investigation, genealogy included, are simply attitudes of one's social formatting. What's more, said formatting is not underpinned on a more primordial, encompassing notion of humanity, let's say, but is contingent, arbitrary, and historical through and through.

The ironic interpretation of genealogy and Nietzsche's *Genealogy*, more specifically, is a thought-provoking yet somewhat problematic reading because if rationality, *en toto*, is merely a product of a peculiar confluence of power, then standards of reason, warrant, and justification are themselves nothing more than emergent epiphenomena emanating from a regime of force. This supposition, if true, would entail that some cultures, or employing Foucault's term *dispositifs*, (power/knowledge apparatus) would have distinct and incomparable definitions of normative epistemic terms. The upshot thereby reveals some startling implications. One such is that all statements, genealogical or otherwise, that purport to be true cannot be decoupled from evaluative claims. A genealogy's commitment, then, to present a more truthful account regarding the origin of some moral phenomenon—assuming this is what a genealogy purports to show—is either meant to be ironic or is a flat-out performative contradiction.[11]

Here, supporters of this position invoke what I call the irony defense. One possible move to offset the seeming incoherency of the situation

[11] Jurgen Habermas quite explicitly makes this very claim in his *Philosophical Discourse of Modernity: 12 lectures* Cambridge Mass: MIT Press, 1985, 281. Paul Bove, in a similar vein, argues the very same point by claiming that genealogy cannot remain critical of power/knowledge once genealogy becomes part of the academic world. Genealogy would, therefore, become part and parcel of the current dispositif. See Bove's article "The End of Humanism: Michel Foucault and the Power of Disciplines" in *Michel Foucault: Critical Assessments*. (Hereafter known as MCFA). Ed. Barry Smart. Volume II. New York: Routledge, 1994, 313–328. Perhaps McCarthy puts this criticism best, writing, "Having become more or less co-extensive with restraint, power becomes all too like the night in which all cows are black". McCarthy concludes that Foucault has a one-dimensional ontology in which truth, knowledge, and subjectivity are reduced in the end to effects of power. See McCarthy, Thomas. "The Critique of Impure Reason." In *Critique and Power: Recasting the Habermas/Foucault Debate*. Ed. Michael Kelly. Cambridge Mass: MIT Press, 1994, 254.

suggests that genealogies are neither any more or any less truthful than the more traditional account they critique, but nor do they claim to be. Nietzschean perspectivism, for example, evacuates the very possibility of taking up a non-subjective stance on the question of morality and, therefore, the question, "Are Nietzsche's genealogies true?" represents a category mistake. Nevertheless, Nietzsche undertakes the investigation in the history of western morality with interest and purpose and indicates this in the very subtitle of *On the Genealogy: A Polemic* (*Eine Streitschrift*).

There are many different stripes of this overall defensive strategy, and the corresponding diagnostic and curative components will differ in kind. I will attempt to draw out the leading players. Under one interpretation, Nietzsche's genealogies are a kind of modern *ephexis (epexetai) (suspension)*; they are tactics aimed at disabusing the reader of a belief once held to be accurate by demonstrating that the traditional stance regarding the origin of some subject matter is rife with problems. They ask that the reader not rush to judgment; readers should hold both narratives (e.g., the Christian account of guilt and Nietzsche's) in a state of equipollence or suspension of judgment.[12] Thus, in looking at the diagnostic purpose and efficacy of Nietzsche's argumentation given this model, the *Genealogy* serves to combat dogmatic beliefs not dissimilar to ancient skeptical models, especially those employed by Democritus, the laughing philosopher or so some defenders of this model hold.[13] The curative value resides in refusing to take moral ideals seriously "…to regard them as if from above and from a great distance and to cast upon them ultimate suspicion."[14] By not taking such beliefs sincerely (e.g. guilt as a punishment from God), we are not subject to deleterious mental suffering.

Another species of this stance holds that genealogies are not self-supporting discourses but are dependent, parasitic as it were, on a more traditional account of morality, which serves as their host, compromising the epistemic and psychological health of the established narrative under investigation. The purpose, then, of genealogy, is to undermine the vigor

[12] "Philology, [Nietzsche writes], as ephexis in interpretation: whether it concerns books, newspaper article, destinies, or facts about the weather—not to mention the salvation of the soul". (Antichrist 52)

[13] Jessica N Berry *Nietzsche and the Ancient Skeptical Tradition*, Oxford University Press, 2011, 171.

[14] Berry, 173.

of the traditional narrative as it were such that and by analogy, its practices, beliefs, and institutions are not taken as seriously as they once were.[15]

This particular version of the ironic defense is incoherent, however. If Nietzsche's genealogies do not have the *imprimatur* of truth or at the very least, justification, then it is hard to see how they challenge their host narratives. Draw out the implications of the parasite metaphor. Under this model, it is presumed that genealogies siphon the creditability from traditional accounts of morality, just as a parasite drinks the blood of its host. Drawing out too much blood leads to a loss of vitality in that host. So too, it is argued, genealogies draw out the living blood of the narrative, the levels of credence fluid, shall we say, that once made it a suitable and engaging human practice. The analogy begins to break down in that the causal mechanism responsible for undermining a narrative has not been identified in contradistinction to the known analog. In the former case, it is clear that the parasite is drawing blood from the host and is causally responsible for the host's debilitation. However, if all narratives are shot through with power and one's diagnosis is corrupted by the very rationality one uses, it is hard to see how credibility in the traditional story is undermined. The curative aspect of this approach is akin to Nagel's discussion of the absurd: "We take back these [narratives] like a spouse who has run off with someone else and then decided to return but we regard them differently."[16] I would argue that we don't really throw off the traditional narrative we are seeking to critique with this reading but rather hold it in a different light.

Another way to interpret the rhetoric model, whose *sine qua non* is the denial of the truth of genealogical claims *simpliciter* but not their truthfulness, is to take up David Owen's position. Owen's stance is that

[15] For more on the parasitic model of the genealogical method, see Jean Granier's, *Le probleme de la Verite dans la Philosophie de Nietzsche*. Paris: Seuil. and Sarah Koffman Nietzsche et la Metaphor Paris: Payot 1972. Daniel W. Conway, in his article, "Genealogy and the Critical Method" argues that, "Genealogical interpretations are always abnormal and reactive, preying upon the normal, authoritative interpretations they challenge. Whatever degree of validity a genealogy acquires is therefore entirely relative to the interpretation it discredits". See Conway, "Genealogy and the Critical Method in On the Genealogy of Morals" in *Nietzsche, Genealogy Morality: Essays on Nietzsche's Genealogy of Morals*. Ed. Richard Schacht (Berkeley California: University of California Press), 318–334, 332.

[16] Thomas Nagel, "The Absurd" in *The Meaning of Life* 4th edition Ed(s). E.D. Klemke and Steven Cahn, Oxford University Press, 2017 143.

genealogies are not ideology critiques but are something else entirely. The purpose of ideology critique is to discover and criticize distorted forms of communication. For this type of emancipatory discourse to be successful, readers must recognize that they suffer from false consciousness/neurosis and that there is a way out from said suffering. Suffering from false consciousness may be defined as follows: (1) an individual has false beliefs which legitimize oppressive social institutions or relationships; (2) an individual is also blocked in some way from recognizing the false beliefs they hold (through the media, the educational system, repressive sexual laws, etc.).[17] Essential to the ideological critique model is the assumption that one may cut through distorted forms of communication, whether of the class type as with Marx or the psychic a la Freud, provided that one has the correct conduit to the truth. Ideology critique acts as a sieve of sorts promising the reader the pure truth undistorted by class or id investment.[18]

However, genealogy militates against the very nature of such promises under this third reading. In contrast to ideology critique, a successful genealogy reveals to its readers that they suffer not from false consciousness, as that would presuppose that there is an accurate picture of the world to be had, but restricted consciousness.[19] Restricted consciousness may be defined as an individual captured by a vision of reality that is neither true nor false in itself but is taken to be the only frame of reference in which questions regarding the truth and falsity of various issues may be legitimately asked.[20] The purpose of genealogy, in general, these authors claim is to free readers from restricted self-consciousness. The advantages of this position are manifold, but they come at a steep cost which I will flesh out below.

[17] David Owen, "Criticism and Captivity: On Genealogy and Critical Theory, "*European Journal of Philosophy* 10: 216–230, 2002, 217.

[18] David Owen "Criticism and Captivity: On Genealogy and Critical Theory", 217.

[19] David Owen "Criticism and Captivity: On Genealogy and Critical Theory", 217.

[20] David Owen "Criticism and Captivity: On Genealogy and Critical Theory", 217.

Model 2: Pragmatic Genealogies: Williams and Queloz Genealogy as Reverse Conceptual Engineering

In his work *Truth and Truthfulness*, Bernard Williams offers a very different interpretation of philosophical genealogy than that typically expounded in the secondary literature. The "Received View" of genealogy holds that it is "documentary grey": it attempts to provide historically well-supported, coherent, but defeasible explanations for the actual transformation of practices, values, and emotions in history. However, paradoxically, the standard interpretation also holds another principle. Genealogies are nevertheless polemical because they admit that any evidence that would serve to justify a genealogical account is indexical to a perspective.

The ironic model places pride of place on the latter, whereas the documentarian template emphasizes the former. As is clear, there is a tension in holding these two claims. The pragmatic approach attempts to resolve this tension in a spectacularly clever way.

In contrast, Williams argues that *all* genealogies provide a functional account for the manifestation of something and further, that a State of Nature story subtends these accounts. "A genealogy, (writes Williams), is a narrative that tries to explain a cultural phenomenon by describing a way in which it came about, or could have come about, or might have come about. Some of the narrative will consist of real history, which to some extent must aim to be, as Foucault puts it, 'gray meticulous, and patiently documentary.'"[21] The key point in this passage is the word "narrative." Genealogies, fundamentally, are stories. They describe how something—whether a concept, practice, value, or feeling—came about. It is critical to note that a genealogical inquiry's target of an investigation is incomprehensible if that same target is extracted from its explanatory context. Expanding on this point, Williams makes it clear that genealogy is not a species of reductive naturalism. He explains: "The genealogy gives no way of translating language that mentions the resultant item into

[21] Williams, *Truth and Truthfulness*, 20.

terms that mention only the original items, nor does it claim that 'justice' or 'property' or 'knowledge' introduces nothing over and above the original items—on the contrary, it shows what new thing is introduced, and why it is new."[22] We might say that genealogies are linguistic non-reductionist types of naturalistic analysis. In explaining the rise of "justice," "morality," or "normalization," we are not explaining these terms in the language of *explicandum* to *explicans*. To put the matter more forcefully, we have a license to say that genealogy is antithetical to physicalist reductionism, a point Williams well-elucidates: "Questions about naturalism (which Williams claims genealogy serves) like questions about individualism in the social sciences, are questions not about reduction but about explanation."[23]

Williams' elucidation of genealogy's methods is introduced with little fanfare which makes the present reconstruction of the pragmatic approach all the more difficult. Only a few passages in Chap. 2 of his major work on the subject of genealogy, *Between Truth and Truthfulness*, clarify his conception of genealogy in any considerable detail. Thus, the reader must perform the heavy lifting of articulating Williams's reconstruction genealogy. I extract two components of Williams's construal of genealogy from this chapter. The first is genealogy's reliance on a State of Nature story. On this point, Williams writes, "Craig's example, like my own State of Nature story, is an example of what I shall call an 'imaginary genealogy'—'imaginary,' because, as I said at the beginning of this chapter, there are also historically true genealogies. Imaginary genealogies typically suggest that a phenomenon can usefully be treated as functional which is not obviously so."[24] The second component of genealogy concerns its functionality. Williams explains what he means by functional in the following: "Second, the account is functional because the relation between the derived, more complex, reason and the simpler, "more primitive" reasons or motivations is rational, in the sense that in the imagined circumstances people with the simpler motivations would welcome, and, if they could do so, aim for a state of affairs (i.e. one other than a State of

[22] Williams, *Truth and Truthfulness*, 36.

[23] Williams, *Truth and Truthfulness*, 23.

[24] Williams, 32.

Nature) in which the more complex reasons would operate."[25] Pinning down a robust articulation of genealogy, from the pragmatic side, involves distilling three additional essential features from these passages and adding them to the description above. These three features are: (1) a genealogy provides a functional account for the emergence of a new thing in history; (2) a State of Nature story subtends this account; (3) the actors in our imaginary State of Nature story are rational, and we as readers of the genealogy are rational too: we can understand and judge the actions and reasons of so-called primitive agents in this State of Nature story. This last point connects the functionality of the genealogy and the normative consequences that follow, from the account. It is because we can judge the behavior of the inhabitants of these State of Nature stories that we may condemn or vindicate their respective decisions.

One of the problems with this model, however, is that there is a limit regarding how far back a genealogy can go. As Williams evinces, genealogy is not a brute naturalism:

> These circumstances are standardly identified in the literature as the environment of our Pleistocene hunter-gatherer ancestors. It is important to the argument of this book that this is not what I mean when I offer the abstract representation of certain human activities and capacities which I call the State of Nature. My story is not intended as a speculation in evolutionary biology or as a contribution to prehistory.[26]

Yet Nietzsche's drive theory militates against placing the actors within a state of nature theory as self-interested and rational, if only quasi-so. This is not to say that one cannot provide a reading of the *Genealogy*, which is predicated on the pragmatic model, of course. My point, rather, is that drive theory is antipodal to the pragmatic reading which is obviously predicated on self-interestedness no matter how obscure or limited the perception of what is truly in one's self-interest happens to be. Put another way, there is no point in postulating a theory of drives if actors always act according to their preferences as they consciously perceive them to be.

[25] Williams, 33–34.

[26] Williams, 30.

The importation of drives—and the Internalization Hypothesis, for that matter—in explaining human psychology would be redundant if one accepted Williams's construal of Nietzsche's *Genealogy*. With that point in mind, I now turn to the substantive or documentary model of genealogy.

Model 3: The Documentary

The third model is often called the documentary or substantive reading in the secondary literature.[27] The purpose of genealogy, when viewed through this lens, is to criticize the traditional interpretations for the rise of some event or thing by providing a more accurate historical etiology for the entity in question. For example, Nietzsche presents three interconnected accounts of morality in his classic work *On the Genealogy of Morals: A Polemic*. Each "story" attempts to explain the origin of some contemporary, feeling-infused behavior. The first gives a rendering of the origin of good and evil intuitions along with the behavior that governs said impulses. The second is a study that seeks to demonstrate how guilt originated. It casts doubt on the prevailing attitude of Nietzsche's time that guilt denoted an innate capacity authored by God himself. The third and final genealogy explains the origin of the ascetic ideal, a seemingly contradictory way of life, at least from the standpoint of the dominant moral and motivational theory of Nietzsche's time, psychological hedonism. Nietzsche's genealogies are gripping, because they are more warranted, so this interpretation holds, than the traditional Christian narrative provided for the emergence of each notion. Nietzsche's evidence is not just wide-ranging (e.g. historical, archeological, linguistic, biological and psychological) but cohesive. Ideally each new genealogical discovery snaps into place with the other pieces forming a well-warranted narrative, a new framing through which to view history.[28]

[27] See my paper Brian Lightbody, "Artificial and Unconscious Selection in Nietzsche's Genealogy: Expectorating the Poisoned Pill of the Lamarckian Reading." *Genealogy*, 34.3 June, 2019 pp. 1–23.

[28] See Chapter 6 of Brian Lightbody *Philosophical Genealogy: Nietzsche and Foucault's Genealogical Method: Vol. 2,* 2011, Chapter 6.

With that said, there is one significant problem with Nietzsche's genealogies when read as attempts to offer a close documentation of history—they do not appear to be well-warranted after all. This criticism is articulated in several ways by three different groups of scholars. The first group includes those scholars who question the historical accuracy and plausibility of the details of Nietzsche's accounts of morality while arguing that the general features are correct.[29] The second group is far more critical. They claim that Nietzsche's hypotheses, while imaginative and entertaining, are, more often than not, wild conjectures with little if any historical and archeological evidence supporting them. Always looking for an opportunity to castigate alternative accounts of human evolution than those purported by Darwin, Dennett as the most compelling member of this camp thinks that "Nietzsche's Just So Stories are terrific … They are a mixture of brilliant and crazy, sublime and ignoble, devastatingly acute history and untrammeled fantasy".[30] Still, other scholars who straddle both camps make the further assertion that Nietzsche's conclusions are predicated on what we now know to be false theories inflected and infected as they were by peculiar nineteenth-century prejudices.[31]

The upshot of these critiques which question the truthfulness of *The Genealogy* as a whole, is that Nietzsche's genealogical conclusions appear

[29] While Prinz takes Nietzsche's historical account regarding the origin of morality seriously, this does not prevent him from finding flaws with Nietzsche's rendering, especially with regard to the timelines of the emergence of slave morality. He writes, "Even if Nietzsche's genealogy of Christian values is mistaken, the basic tenets of his approach can be defended". Jesse Prinz, *The Emotional Construction of Morals*. Oxford: Oxford University Press, 2007, 219. Jesse Prinz, "Genealogies of Morals: Nietzsche's Method Compared" *Journal of Nietzsche Studies* 47: 2016, 180–201, 194. However, Mark Migotti's recent article, "History, Genealogy, Nietzsche: Comments on "Jesse Prinz's Genealogies of Morals: Nietzsche's Methods Compared", *Journal of Nietzsche Studies* 47: 2016, 212–227 demonstrates, quite brilliantly, that Prinz badly misreads the first and second essays of *the Genealogy*. Migotti claims, "Prinz's mistaken identification of the slave revolt in morality with the emergence of the Christian religion leads him to think that he is improving on Nietzsche, when in fact he is simply following suit … But, as we have seen, Nietzsche's view is not that Christianity began with the slave revolt, but that it was born of it". (223).

[30] Daniel Dennett, *Darwin's Dangerous Idea: Evolution and the Meanings of Life*. London: Allen Lane and Penguin Press, 1995, 464.

[31] Their work (Nietzsche's contemporaries who were also interested in degeneration, decadence, and eugenics) also lacks the fundamental contradictoriness of Nietzsche's position—a nineteenth-century faith in the institutional authority of the biological sciences which co-exists uneasily with a belief that these same disciplines are infected with false values: the characteristic hovering between literalness and metaphor, sincerity and irony". Gregory Moore, *Nietzsche, Biology, Metaphor*, 211.

dubious and indeed sophomoric when compared to the sort of work conducted by contemporary ethical naturalists whose own research is informed by the very best archeological, historical, psychological, neuroscientific, biological, and linguistic evidence.

My way to maneuver around these sorts of objections is twofold: one is to accept that Nietzsche's stories are not, as Williams remarks, accurate depictions of the Paleolithic or even Neolithic eras. But neither are they merely speculative models one might use to flesh out an alternative story regarding the formation and evolution of humanity, as Williams and Queloz hold. In my view, *The Genealogy* is not comparable to Humean armchair models of genealogical theorizing because the very cognitive faculties responsible for speculation, insight, and reason (whether instrumental or moral) are reflexively conditioned by biological and, to a lesser extent, cultural factors and constraints. I will say much more about this below.

My way of looking at genealogy is similar in some respects to Foucault's warning in "Nietzsche, Genealogy History" to separate *Ursrpung* (source in the metaphysical sense) from *Herkunft* (lineage, descent). In other words, a genealogy, no matter how well-documented, historically speaking, should not assume it is arriving at the origin of some belief, value, or practice. An important passage from Foucault's text to keep in mind is the following:

> We believe, in any event, that the body obeys the exclusive laws of physiology and that it escapes the influence of history, but this too is false. The body is molded by a great many distinct regimes; it is broken down by the rhythms of work, rest and holidays… "Effective" history differs from traditional history in being without constants. Nothing in man—not even his body—is sufficiently stable to serve as the basis for self-recognition or for the understanding of other men.[32]

The basic tenet of implexic genealogy embraces the '*Herkunft*' or the stock and descent of values rather than a desire to discover their ultimate source or '*Ursprung*.'

[32] Foucault, "Nietzsche, Genealogy, History", 153.

However, the novelty of my position is that our faculties, whether construed as virtues or limits, were not simply responses to the environment of our ancestors or are unknowable *simplicter* as Foucault suggests above but were amplified. In keeping with this approach, I demonstrate that Nietzsche's Internalization Hypothesis is accurate (when viewed under the right framework). I then elucidate how the Internalization Hypothesis informs Nietzsche's drive theory.

To be more precise, I argue that Nietzsche's philosophical psychology cannot be fully appreciated nor rendered coherent without putting pride of place on the story that Nietzsche provides for the origin of the housing of drives, as it were: the psyche. According to those who approach *the Genealogy* from a documentarian standpoint (see above), the purpose of sections 16–18 of GM II, is to provide a pre-historic account for the transformation of animal instincts into drives, which then are responsible for carving out human subjectivity. I think this is interpretation is a fatal mistake and occludes the real intention and profundity of this section. My view is that the Internalization Hypothesis is symbolic and best interpreted as a prism genealogists may use to discover other truths about historical phenomena. I then use this lens (along with two others), to propose a new understanding of what drives are, their role in Nietzsche's moral psychology, and their significance. The three lenses on offer are (1) the separation between the meaning of some bodily practice and, especially torture, from the mechanism used to administer said torture. I call this method the Separation Thesis. (2) The Rule of Conceptual Transformation; (3) GM II 16 the original Internalization Hypothesis. All three methods share a common trait: they demonstrate that practices tied directly to the body: torture, internment, diet, and hygiene are reinterpreted to new ends. Behind these practices are drives, but the 'drives' themselves become twisted and distorted by the very practices they help to motivate and steer.

These techniques, however, are ways of operationalizing a more basic hypothesis, namely, the will to power. There are many interpretations of will to power in the secondary literature: some are relatively robust, while others embrace minimalist and naturalistic analyses.[33] My starting point is section GM II: 12. In that section, Nietzsche introduces the principal schema for interpreting the *Genealogy*. He writes, "I emphasize this major point of historical method all the more because it is in fundamental opposition to the now prevalent instinct in taste which would rather be reconciled even to the absolute fortuitousness, even the mechanistic senselessness of all events than to the theory that in all event a will to power is operating." (GM II 12)

The prevalent instinct Nietzsche is chastising here is the idea that the environment alone determines the form an organism will take. He considers this supposition a "democratic tendency" because it entails that the entity is a passive plaything of its ecosystem. Nietzsche makes clear, however, that his approach to understanding life in all its many manifestations will emphasize activity, which he claims is the essence of life of itself. Neglecting the spontaneity of life is a grave mistake—so thinks Nietzsche. He notes:

> Thus the essence of life, its will to power, is ignored; one overlooks the essential priority of the spontaneous, aggressive, expansive form giving forces that give new interpretations and directions although "adaptation" follows only after this; the dominant role of the highest functionaries within the organism itself in which the will to life appears active and form-giving is denied. (GM II 12)

[33] There are many different interpretations of will to power in the secondary literature. I cannot explore all of them here. For metaphysical accounts of will to power, see Daniel Ahern, *Nietzsche as Cultural Physician*, (Pennsylvania: Pennsylvania University State Press), 1995. Linda Williams, *Nietzsche's Mirror, The World as Will to Power*, (Lexington MD: Rowman and Littlefield), 2000. Christopher Janaway and John Richardson argue for what I call minimalist interpretations of will to power. See Christopher Janaway *Beyond Selflessness: Reading Nietzsche's Genealogy* (Oxford University Press, 2007). See John Richardson *Nietzsche's New Darwinism*, (Oxford University Press), 2004 For linguistic/ pragmatic accounts see Christoph Cox, *Nietzsche, Naturalism and Interpretation*, (Berkeley California: University of California Press), 1999. For Pragmatic/Naturalist accounts see Brian Lightbody *Nietzsche's Will to Power Naturalized: Translating the Human into Nature and Nature into the Human* (Lanham Maryland: Lexington Books, 2017). Also see Brian Lightbody "Hermeneutics vs. Genealogy: Brandom's Cloak or Nietzsche's Quilt?" *The European Legacy*, Vol. 25. Issue 6, 2020, 635–652 Finally for a recent "transcendental" account see Tom Bailey "Will to Power: Nietzsche's Transcendental Idealism" *The Journal of Nietzsche Studies* (2021) 52 (2): 260–289. Bailey also provides a helpful summation of the naturalistic interpretations of will to power in the secondary literature (even though his interpretations of some of the positions are not entirely correct.)

This project will explain what I take to be Nietzsche's universal genealogical hypothesis, as expressed here. The shorthand for this hypothesis I will call will to power. Will to power is not, however, something that can be conceptualized; if it can be understood it at all it is only through its operation. Let me explain.

To concretize the above point, I now turn to Heidegger. As Heidegger correctly noted a half-century ago, Nietzsche's attempt to "permanentize" being *is* will to power. "Certainly, Nietzsche wants Becoming and what becomes, as the fundamental character of beings as a whole; but he wants what becomes precisely and before all else as what remains, as 'being' proper, being in the sense of the Greek thinkers."[34] Yet *pace* Heidegger Nietzsche is not the last metaphysician because will to power is not the word for "the Being of beings, as such the *essentia* of beings." As indicated in the introduction, will to power is dehiscent: it refers to the ever-churning movement of life itself, which may only be conceptualized, symbolically, once it becomes crystallized in a stable form. Yet to articulate will to power in this way is also to falsify it. The best way to understand will to power, then, is operationally. I argue that we get a better sense of its use through the methods that are extracted from it. These methods then serve to illustrate the dehiscent nature of will to power.

Section III: Implexic Genealogy Three Methods

Sections 12–13 of GM II are the focal point of this project. The methodological rule I extract from these sections can be reapplied to a genealogical investigation in general and to Nietzsche's genealogies in particular, over and over again. In those sections, Nietzsche famously divides punishment into two components: a stable element and a fluid element. As Nietzsche explains: "Second in accordance with the previously developed major point of historical method, it is assumed without further ado that the procedure itself will be something older, earlier than its employment in punishment, that the latter is projected and interpreted *into* the

[34] Martin Heidegger, *Nietzsche* 3 Volumes Trans. Joan Stambaugh, David Farrell Krell, and Frank A Capuzzi (San Francisco: Harper and Row, 1987), 156.

procedure which has long existed but been employed in another sense" (GM II 13). It is critical to keep these two components distinct, namely, in this specific case: (1) the procedures of punishment, and (2) its meaning, when performing an investigation. Indeed, there is not much disagreement regarding the passage's interpretation in the secondary literature, at least when viewed in the absence of a larger interpretative context.[35] The lesson to be learned, so Nietzsche evinces, is that the separation between bodily practices and their meaning can be reapplied to other examples.

Although the historiographical lesson is well-defined, a critical aspect is missing from the glosses of this passage in the scholarship. Section 13, at least as I read it, is Nietzsche's attempt to clarify and concretize a more *general* theory discussed in the preceding section concerning how one should investigate historical scholarship. It exemplifies a fundamental technique and lesson regarding genealogy itself. The connection between sections 12 and 13 is found in the first paragraph. Notice that in the above quote, Nietzsche begins by asserting "in accordance with the major point of historical method" The method Nietzsche is referring to stems from the section preceding it. In its most distilled form, that method argues that, "Purposes and utilities are only signs that a will to power has become master of something less powerful and imposed upon it the character of function" (GM II 12). Thus section 13, what I am referring to as the "Separation Thesis," is meant to *clarify* Nietzsche's universal genealogical hypothesis advanced in section 12. The correct understanding of the relationship between these two is that between theory and its application. Section 13, to put it bluntly, operationalizes will to power. More perspicuously stated, the Separation Thesis construes will to power negatively; when section 12 is viewed through the framework of the Separation Thesis, the reader is meant to understand that whatever function a thing once had becomes transformed into something altogether different.

Ciano Aydin in his "Nietzsche on Will to Power; an Organizationist-struggle Model" provides much needed clarity in fleshing out this view

[35] See Conway, Nietzsche *On the Genealogy of Morals*, 74–75 and Brian Lightbody "Twice Removed: Foucault's Critique of Nietzsche's Genealogical Method" Chapter 7 *Foucault and Nietzsche: A Critical Encounter*, Ed(s). Alan Rosenberg and Joseph Westfall, London: Bloomsbury, Press, 2018, 167–182, 169–170.

although, as I will duly note, there will be points of divergence between Aydin and my understanding of will to power. According to Aydin, will to power manifests itself in ground forms. "Ground forms," he writes, "are manifestations of 'will to power' organizations that are ordered in such a way that subduing other organizations is possible. These are incorporated because they have proven themselves to be 'means' that can preserve a certain kind of life, on the basis of which a 'will to power' organization can become stronger."[36] Ground forms, as Aydin explains, are hierarchical bundles of quanta-power that have been so organized as to produce structure in an ever-becoming multiplicity.[37]

A ground form of biological organization, for example such as, in the words of Nietzsche, the system in which organs are connected via "chains of nutrition" allows the organism to exercise greater domination in its environment, than, say, a single-celled amoeba. Ground forms are underwritten by power, while power perpetually engages in a gain of function strategy. The initial purpose or utility of the phenomenon being investigated is obliterated with the consequence that a new, more significant function, platformed as it must be by some organism, emerges to take its place. Once again, I turn to Aydin for further perspicuity.

> Furthermore, Nietzsche's concept of power implies that reality is dynamic in the strongest meaning of the word. Power, in Nietzsche's view, entails a directedness or causation without there being something (durable), a fixed cause, that can be separated from that directedness or causation; power is in its essence "something" that does not coincide with itself. It is an always-being-on-the-way. Additionally, this structure implies that power must be understood as a necessary striving for more power (see KSA 13:14[82]). Power is a necessary striving to expand itself. Power is only power insofar as it can maintain itself against other powers and strives to predominate over them.[38]

[36] Ciano Aydin, Nietzsche on Will to Power Towards and Organizationist -Struggle Model," *Journal of Nietzsche Studies*, 33:1, 2007 25–48, 39.

[37] Aydin, 41–42.

[38] Ciano Aydin, "Nietzsche on Will to Power Toward an Organization-Struggle Model" *Journal of Nietzsche Studies,* 33. 1 25–48, 2007, 26.

This framework that Aydin delineates here is well-supported when one turns to GM II 12. Consider what Nietzsche writes about the organic world "All events in the organic world (*organischen Welt*) are a subduing, a becoming master, and all subduing and becoming master involves a fresh interpretation, an adaptation through which any previous 'meaning' and 'purpose' are necessarily obscured or even obliterated ... Thus the essence of life (*Wesen des Lebens*), its will to power, is ignored; one overlooks the essential priority of the spontaneous, aggressive, expansive, form-giving forces (*Gestalatenden Kraft*) that give new interpretations and directions." (GM II 12)

Aydin provides a positive spin on the will to power in relating the idea to ground forms. In contrast, I emphasize and explain will to power negatively. Will to power is a reminder that all attempts to understand a thing or historical event in terms of its function or utility are destined to fail. The true purpose of the Separation Thesis, or so I hold, is to instrumentalize Nietzsche's will to power hypothesis by thinking of it in terms of refutation of function; the Separation Thesis clarifies the implexic understanding of the object I highlight as the essence of a genealogical investigation. Let me explain.

On the one hand, the means of torture from era to era remain relatively the same. There are only so many ways one might inflict pain on a body after all. However, the process, as a whole, is dynamic and cumulative: will to power continually seeks domination by employing the current function of a ground form to better harness and control multiplicity. For example, torturing bodies and connecting these procedures (e.g. burning someone alive at the stake) to a narrative like Christianity, alters the body undergoing punishment. The individual is not just a suppliant, begging for mercy, but a witch undergoing trial or a heretic who is receiving his just desserts. These new narratives not only justify ancient somatic practices but transform them, allowing for novel tactics to dominate bodies. Will to power is the singular red thread that weaves its way through whatever new narrational tapestry a dispositif (power/knowledge apparatus) produces. By reading section 13 as an operationalization of Nietzsche's refutation of function hypothesis, I hope to understand what Nietzsche is attempting to do and thus clarify what I mean by "implexic genealogy."

To flesh out this novel interpretation of section 13, I begin by examining the passage's meaning independently of section 12. Thus, starting with section 13, Nietzsche writes: "To return to our subject namely *punishment*, one must distinguish two aspects: on the one hand, that in which is relatively enduring, the custom, the act, the 'drama,' a certain strict sequence of procedures; on the other that in it which is *fluid*, the meaning the purpose the expectation associated with the performance of procedures." (GM II 13) The first aspect of punishment Nietzsche posits is the enduring part. It is the stable element; it is the practice stripped of any functionality, symbolism, or utility. Nietzsche provides several descriptors to capture what he means to convey: "It is the custom, the act, the 'drama'; a certain strict sequence of procedures…" Why does Nietzsche take such pains to explain what this first aspect is?

What Nietzsche is communicating here that we cannot get at what this aspect is *simplicter*. We may strip down the meaning of punishment, for example, to examine how a regime of force or *dispositif* to use Foucault's parlance, disciplines the body, but even here we cannot be sure that it is the body that is targeted. "Today it is impossible to say for certain why people are really punished: all concepts in which an entire process is semiotically concentrated elude definition; only that which has no history is definable… The form is fluid, the meaning even more so." (GM II 13) In reading the Separation Thesis in light of the reduction of function thesis, I will demonstrate that the standard analysis of section GM II: 16, which I will examine in more detail below, is just another projection of purpose onto the process of will to power. A deeper reading can be rendered.

The other aspect is the fluid element; it is projected onto the older component. It changes, Nietzsche suggests, depending on the culture that views the procedures. Let me explain. Again, Nietzsche provides a multitude of descriptions to capture how we may untangle the threads of a seemingly singular phenomenon (e.g. punishment) such that a genealogy of these individual threads reveals how these strands came together and therefore how they can come apart. For example, a historian looking at the ancient Roman punishment of "cutting shares" might conclude that the punishment is meant to deter; debtors who take on loans with no intention or means of repaying will have a pound of flesh removed to cover the debt.[39] That is one possible meaning for the Roman practice. But Nietzsche says there could be another interpretation. Indeed, in GM II 13, Nietzsche provides no less than 9 different interpretations of 'punishment.'[40]

Nietzsche then concretizes the need to separate meaning from the action by providing an extensive commentary on Roman punishment. The purpose, in part, is to ensure that the reader moves past the feelings of empathy she has for the debtor. Such feelings of empathy are dangerous for two reasons. First, they obscure truth. They prevent us from recognizing the terrible and cruel reality of our pre-history. This impediment to grasping a deeper genealogical connection between skeins of practices is well-put by Christopher Janaway. He notes that cognition is often entangled with affect. Janaway then concludes that the primary purpose of genealogy is to work through our inherited emotions. As he explains:

> More precisely, in order to grasp the real history of our values we require, then, some process that dissolves or explodes our apparently unified present-day concepts into their more primitive psychological components. Because our moral concepts are post facto rationalizations of inherited affects, to whose explanatory role we may be blind, our feelings for and against need to be aroused and questioned, if we are to grasp the variegated psychological truth behind our concepts.[41]

Second, and most importantly, our inherited values keep us from experiencing those uncomfortable feelings, which will help us arrive at greater truths. Distressing emotions are challenging to work through for two reasons: (1) we have been trained to think the affects have no epistemic role to play vis-a-vis conducting a philosophical investigation. (2) Because they are painful, we are averse to analyzing them. However, it is only in recognizing such painful truths about our history, so Nietzsche argues, that allows us to incorporate that other aspect of genealogy, namely, the curative component.

---

[39] Nietzsche examines this specific Roman practice as drawn from the Twelve Tables Rome in GM II: 5.

[40] The list can be found at the conclusion of GM II 13.

[41] Janaway, "Naturalism and Genealogy", 349.

To concretize Janaway's interpretation, consider thinking through and, critically, "feeling through" what Nietzsche takes to be the Roman need for the Twelve Tables. Nietzsche writes:

> Let us be clear as to the logic of this form of compensation: it is strange enough. An equivalence is provided by the creditor's receiving, in place of a literal compensation for an injury (thus in the place of money, land, possessions of any kind), a recompense in the form of a kind of pleasure---the pleasure of being allowed to vent his power freely upon one who is powerless, the voluptuous pleasure "*de faire le mal pour le plaisir de faire*" (Of doing evil for the pleasure of doing it), the enjoyment of violation. (Nietzsche's Italics) (GM II: 7)

According to Nietzsche, the enjoyment the creditor receives from violating the body of the one indebted to him is more than just a repayment of the original debt. It is a return to "the right of the masters … a warrant for and title to cruelty." (GM II 7) This equation of gaining power = pleasure= making another suffer = repayment of funds, property, goods, and so on, may again sound strange to modern ears, but Nietzsche shows that it has its own logic. We may make sense of this logic by returning to the Twelve Tables of Rome. A common interpretation of the Twelve Tables is that it was a strategy the Plebs could use to guarantee that their recent struggle with the Patrician class for greater rights and privileges would be codified to be preserved and retained. However, under Nietzsche's interpretation, the Twelve Tables is shot through with at least two different power investments. It serves to mark the rise of the Plebians, but it also entrenches the power of the Patricians by providing the noble classes of Rome the right to treat those in their debt (most likely the plebs) in whatever manner they so desired.[42] Thus, the *Twelve Tables* is an historical emergent representative of the agonic nature of power. It is a concretization of the general method of refutation of function. It is a reminder that no matter how transparent a historical document's purpose appears to be it is always polysemous and perspectival: the goals of a

[42] *The Cambridge Ancient History Volume VII: The Hellenestic Monarchies and the Rise of Rome* (Ed. S.A. Cook, E.E. cock, and M.P. Charlesworth (Cambridge: University of Cambridge Press, 1954), 456–467.

document are indexicals. They only have meaning through the perspective in which they are viewed.

What is clear is that The Twelve Tables marks a clear power struggle between two groups in history that may be interpreted differently according to one's perspective and embodiment. The document demonstrates that power is fluid—historical documents are shot through with conflicting agendas and interpretations.

To summarize, Nietzsche presses into service the Separation Thesis initially as a warning to his readers: avoid thinking that the purpose of punishment is directly connected to the origin of its procedures. In other words, we should avoid taking up the viewpoint that entails thinking that the utility of punishment, like correction or deterrence, is the reason for the torture that befalls a body. This is a mistake, epistemically speaking. Nietzsche is suggesting that ancient peoples would not draw this conclusion.

The above interpretation of GM II 13 is one that is widely endorsed in the secondary literature. Brian Leiter in *Nietzsche on Morality* suggests: "The genealogy is not only a history of morality that rejects the evidential value of morality's present meaning for discovering its origin, but it is also a distinctively naturalistic history, an account of the origins of morality without appeal to supernatural causes."[43] Daniel Conway also claims that the Separation Thesis attempts to reduce the emergence of punishment itself to a more natural explanation: "As we shall see, Nietzsche hypothesizes that punishment originated in a particular expression of spontaneous, form-giving animal aggression, which he attributes to 'artists' who were indifferent and perhaps oblivious to the victims of their aggression."[44]

Conway comes closest to getting at the point I am making. On the first point, Nietzsche is suggesting that we should not take at face value what the representatives of a culture say about a particular practice. One interpretation of the passage is in an epistemic key. The distinction between the means of punishment and its meaning highlights the

[43] Brian Leiter, *Nietzsche on Morality*, London: Routledge, 2002, 172.

[44] Daniel Conway, *Nietzsche's on the Genealogy of Morals A Reader's Guide* (Lanham Maryland Rowan and Littlefield, 2008), 74–75.

importance of practices that orbit the body because it is the somatic and not the semantic, which provides the external or non-doxastic link between different historical regimes. An external link between time periods is required because a genealogist needs clear (vertical) lines of descent in order to trace a practice from era to era. After all, if the genealogist contends that concepts are completely fluid in that the particular culture assigns them a specific meaning, then tracing a concept's history will not provide us with the stability required for a genealogical investigation. For this reason, the body serves as the primary document for any genealogical inquiry.[45]

The above interpretation of the method of separation, I hope, is uncontroversial. However, it is when we examine the thesis as an operationalization of will to power that informs and reorients this interpretation. It is in viewing the Separation Thesis in a methodological key that is new. When viewed from the refutation of function framework, which I argue is the core notion of will to power as displayed in GM II 12, the Separation Thesis is reflexive: it demonstrates that purpose, meaning, design, form, and so on, is *always* projected onto some object. Thus, we must not assume that we have uncovered the genuine function of the practice itself when distinguishing the meaning of some event from its drama. (GM II 13) The actual purpose is elusive. We can only interpret some action in terms of its *signs* and forms.

Foucault remains, arguably, the most insightful commentator in this regard. His interpretation of The Genealogy is instructive, especially when one turns to analyze the material that makes the very tracing of past punishments possible: the body. The body Foucault tells us is, "the inscribed surface of events (traced by language and dissolved by ideas), the locus of a dissociated self adopting an illusion of substantial unity and

[45] Foucault is perhaps the best interpreter of this method. He writes *in Nietzsche Genealogy History* that "Descent (*Enstehung*) attaches itself to the body. It inscribes itself in the nervous system, in temperament in the digestive apparatus." (147) And further in *Discipline and Punish*: "Try to discover whether this entry of the soul on to the scene of penal justice, and with it the intention in legal practice of a whole corpus of 'scientific' knowledge, is not the effect of a transformation of the way in which the body is invested by power relations (28)) For more information regarding the need for this non-doxastic element in genealogy. See Brian Lightbody *Philosophical Genealogy: An Epistemological Reconstruction of Nietzsche and Foucault's Genealogical Method Volume 1 and 2.* (New York, Peter Lang), 2010 and 2011.

a volume in perpetual disintegration."[46] Systems of power score the body attempting to mark and thereby track its productive pathways:

> The body is … directly involved in a political field; power relations have an immediate hold upon it; they invest, mark it, train it, torture it … This political investment of the body is bound up, in accordance with complex reciprocal relations with its economic use; it is largely as a force of production that the body is invested with relations of power and domination; but, on the other hand, its constitution as labor power is possible only if it is caught up in a system of subjection … [T]he body becomes a useful force only if it is both a productive body and a subjected body.[47]

Foucault in *Discipline and Punish* puts the Separation Thesis to work by demonstrating that the penitentiary was never about penance *per se*; the criminal's soul was never the true target of power. Instead, it was always about reformatting the body. As Foucault provocatively put it, "the soul is the prison of the body."[48]

However, notice that even here, in Foucault's most quoted perfect encapsulation of his genealogy of the prison, the meaning of punishment remains; it is the singular body that is punished. Even Foucault cannot escape assigning meaning to the mechanics of torture, as it were. Foucault coaxes his readers to reframe what power/knowledge targets, but in tracing the lines of descent that comprise our present carceral regime, he may only assign them function by giving them form. The individual's labor (and reproductive energies) and not his soul are reconditioned and harnessed by bio-power.

Implexic genealogy argues that such a predicament is ineluctable: vertical lines of inheritance become comprehensible only when they are woven into a narrative. Indeed, as I demonstrate in Chap. 4, Foucault is in good company: many scholars in the secondary literature are guilty of conflating the nine Germanic punishments Nietzsche lists in GM II 5 as analogs for pre-civilized forms of torture. In that section, Nietzsche seems to hypothesize that the origin of the "bad conscience" was the

[46] Foucault, *Nietzsche, Genealogy, History*, 83.

[47] Foucault, *Discipline and Punish*, 25–26.

[48] Foucault, *Discipline and Punish*, 30.

consequence of two mechanisms: torture and internment. The standard view stipulates that the half-animal half-human creatures had the first laws of civilization (its "thou shalt nots") burnt into them via the horrendous brutal methods of punishment in what we might call today the Neolithic period. One of the issues with this explanation is epistemic; it presupposes a Lamarckian mechanism, but Nietzsche's story also violates the very rule of separation, or so it would appear. The assumption is that warrior artists inflict punishment on a body, an individual whole, an organism. Thus whether one tortures a human or (semi-animal), we take this as a *sign* that it is the organism in each case that suffers. My interpretation of this passage, which I will present in detail in Chap. 4, argues that torture, at least initially, is not a means of punishment but of culling—it excludes those traits which are not desirable. They are neither consciously nor unconsciously selected for.

Thus, a different account of GM II 5 and its complementary passage GM II 16 emerges by interpreting the Separation Thesis as a methodological principle instead of an epistemic one. On that note, I now turn to GM II 16.

Method II: Nietzsche's InternalizationHypothesis

On the surface, Nietzsche provides a rich and profound account regarding the origins of memory, conscience, and agency in sections 1–18 of GM II. But Nietzsche's conclusions have loftier ambitions; they extend further, becoming incredibly significant regarding his overall philosophy of psychology. Nietzsche's genealogical investigations serve as a springboard for, and foundation of, important moral and psychic truths that represent Nietzsche's psychology. Indeed, these explorations regarding the primal unconscious of future humans may be distilled to a fundamental psychological principle that, seemingly, applies to the entire scope of past, present, and future human behavior. That principle is the Internalization Hypothesis. This eventual lodestone for Nietzsche's philosophy of action is best expressed in GM II, 16:

> All instincts that do not discharge themselves outwardly (*Aussen*) turn inward—this is what I call the internalization (*Verinnerlichung*) of man: thus it was that man first developed what was later called his "soul." (*Seele*) The entire inner world, originally as thin as if it were stretched between two membranes, expanded and extended itself, acquired depth, (*Tiefe*) breadth, (*Breite*) and height (*Höhe*), in the same measure as outward discharge, was inhibited.

The Internalization Hypothesis becomes a powerful explanatory tool when it is connected to Nietzsche's drive theory, a veritable cottage industry in the secondary literature. The basic tenets of this theory hold that primordial drives like sex and violence always take targets for their expression. As Peter Poellner puts it, "Nietzsche ultimately treats drives not as attributes of agents (like desires) but as agents themselves."[49] Drives, moreover, that are not always expressed in terms of their original objectives (e.g. sex) will find some other avenue for their successful manifestation. Thus, drives that do not find outward expression turn inward, leading to new dispositions and, according to some scholars, new emotions. John Richardson states the nature of drives well when he writes, "A drive is a plastic disposition … inasmuch it tends to produce different behaviors in different circumstances, in such a way that the same outcome is reached, by different routes, in all of them … Such plasticity depends on a capacity to 'respond' to circumstances … in some minimal way."[50]

As expressed in many of his works (See *Human and all Too Human*, I. 32, *Daybreak* 119, GM III: 24) Nietzsche's drive theory is well-complemented with a rich, mature, and profound articulation of the theory in the secondary literature. Chapter 3 investigates several interpretations of Nietzsche's theory of drives in the scholarship. Although there are dozens of different articulations of the theory in the literature, one common thread runs through these frameworks: drives motivate behaviors and take an object as the drive's target. They are, then, the bedrock for Nietzsche's system of values and psychology. Nietzsche intends his

---

[49] Peter Poellner, *Nietzsche and Metaphysics*, (New York: Oxford University Press), 1995, 174.

[50] John Richardson, Nietzsche's New Darwinism, (New York: Oxford University Press), 2004, 75.

drive theory not only to explain our initial evaluations as to why some objects should be pursued or avoided but indeed to explain the reflective value judgments we come to have on said evaluations. As Paul Katsafanas summarizes its role, the drive is, "Nietzsche's principle explanatory token within psychology."[51]

Yet, given the apparent importance of Nietzsche's drive theory to his ethics and psychology, it is perplexing that scholars have not focused on challenging the very historical foundation for the idea itself, which is I.H. In order to fully capture Nietzsche's theory of drives, it is critical to examine the role the I.H. plays in this regard—an examination to which I now turn.

The I.H. performs two functions in Nietzsche's theory of mind. First, it explains how human beings acquired a bad conscience and later a more fully developed sense of agency and moral being. The standard reading of GM II 16, which I will detail in Chap. 4, holds that the creation of the soul or agency was a consequence of the internalization of instinctual animal drives. The I.H., therefore, plays a grounding role in naturalizing the process of transformation from that of our animal ancestors to the contemporary, rational, and free agents we assume ourselves to be today. Second, Nietzsche's explanation is biological or, indeed, zoological in that it purports to show how we were transformed into a different species than we once were.

However, the theory also plays a different psychological role than the one noted above; it attempts to explain the reasons agents use to explain/rationalize their behavior. For example, it underpins Nietzsche's development of slave versus noble values as described in the *Genealogy's* first essay. Also, it plays a significant explanatory role concerning Nietzsche's account of what he diagnosed as the substantial sickness in the current age, nihilism. In this latter role, the Internalization Hypothesis attempts to reduce matters of what Kant would call *quid Juris* (or justification concerning one's reasons) to a mere *quid facti* or etiological approach. I submit that the Internalization Hypothesis is the lynchpin connecting Nietzsche's reductionist biological naturalism with his philosophy of psychology.

---

[51] Paul Katsafanas, *The Nietzschean Self: Moral Psychology, Agency and the Unconscious*, Oxford University Press, 2016, 74.

In broad brushstrokes, Nietzsche argues that moral psychology is either directly reducible to primal drives or instincts (e.g. sex, violence) or is indirectly answerable to the historical transformations (e.g. ressentiment) thereof. Drive theory is well-complemented with a fecund, profound, and lucid exposition of the concept in the secondary literature.

Yet, there remains a glaring lacuna for all the discussion of drive theory in the scholarship. The secondary literature is delinquent; it fails to explain how these same drives became housed in their present container (i.e. the psyche). As I demonstrate, there is a gap in the research surrounding the formulation and genesis of this psychical 'housing.' Scholars have placed emphasis on articulating what drives are in themselves independently of their enclosing, (i.e. the Internalization Hypothesis). This is wrong. Using Nietzsche's analogy, understanding how drives were digested is essential in understating the function of a drive and what or whom it targets and further explains the process of psychical integration. Any commentary that examines drives without placing pride of place on the Internalization hypothesis, or so I argue, cannot offer a fulsome explanation of drive theory.

With the above in mind, it is vital to carefully examine how internalization works and how to secure the foundation for this hypothesis. My argument is that the true meaning of I.H is revealed only when one reads it through the lens of the Separation Thesis. Chapter 4 provides a more in-depth reading of GM: II 3 than that typically offered in the secondary literature to demonstrate the epistemic obstacles that underpin a traditional reading of I.H in GM II: 16, namely, its seeming reliance on the false scientific theory of Lamarck's. More importantly, I demonstrate that the process of internalization is just another sign—it is symbolic and therefore capable of further dissection. This interpretation is not only consistent with the full application of the Separation Thesis but is supported by Nietzsche himself: "In general, the word drive is only a convenience and will be used everywhere that regular effects in organisms are still not reducible to chemical and mechanical laws." [KSA 8 23 1876–1877]. In other words, drives do not become internalized because drives do not exist—drives, too, are simply a symbolic struggle between two modules of mind: the cognitive and the affective. Drives are implexes: they are simply the name given to the intersection of biological and cognitive processes. A drive is an interpretation of our psychological make-up.

My analysis will demonstrate that the mystery surrounding internalization, at least in terms of the core biological component of Nietzsche's drive theory, is resolved because it dissolves into a more stable process: genetic inheritance and affective trauma. I solve the puzzle concerning how values, emotions, and rational thinking become 'housed' in a psyche by employing Foucault's term of subjectivization. Foucault defines subjectivization as "the procedure by which one obtains the constitution of a subject or more precisely of a subjectivity which of course is only one of the given possibilities of organization of self-consciousness"[52] My assertion holds that contemporary subjectivizing processes are the result of the intersection of two vectors: cognitive and affective.[53] This argument will be carefully unfolded in Chaps. 3, 5, and 6.

Rule 3: The Rule of Conceptual Transformation

I argue that the Rule of Conceptual Transformation is another reiteration of the Separation Thesis. Unlike the other methods in the *Genealogy*, it is clearly articulated by Nietzsche: "A concept denoting political superiority always resolves itself into a concept denoting superiority of soul" (GM I 6) This phrase is referred to as the rule of conceptual transformation in the secondary literature.[54] (This rule, however, is initially just an hypothesis that must be operationalized to be employed, so the spirit of my book argues. It is, in this vein, that we should interpret Nietzsche's fundamental insight (*Wessenlich ensicht*): his reliance on the etymological roots of evaluative words). As Nietzsche puts this insight: "The signpost to the right (*Rechten*) road was for me the question: what was the real etymological significance of the designations for 'good' coined in the various languages?" (Nietzsche's emphasis). (GM I 4) Nietzsche's great discovery

[52] Michel Foucault, The Return of Morality", L. Kritzman (Ed.) *Michel Foucault-politics, philosophy, culture: interviews and other writings* 1977–1984 L. Kritzman Ed (London, Routledge), 242–254.
[53] Michel Foucault "The Return of Morality", 253.
[54] Conway, *Nietzsche's Genealogy of Morality a Reader's Guide*, 34–35.

is in connecting etymological evidence and the past's entanglement of evaluative and descriptive terms. The standard interpretation of this rule argues that etymological evidence allows him to move beyond our preconceived liberal sensibilities when viewing the past to reveal how ancient peoples thought of themselves.[55] In keeping with the Separation Thesis, however, I argue that Nietzsche's true purpose is to demonstrate that terms used to designate superiority of spirit (e.g. goodness, noble soul, purity) or pejoratives that denote the opposite (e.g. impurity, evil, etc.) are meanings that come later in history. Moral interpretation is a conceptual transformation of a descriptive term, but the descriptive word, so transformed, was initially underwritten on a somatic platform.

There are at least two ways Nietzsche recommends using this insight. (1) Genealogists should look at commonalities between words. GM: II 8–12 provides a paradigm case, which I will treat in more detail immediately below. (2) Genealogists should examine the variegated ways evaluative terms are used. The paradigm case for this method may be found in sections 3–8 of the first essay. I will turn to outlining the first method before treating the second.

In GM: II 8–12, Nietzsche signals to his audience that when highly charged evaluative and psychological affect words such as guilt, (*Schuld*), are closely related to terms that offer bare descriptions like debt *Schulden (debt)* the resemblance is significant. It is not a mere coincidence. In utilizing the Separation Thesis—which comes just after this section, and one may suggest the discussion regarding the close etymological relationship between *Schuld* and *Schulden* is a distillation of the method itself—Nietzsche proceeds to uncover the origin of guilt. The upshot of this inquiry is summarized in section GM I 10: "To return to our investigation: the feeling of guilt or personal obligation, had its origin, as we saw, in the oldest and most primitive personal relationship, that between buyer and seller, creditor and debtor" There is something essential to notice with this summation. Notice that Nietzsche claims that it isn't just *the term* that has its origin in an older practice but *the feeling* itself. Guilt, as a feeling, is a transformation of some older affect. It is also, and this is critical, internalized. It is this process of internalization that is at issue

[55] See Simon May *Nietzsche's Ethics and his War On Morality*, Oxford Clarendon Press, 1999 51.

here. The etymological evidence, returning to the refutation of function hypothesis, is simply a sign of a will to power that underlies the historical process of this transformation. In these sections, Nietzsche demonstrates how feelings associated with our most profound sense of agency, like guilt, are produced via a mechanical non-psychological process; the infrastructure of guilt is simply the recording of debits and credits and the means to enforce them. Thus the Rule of Conceptual Transformation is just another manifestation of the Separation Thesis.

The reading above which reduces guilt to debt is non-tendentious. I now return to GM I sections 5–7, where I will demonstrate that Nietzsche employs the same method, namely, the Separation Thesis, to analyze the origins of knightly or priestly aristocracies. It is this application that is novel. Let me explain.

My argument is that signs of internalization are symbolic and therefore betray an older relation of power. The Separation Thesis tasks genealogists with discovering the older, more stable infrastructure subtending the practice being analyzed. Therefore, any investigation that rests on the symbolic is premature, or so my Foucauldian-inspired reading of the *Genealogy* holds. For instance, Conway's interpretation of the above sections is a clear example of curtailing the genealogical investigation prematurely. He writes:

> He (Nietzsche) detects a parallel development with respect to the transformation of concepts denoting low social standing e.g. common plebeian into concepts denoting a vulgar or base moral condition e.g. bad he thus concludes that the origins of the moral designations under investigation can and should be traced to the pre moral I.E. social and political designations from which they are derived.[56]

Turning to Owen, in his *Nietzsche's Genealogy of Morality*, it is clear he agrees. He notes:

> The first step in this account hangs on the combination of a historical assumption and a psychological claim the historical assumption is that a

[56] Conway, *Nietzsche On Genealogy of Morals: A Reader's Guide*, 31.

> post tribal political community for Nietzsche a state is characterized by a political hierarchy and order of rank which differentiates at least between nobles and slaves. The psychological claim is the rule that the political concept of rank always transforms itself into a spiritual concept of rank. Nietzsche's thought is that the nobles as the highest political rank are characterized by the pathos of nobility and distance the enduring dominating and fundamental feeling of a higher ruling kind in relation to a lower kind to below a path that is unreflectively internalized as a feeling of spiritual IE ethical superiority and expressed as the valuing of what the nobility identify as their own typical character traits.[57]

These analyses are not inaccurate *per se*, provided they remain in their proper scope. The scope, in this case, would be either psychological agency, which for Nietzsche, at minimum, is an internalization of affect and drive a la Owen, or social designation for Conway. I argue that there is another way to employ the rule of conceptual transformation. We can trace the groundwork stabilizing either internalization or social role as the case may be, to an even older, more visceral setting.

There is support for the above interpretation. In the second paragraph of section 5, Nietzsche discusses a feeling of ethical superiority the nobles have over, what will be their rivals, the common. This feeling, as Nietzsche demonstrates, is an accurate depiction of the ancient Greek psyche of 600 BCE. Nietzsche draws on Theognis, which supports Owen's and Conway's contention:

> They call themselves for instance the "truthful" this is so above all of the Greek nobility whose mouthpiece is the Megarian poet Theognis. The root of the word coined for this *esthlos*, signifies one who is, who possesses reality who is actual who is true; then, with a subjective turn, the true as the truthful: in this phase of conceptual transformation it becomes a slogan and catchword for the nobility and passes over entirely into the sense of noble as distinct from the lying common man. (GM I 5)

[57] David Owen, *Nietzsche's Genealogy of Morality*, (Montreal: McGill-Queen's University Press, 2007, 77.

Furthermore, Kaufmann's commentary on this passage is instructive and provides additional backing to Nietzsche's analysis. He borrows from Gerald Else's *Aristotle's Poetics: The Argument.* In regard to Theognis Else writes:

> Greek thinking begins with and for a long time holds to the proposition that mankind is divided into 'good' and 'bad', and these terms are quite as much social, political, and economic as they are moral… The dichotomy is absolute and exclusive for a simple reason: it began as the aristocrats' view of society and reflects their idea of the gulf between themselves and the 'others.' In the minds of a comparatively small and close-knit group like the Greek aristocracy there are only two kinds of people, 'we' and 'they'; and of course 'we' are the good people, the proper, decent, good-looking, right thinking ones, while 'they' are the rascals, the poltroons, the good for nothings[58]

On the surface, Nietzsche's use of Theognis and the subsequent commentary buttresses the interpretation above.

But there is something else to notice in Else's commentary. Observe that "good-looking," "proper," and "right-thinking" are synonymous terms for nobility, at least according to Theognis. Where we, as modern readers, might see a tension with these concepts, the nobles of Theognis's day see them as inseparable. Indeed, the very fact that these distinct concepts are intermingled in the same word, "*Esthlos*" indicates a refinement of cognitive thinking, that the Greeks did not have, or so Nietzsche thinks. But more critically, it points to the second way Nietzsche utilized his etymological method. Let me explain.

For the implexic genealogist, then, the traditional analyses of this section are limited. I argue that Nietzsche provides a richer analysis of these claims. Therefore, and in keeping with the significance I attribute to the Separation Thesis, a more precise interpretation can be gleaned, clearly distinguishing the stable element from that which is more fluid. Nietzsche employs the Rule of Conceptual Transformation to reveal that there is a

[58] Gerald Else *Aristotle's Poetices: The Argument*, (Cambridge Mass, Harvard University Press, 1957) 75.

somatic platform to these moral designations, such as good, evil, and the like, just as he did with guilt.

Nietzsche's analysis begins by operationalizing his conceptual rule of transformation, etymologically, just as he did in GM II. What he discovers is that in tracing the etymological roots of the Latin *Bonus* (good) reveals, rather ironically, that contemporary notions of goodness are corrupt: goodness was initially used as a descriptor to mark out high-status or character (two ways one might interpret social or political standing and even earlier, the man, or more precisely put, "body of action"). Near the end of section GM, I 5, Nietzsche provides a genealogical account that goes well beyond an internalized understanding of some word. Nietzsche writes, "I believe I may venture to interpret the Latin *bonus* as the warrior provided, I am right in tracing *bonus* back to an earlier *duonus* (compare bellum=duellum=deun-lum, which seems to me to contain *duonus*). Therefore bonus as the man of strife, of dissension (duo) as the man of war" (GM I 5) Notice that Nietzsche's warrior is not just a person with a political designation but a somatic description; warriors—those defined by their physical attributes and abilities—were deemed *duonus*.[59] This reading is not to discount what Conway, Owen and others argue, namely, that political and social designations resolve themselves into spiritual designations. That is a correct reading, but rather that one can extend the analysis, historically speaking, such that what Nietzsche means by "political superiority" can be further separated into a fluid and stable element.

Moreover, this reading is further supported when we turn to examining two different kinds of primordial aristocracies: noble and priestly. In the former Nietzsche notes that "in the majority of cases, they designate themselves simply by their superiority in power (as 'the powerful', 'the masters', 'the commanders') or by the most clearly visible signs of this superiority as 'the rich', as 'the possessors'" (GM I 5). Notice that what is more basic, conceptually, for noble designation is not social or political standing. Nor is it the feeling of superiority *per se*—all these notions

[59] Nietzsche's etymological method of tracing is similar to the argument advanced by the Roman writer Varro in his *On The Latin Language Varro: De Lingua Latina.* With an English translation by Roland G. Kent. Two volumes. Pp. 1+676. (Loeb Classical Library.) London: Heinemann, 1938.

come later, indeed much later—but rather capacity in the raw. Nietzsche offers a genealogical analysis that goes beyond internalization writ large. What comes first, both temporally and ontologically are the bodily signs that one is powerful; one is muscular, commanding, and capable of battle, of killing or, in the second way of treating the term, one has the valuable things in a community (livestock, slaves) and these objects circle the body.

Further proof for Nietzsche's stance can be gleaned from analyzing the Old English word, caitiff (coward or wretch). In Shakespeare's *Measure for Measure Act II Scene 1*, for example, Elbow says to Escalus, "O thou caitiff! O thou varlet! O thou wicked Hannibal!" Shakespeare uses the term as a moral designation and a pejorative one at that! But what's critical to notice about this word is that it is an internalized feeling. However, the origin of the word denotes something more straightforward—it is derived from the Latin for captive (*captivus*)—a designation that orbits the body. So once again, the etymological evidence points to a process that Nietzsche is at pains to figure out: how did a distinct, subjectively felt mental state originate from a social, external, and more primitive bodily designation?

As previously mentioned, however, this isn't the only way Nietzsche employs his fundamental insight. This leads to the second way of interpreting the etymological evidence. It was something that was hinted at before. What Nietzsche asks his readers to notice this time, are not the etymological commonalities between evaluative concepts and descriptive terms (as he did with *Schuld* and *Schulden* or *Bellum* and *duellem*), but to pay attention to the variegated meanings the same word might have. Put another way, the longer words are removed from the somatic platform that grounds them, the less literal, more symbolic and metaphorical they become. Recall what Else mentioned earlier; the qualitative descriptors like "good-looking," "proper" and "right thinking" are all concepts contained in "*Esthlos*." Mark Migotti in his majestic "Slave Morality, Socrates and the Bushmen" explains how this second method of interpreting etymological evidence works and lends support, indirectly, to my argument. He elaborates that the purpose of Nietzsche's employment of etymology is to uncover multi-layered meanings surrounding terms like 'nobility', 'common', 'good' and the like. Such strong evaluative words are shot through with ambiguity. This ambiguity demonstrates, according to Migotti, the ancestral remnants of, what were once primitive noble ideas that become exapted once the slave-revolt in morality takes hold.[60] To concretize his investigation, Migotti examines the multifarious meanings of nobility. He lists no less than 14 definitions of the term according to the O.E.D. and notices that, conceptually, there is no clear connection, notionally speaking, between the second definition of nobility ("of illustrious rank or birth") and the fourth ("having high moral qualities or ideals"). The question Nietzsche is asking, so Migotti thinks, is: What connects these disparate definitions? Let us now take a look at several possible answers.

The first solution to this problem is a Socratean approach. However, a Socratic investigation that connects the above two is a non-starter: one cannot provide an answer to the Elenchusly formatted question: "What is nobility?" A generic answer that would satisfy these two very different definitions is not in the offing. One has to take a different approach, a genealogical approach. As Migotti puts it: "According to the slave revolt hypothesis, these ambiguities as what the English anthropologist E. B. Taylor calls "survivals": remnants of a time before good and evil…What today might seem a grossly tendentious *yoking* of disparate senses was once, according to Nietzsche, a perfectly natural conceptual mixture."[61]

Unlike Owen and Conway, Migotti suggests that Nietzsche traces noble virtues to an earlier, more naturalistic setting: "The early nobles are too intellectually primitive to be able to defend, or even articulate, their sense that their several virtues naturally belong together, and it is just this incapacity that will render their world vulnerable to the corrosive influence of slave morality."[62] This analysis goes deeper, than the interpretations put forward by Conway, Owen and others. Notice that social

---

[60] Mark Migotti, "Slave Morality, Socrates, and the Bushmen: A Critical Introduction to On the Genealogy of Morality, Essay 1" in *Nietzsche's On the Genealogy of Morals, Critical Essays* Ed.d Christa Davis Acampore, Lanham Maryland: Rowman and Littlefield, Press, 2006, 109–129, 118.

[61] Migotti, "Slave Morality, Socrates and the Bushmen," 118.

[62] Mark Migotti, "Slave Morality, Socrates, and the Bushmen: A Reading of the First Essay of On the Genealogy of Moral", *Philosophy and Phenomenological Research* Vol. 58, No. 4 (Dec., 1998), pp. 745–779 751.

hierarchy is not predicated on an internalized mutually reflexive understanding of what it means to be a noble, as Owen in particular emphasizes. The nobles of the early knightly aristocracies pre-600 BCE, remain a community even if the notion of a "we," a *Gemeinschaftsgefuele* or "community feeling," is absent. Evidence for this conclusion is found in the section where Nietzsche intimates that the powerful physicality of the warrior class is in harmony with their, "crude, coarse, external, narrow, straightforward, altogether unsymbolical" psychology. (GM I 6). Furthermore, in section 7, Nietzsche claims that "The knightly-Aristocratic value judgments presupposed a powerful physicality a flourishing abundant even overflowing health together with that which serves to preserve it: war, adventure, hunting, dancing war games and in general all that involves vigorous, free joyful activity." (GM I 7)

I submit that what Nietzsche is demonstrating is a very slow transformation of what the nobility designates. In keeping with the operationalization of the reduction of function hypothesis (will to power), namely, the Separation Thesis, Nietzsche is carefully decoupling the idea of nobility from its standard narrative. The contemporary understanding of what it means to be noble is completely subjectivized, or so Nietzsche thinks. A noble soul, is a Christian soul, it denotes one who is truthful, God fearing, loving, and so on. But an earlier manifestation of the concept of nobility denotes those who possess truth, that is, reality. Nietzsche musters Theognis as proof to unearth a lower stratum as it were of the noble transformation.

However, there is also reason to think that Nietzsche is asking us to envision an even earlier period, what we may call a proto-knightly aristocratic rule. Perhaps the first possessions of this proto-noble group would be livestock, tools, slaves, and so on. But notice that here, too, the idea of possession is rather sophisticated which belies an even earlier understanding of nobility, a speculative UR- nobility which presents will to power in its almost naked form: noble designation, in pre-historic warrior aristocracies at least, starts with the bodies that are thought to be powerful.

This reading is supported when we turn to Nietzsche's summation of the rule. He states at the beginning of section 6: "To this rule that a concept denoting political superiority always resolves itself into a concept denoting superiority of soul it is not necessarily an exception (although it provides occasions for exceptions) when the highest caste is at the same time the priestly caste" (GM I 6) Nietzsche then proceeds to elucidate that, "All concepts of ancient man were rather at first incredibly uncouth, coarse, external, narrow, straightforward, and altogether *unsymbolical* in meaning to a degree that we can scarcely conceive." (GM I 6) Turning to the priestly type of aristocracy, Nietzsche there explores the conceptual distinction between "pure" and "impure" ideas. These moral designations do not refer to notions like "soul" for ancient peoples because these concepts, being more abstract and complex, arrive later on the scene or so the Separation Thesis tells us. Indeed even "character" or perhaps the more primitive "social standing" (e.g. chief, shaman, warrior, etc.) as social designations are still too fluid; they are still too shot through with a society's self-assessment. They are not in keeping with the lesson of GM: II 12: they are too symbolic. A better way to understand these terms is to trace practices that, once again, orbited the bodies of ancient peoples. In that vein, Nietzsche informs his reader that there is an even more forthright rendering: "The "pure one" is merely a man who washed himself, who forbids himself certain foods that produce skin ailments, who does not sleep with the dirty women of the lower strata, who has an aversion to blood–no more, hardly more!" (GM I 6)

To summarize, there are, then, two methodological practices contained within the same rule. The first is empirical: the rule stipulates that genealogists, when tracing the roots of value words, should see if the word is derived from a root that describes bodies, as is the case in *bellum* and *duellum*. This tracing exposes the different semantic evolutions of an evaluative word. In exposing the transformation of this long sign chain of evaluative words, the most basic of which are good and bad, Nietzsche seeks to annihilate any attempt to conceptualize such notions philosophically. However, the second method is more intriguing. The second method is more speculative in nature. Following Migotti's insight that evaluative words denote a constellation of unrelated meanings, such words point to a site of contestation—that is will to power, a battle of competing values, utilities, and beliefs. Nothing further can be stated at this point of the analysis because we are no longer dealing with the symbolic: we may only understand what emerges from the chrysalis of will to power, its ground form, a la Aydin.

The above elucidation of the methods of genealogy demonstrates a novel cohesion of approaches never specified before until now. My purpose, now that the principal methods of implexic genealogy have been introduced, is to put them to work. In Chap. 3, I analyze Nietzsche's drive theory. Drive theory is a rich popular field of inquiry in the secondary literature. Offering an analysis of the many ways drive theory has been interpreted in the literature itself would necessitate several volumes. Thus, what I intend to do is to use Tom Stern's article "Against Nietzsche's Theory of Drives" as a litmus test. Stern claims there are several problems with Nietzsche's drive theory. I show that the current view of drives fails to resolve the above issues Stern identifies. Instead, I use the Separation Thesis as a filter; drives come into sharper focus when one understands them as implexes: they are the meeting point of cognitive and affective threads that various confluences of power have formatted. I then complete this purified conception of drive by providing a new interpretation of the Internalization Hypothesis in Chap. 4.

References

Ahern, Daniel. *Nietzsche as Cultural Physician*. Pennsylvania: Pennsylvania University State Press, 1995.

Aydin, Ciano. "Nietzsche on Will to Power Toward an Organization-Struggle Model." *Journal of Nietzsche Studies*, 33:1, 2007, 25–48.

Berry, Jessica. 2011. Nietzsche and the Anti-Skeptical Tradition. Oxford: Oxford University Press.

Blondel, Eric. *Nietzsche: The Body and Culture. Philosophy as a philological Genealogy*. Trans. Sean Hand. Stanford, California: Stanford University Press, 1991.

Blondel, Eric. The Question of Genealogy." *In Nietzsche, Genealogy, Morality: Essays on Nietzsche's Genealogy of Morals*. (Hereafter NGM). Ed. Richard Schacht. Berkeley, California: California University Press, 1994.

Bove, Paul A. "The End of Humanism: Michel Foucault and the Power of the Disciplines" in *Michel Foucault: Critical Assessments* Ed. Barry Smart, Vol. II New York Routledge, 1994.

Brown, Richard S. G. "Nihilism: "Thus Speaks Physiology" in *Nietzsche and the Rhetoric of Nihilism: Essays on Interpretation, Language and Politics*. Ed(s).

Tom Darby, Bela Egyed and Ben Jones. Ottawa: Carleton University Press, 1989.

Brown, Richard S. G. “Nietzsche: That Profound Physiologist.” *Nietzsche and Science* Ed(s) Gregory Moore and Thomas Brobjer Aldershot: Ashgate Press, 2004.

Conway, Daniel. “Genealogy and the Critical Method in *On the Genealogy of Morals*” in *Nietzsche, Genealogy Morality: Essays on Nietzsche's Genealogy of Morals*. Ed. Richard Schacht (Berkeley California: University of California Press, 318–334.

Conway, Daniel. 2008. N*ietzsche's on the Genealogy of Morals: A Reader's Guide.* Lanham Maryland: Rowman and Littlefield, 2008.

Cox, Christoph. *Nietzsche, Naturalism and Interpretation*. Berkeley California: University of California Press, 1999.

Craig, Edward. *Knowledge and the State of Nature* Oxford University Press: 1990.

Dennett, Daniel. 1994. *Darwin's Dangerous Idea*. New York: Simon and Schuster.

Else, Gerald. *Aristotle's Poetices: The Argument*, (Cambridge Mass, Harvard University Press, 1957.

Foucault, Michel. 1977. “Nietzsche, Genealogy, History.” In *Language, Counter-Memory, Practice Selected Essays and Interviews by Michel Foucault*. Edited by Donald F. Bouchard. Ithaca and New York: Cornell University Press.

Foucault, Michel. The Return of Morality”. L. Kritzman (Ed.) *Michel Foucault-Politics, Philosophy, Culture: Interviews and other Writings* 1977–1984 L. Kritzman Ed (London, Routledge), 1988, 242–254.

Granier, Jean. *Le probleme de la Verite dans la Philosophie de Nietzsche*. Paris: Seuil. 1966.

Habermas, Jurgen. *Philosophical Discourse of Modernity*. Translated by Fredrick Lawrence. Cambridge: MIT Press 1985.

Heidegger, Martin. *Nietzsche,* Volume 3: *The Will to Power as Knowledge and as Metaphysics*. Trans. Joan Stambaugh, David Farrell Krell and Frank A. Capuzzi. New York: Harper and Row 1987.

Higgins, Kathleen Marie. “On the Genealogy of Morals—Nietzsche's Gift.” In NGM, 1994.

Hobbes, Thomas. *Leviathan*, Edited by Michael Oakeshott (New York: Collier), 1966.

Hume, David. *A Treatise of Human Nature*, edited by L. A. Selby-Bigge, 2nd ed. revised by P. H. Nidditch, Oxford: Clarendon Press, 1975.

Janaway, Christopher. “Naturalism and Genealogy”. *In Blackwell's Companions to Philosophy: A Companion to Nietzsche*. Edited By Keith Ansell Pearson. Blackwell Publishers, 2006, 337–353.

Janaway, Christopher. *Beyond Selflessness: Reading Nietzsche's Genealogy*. Oxford: Oxford University Press, 2007.

Katsafanas, Paul. *The Nietzschean Self: Moral Psychology, Agency and the Unconscious*, Oxford University Press, 2016.

Klein, Wayne. *Nietzsche and the Promise of Philosophy*, Albany, NY: State University of New York Press, 1997.

Koffman. Sarah. *Nietzsche et la Metaphor* Paris: Payot 1972.

Lightbody, Brian. *Philosophical Genealogy: An Epistemological Reconstruction of Nietzsche and Foucault's Genealogical Method.* New York: Peter Lang, vols. 1 and 2. 2011 and 2011.

Lightbody, Brian. *Nietzsche's Will to Power Naturalized: Translating the Human into Nature and Nature into the Human*. (Lanham Maryland: Rowman and Littlefield, Lexington Books), 2017.

Lightbody, Brian. "Twice Removed: Foucault's Critique of Nietzsche's Genealogical Method" Chapter 7 *Foucault and Nietzsche: A Critical Encounter*, Ed(s). Alan Rosenberg and Joseph Westfall, London: Bloomsbury, Press, 2018, 167–182, 169–170.

Lightbody, Brian. "Artificial and Unconscious Selection in Nietzsche's Genealogy: Expectorating the Poisoned Pill of the Lamarckian Reading." Genealogy, 34.3 June, 2019 pp. 1–23.

Lightbody, Brian. "Hermeneutics vs. Genealogy: Brandom's Cloak or Nietzsche's Quilt?" *The European Legacy*, Vol. 25. Issue 6, 2020, pp. 635–652.

Lightbody, Brian. "The Passive Body and States of Nature: An Examination of the Methodological Role State of Nature Theory Plays in Williams and Nietzsche" in the Special Issue *Philosophical Genealogy from Nietzsche to Williams, Genealogy* MPDI (5) 2, 38, 2021 1–15, 6–7.

May, Simon. *Nietzsche's Ethics and His war on Morality*, Oxford Clarendon Press, 1999.

McCarthy, Thomas. "The Critique of Impure Reason." In *Critique and Power: Recasting the Habermas/Foucault Debate*. Ed. Michael Kelly. Cambridge Mass: MIT Press, 1994.

Migotti, Mark "Slave Morality, Socrates, and the Bushmen: A Reading of the First Essay of On the Genealogy of Moral", *Philosophy and Phenomenological Research* Vol. 58, No. 4 (Dec., 1998), 745–779.

Migotti, Mark. "Slave Morality, Socrates, and the Bushmen: A Critical Introduction to On the Genealogy of Morals, Essay I" in *Nietzsche's on the Genealogy of Morals: Critical Essays.* Lanham Maryland: Rowman and Littlefield, 2006 pp. 109–131.

Migotti, Mark. History, Genealogy, Nietzsche: Comments on Jesse Prinz's Genealogies of Morals: Nietzsche's Methods Compared. *Journal of Nietzsche Studies* 47: 2016 212–227.

Moore, Gregory. 2002. *Nietzsche, Biology, Metaphor*. Cambridge: Cambridge University Press.

Muller-Lauter, Wolfgang. *Nietzsche: His Philosophy of Contradictions and the Contradictions of his Philosophy*. Trans. David J. Parent. University of Illinois Press, 1999.

Nagel, Thomas. "The Absurd" *The Meaning of Life* 4th edition Ed E.D. Klemke and Steven Cahn Oxford: Oxford University Press, 2017.

Owen, David. Criticism and Captivity: On Genealogy and Critical Theory. *European Journal of Philosophy* 10: 2002, 216–230.

Owen, David. *Nietzsche's Genealogy of Morality*. Montreal: McGill-Queen's University Press 2007.

Prado, C.G. *Searle and Foucault on Truth* Cambridge University Press: 2006.

Prinz, Jesse. *The Emotional Construction of Morals*. Oxford: Oxford University Press, 2007.

Queloz, Mathieu. *The Practical Origin of Ideas: Genealogy as Conceptual Reverse-Engineering* Oxford University Press, 2020.

Queloz, Mathieu, "Tracing Concepts to Needs", *The Philosopher*, 109, (3) 34–39, 2021.

Poellner, Peter. *Nietzsche and Metaphysics* (New York: Oxford University Press), 1995.

Rajchman, John "The Story of Foucault's History" In *Michel Foucault: Critical Assessments* Ed. Barry Smart. Volume II. New York: Routledge, 1994, 389–411.

Richardson, John. *Nietzsche's New Darwinism*. Oxford: Oxford University Press, 2004.

Varro on *the Latin Language* (Varro: *De Lingua Latina)*. With an English translation by Roland G. Kent. Two volumes. Pp. 1+676. (Loeb Classical Library.) London: Heinemann, 1938.

Williams, Bernard. *Truth and Truthfulness: An Essay in Genealogy*. Princeton and Oxford: Princeton University Press, 2002.

Williams, Linda. *Nietzsche's Mirror, The World as Will to Power*. Lexington MD: Rowman and Littlefield, 2000.

3

Drives in the Secondary Literature

This chapter examines Nietzsche's theory of drives separately from the Internalization Hypothesis. According to the secondary literature, drive theory best describes Nietzsche's moral psychology. Drives are the true workhorses of Nietzsche's philosophy, so it is argued, because he treats them as fundamental albeit dynamic psychological—and, in some texts—metaphysical elements.[1] From the standpoint of the psyche, drives not only explain the diversity and complexity of human behavior, but in addition, they serve to illuminate the processes behind so called rational decision making.[2]

[1] For psychological accounts of drives, see BGE 117, GS 49, HH1 138. For biological accounts, obviously GM II 16, D 119, BGE 13 and GS, 349 and GS 1. For metaphysical accounts, see the infamous passage of BGE 36 and WP 461. There are secondary works that explore each of these readings. In the main, I explore the principal psychological accounts of drives in this chapter.

[2] The causal relationship between drives and agency is difficult to navigate. There are, what I would call reductive accounts where agency is causally reducible to the collection of drives which make up the physiological/mental confluence that is the person. Then, there are softer, causal theories which suggest that drives are merely persuasive in that they direct what we find choice-worthy and in addition influence the process of decision-making in evaluating actions deemed worthy of choosing. I explore two representative interpretations (i.e. Leiter for the former and Katsafanas for the latter) from each camp below.

B. Lightbody, *A Genealogical Analysis of Nietzschean Drive Theory*,
https://doi.org/10.1007/978-3-031-27148-9_3

Yet the literature is delinquent when it comes to elucidating the context of drive theory which is of course the Internalization Hypothesis. In what follows I explain the main tenets of drive theory in the secondary literature. I utilize and further flesh out Mattia Riccardi's fivefold aspectual sketch of drives as elucidated in his article; "Virtuous Homunculi: Nietzsche on the order of drives."[3] Riccardi's article ably manages to distill the vast discussion on drive theory in the secondary literature into a wieldy and discernible form.

The justification for Riccardi's refinement relies on three supports: (1) the primary literature: what Nietzsche writes about drives throughout his substantial and impressive *oeuvre;* (2) the predecessors whom Nietzsche read who themselves utilized drives to explain and justify their own psychological models; and (3) *prima facie* intuitions about what drives are. I flesh out these aspects in the following by examining each from the interrelational tripartite supports mentioned above. In addition to expositing, I analyze how each feature has been understood by other writers working in the secondary literature in order to bring into sharper relief the nuanced views of each component.

There is something else that I do. More than simply recapitulating these aspects of drive theory, I go to more extraordinary lengths to discuss the consequences and problematic features of each facet of drives as identified by Riccardi. To assist me with that critical endeavor, I employ Tom Stern's incisive and powerful article "Against Nietzsche's Theory of Drives" and Christopher Fowles's fecund "The Heart of the Flesh: Nietzsche on Affects and the Interpretation of the Body." When brought together these two articles problematize what seems to be at least on the surface a cogent and non-tendentious paradigm of the psychological. The Stern article is destructive, while Fowles is reconstructive. Stern argues that it is impossible to reconstruct a coherent understanding of Nietzsche's drive theory. He minces no words and provides the clearest articulation of the problem to be found anywhere in the secondary literature: "For the things Nietzsche says about drives what they are what we could know about them and what their relationship to actions is are so deeply and centrally

[3] Matias Riccardi, "Virtuous Homunculi: Nietzsche on the Order of Drives", *Inquiry an International Journal of Philosophy*, 61 (1) 21–41 (2018).

conflicting in so many ways that no coherent position can be formed without ignoring significant published passages."[4] I use Stern's article as an acid of sorts; its corrosive properties eat through any attempt in the scholarship to provide some platform from which a substantive theory of drives may be built. What is revealing about this quotation, however, is the last phrase "without ignoring significant published passages." Unknowingly, Stern signals what a coherent position requires in this very phrasing—far from ignoring passages, one should instead privilege some sections over others. This is precisely the path I take by favoring the Separation Thesis and I.H.

Turning to Fowles' article, I use it as a probe of sorts highlighting which features of the standard view are underdetermined. For example, it is clear that drives induce agents to undertake some action as opposed to some other. However, actions are accompanied by a feeling; if the hunger drive causes me to find food, and I remember I have a left-over piece of cheesecake in the fridge, I become excited. This excitement would seem to be part of the causal etiology to explain the action of eating the cheesecake. Yet feelings in the secondary literature are often not sufficiently discussed when explaining Nietzsche's drive psychology. Thus, Fowles's main task is to connect emotions to drive. Fowles's article, then, is vital for two reasons: first, he explains the causal relationship between drives and affects for Nietzsche. But of paramount importance, he grounds this causal interpretation on a somatic platform. In Chap. 5, I operationalize Fowles' insightful somatic solution to bridge drives' mental and bodily sides. The relationship between the mental aspect of drives (drives represent features of the world) and their physical platforming is a mystery that continues to haunt the secondary literature.[5]

The conclusion of this chapter will mark the path forward; this path is one where a clear connection is made between the Internalization Hypothesis and drives. I argue that drives have both a mental qua representational and biological feature and, because of this schism, it leads to a seeming irreconcilable dichotomy. My solution to what appears to be

---

[4] Tom Stern, Against Nietzsche's Theory of Drives *Journal of the American Philosophical Association* Vol 1. Issue 1 Spring (2015) 121–140, 122.

[5] Christopher Fowles, "The Heart of Flesh: Nietzsche on Affects and the Interpretation of the Body" *Journal of the History of Philosophy*, Volume 58, Number 1, January 2020, 113–139.

just another mind/body dualism problem is to treat drives as implexes: they are the interstice where cognitive and affective vectors meet. It is from this interpretation that a new path toward resolving the many paradoxes relating to drives may be staked out.

Section I: Five Characteristics of Drives

Characteristic 1: Drives are Rooted in Our Biology

The first aspect claims that drives are grounded—in some capacity—in one's biological constitution. Whether all drives are remnants of animal instincts and in what sense instincts are different from drives is an open question. For example, in his recent book, *Nietzsche's Moral Psychology*, Mark Alfano makes a persuasive case for arguing that instincts are a subset of drives: "I now want to argue that instincts are a species of drive: instincts are innate drives."[6] However, and in keeping with Nietzsche's naturalistic hypothesis, I will treat drives (*Triebs*) and instincts (*Instinkts*) as co-referential: both are expressions of a physical need or a transformation thereof.

The scholar who has done the most and, in my opinion, best work in stressing the biological substrate that subtends drives is John Richardson. As Richardson puts it in his *Nietzsche's New Darwinism*, "I claim that we can't understand his (Nietzsche's) views on our values without seeing first and precisely how he thinks we are animals with drives".[7] This way of putting the matter will be a refrain to which I return. Moreover, Richardson makes a strong case for suggesting that one cannot provide a coherent view of drive theory without taking seriously what Nietzsche has to say about breeding (*züchten*)—a polysemous term for Nietzsche that includes both inculturation and biological inheritance.

Richardson's task is truly herculean; he attempts to provide a feasible explanation for explaining how humans became rational, moralistic animals. Under Richardson's narrative, drives remain the elemental conduit

[6] Mark Alfano, *Nietzsche's Moral Psychology* Cambridge University Press, 2019, 69.

[7] John Richardson, *Nietzsche's New Darwinism*, (Oxford University Press, 2004), 11–12.

of lineage for Nietzsche, yet they can be exapted for different purposes. "Thus drives can retain an end, but this end need not be conscious; nor is the end non-revisable. In better moments he treats drives as designed by selection. They are so designed simply qua drives, in that organisms are crucially rendered fit by being equipped with plastic dispositions (drives) physical set ups with causal tendencies that are plastic toward certain ends."[8] In worse moments, which Richardson avers are far more often, Nietzsche treats drives as little homunculi or (little agents), a problem I will address at length toward the end of this chapter.

In thinking about Alfano's and Richardson's respective viewpoints regarding the biological footing of drives and its subsequent zoological transformation, it is crucial to think through their individual implications. Tom Stern explores these implications pertaining to the physical rootedness of drives in his article. He discovers that even this seemingly non-contentious claim, that drives have an animal base, is puzzling. He writes:

> I have already suggested that the biological model of drive or instinct, based on the animal case, tells us very little about humans. But note that many 'drives' certainly do not obviously relate to physiological processes, do not seem standard features of every human let alone non-human animal, are not the sorts of things that we'd be inclined to say are naturally seeking expression … An adequate discussion would digress, but, taken as a whole I can find nothing *distinctively* 'naturalistic' about the drive pantheon or Nietzsche's approach to constructing it.[9]

To take but one example that Stern mentions but does not treat in full consider the instinct for "luxury." In GM III 8 Nietzsche claims that inventive spirits throughout the ages have had to resist natural instincts toward "a love of luxury and refinement or an excessive liberality of heart and hand." (GM III 8) Moreover, these instincts were checked because of a more dominating spiritualizing instinct: "The three great slogans of the ascetic ideal are familiar: poverty, humility, chastity. Now take a close look at the lives of all the great inventive spirits: you will always encounter all three to a lesser degree."

[8] Richardson, *Nietzsche's New Darwinism*, 40.

[9] Stern, "Against Nietzsche's Theory of Drives", 127.

(GM III: 8) But as Nietzsche explains, these dispositions toward the finer things in life are negated not through the imposition and implementation of virtue, whether construed as Greek *Arete* or Christian moral practices or even in a more ordinary sense like Sartre's mantra "never a day without a line" but rather because of a dominating spirit. "It was the dominating spirit whose demands prevailed against those of all the other instincts–it continues to do it; if it did not do it, it would not dominate. There is thus nothing of virtue in this." (GM III: 8) The difficulty here is in coming to terms with the biological basis for the drive to pursue, let's call it, "the finer things in life." To be clear about the problem, it is not that persons may be drawn to pursue such things unconsciously—Marcuse in *Eros and Civilization* for one provides an illuminating account of how a subject's libidinal desires may be harnessed and redirected toward some commercial product.[10] The point I return to is the one made by Alfano and Richardson above. How is one expected to view the drive for luxury through the framework of an animal with defined instincts whose purpose allows the animal to thrive in its particular environment? One may make the case that such drives were instilled via culture at some point in our collective prehistory, but that tells us nothing about that very transitional stage—the interval between animal and human. It is this very stage about which we are inquiring.

As I will argue in Chap. 4, a genealogical solution to this problem argues that drives are implexes; they are the symbolic intersection of cognitive and affective systems. This framework allows for a new understanding of Nietzsche's bad conscience. Chapter 4 demonstrates how the twin mechanisms of artificial and unconscious selection came to produce this traumatic memory. Neo-Darwinism explains, at least in part, how the excising of specific drives came about and how other cognitive capacities, like one-shot learning, came to be.[11] What is impor-

---

[10] Far more on this see my paper, Brian Lightbody, "Can We Truly Love That Which is Fleeting? The Problem of Time in Marcuse's *Eros and Civilization*." *Florida Philosophical Review* (1) 25–42 2010.

[11] According to Peter Tse, one-shot learning is the unique human, all too human ability. "to make associations among arbitrary categories of things and events." As Tse concretizes the idea: "In contrast, (to animals), a three-year old child can pretend that a block is a truck and then, a moment later, pretend that it is a monster. This capacity to instantly remap the referent of an object file is unique to humans and is at the heart of why our cognition can be truly symbolic." Tse, Peter, Ulric. "Symbolic Thought and the Evolution of Human Morality." *Moral Psychology: The Evolution of Morality: Adaptations and Innateness* Vol. 1 Ed. Walter Sinnott-Armstrong. MIT Press, 2008, 269–297, 269–271.

tant to grab onto as we make our way through these aspects is that this first component takes a drive as a pre-conscious, biological, and therefore unreflective vehicle for the expression of some definite aim—the second aspect of drive theory.

Charactertistic 2: Drives Have Definite Aims

Secondly, drives seek to express themselves. As Nietzsche puts it in GS 360: Drives are "a quantum of dammed up energy waiting to be used up somehow." To think about drives as a desire for expression is almost tautologous. According to scholars in the literature, drive expression has both an aim and an object. The aim of the drive is fixed, and for most scholars the object of the aim may change. For example, the sex drive leads a subject to find a suitable mating partner. But according to the majority of scholars, the object or in relation to the sex drive, the specific partner is unessential. As Alfano puts it, "a drive is a disposition to activate behavior of a particular type though not necessarily with respect to any particular intentional object."[12] Alfano's example of the expression of the sex drive is constructive in enlarging this detail. He continues, "someone's sex drive might lead them to engage in sexual congress with one person today to perform a different sex act with a different person tomorrow or to masturbate alone the next day."[13]

In an earlier article, Paul Katsafanas echoed this sentiment. Drives he argued do not aim at the achievement of some determinate state of affairs. To concretize this a bit more, Katsafanas claims that, "Drives do not simply arise in response to external stimuli; they actively seek opportunities for expression sometimes distorting the agent's perception of the environment in order to incline the agent to act in ways that give the drives expression."[14] Katsafanas' explication may appear convoluted; it is diffi-

[12] Alfano, *Nietzsche's Moral Psychology*, 51.

[13] Alfano, 51.

[14] Paul Katsafanas, "Nietzsche's Philosophical Psychology", 752.

cult to maintain that a drive's expression is fixed, yet its aim might change. To take animalistic drives such as the thirst, shelter, sex, and hunger drive, the drives are distinct (we understand how each drive may pursue objects for its expression), and yet the aim of these drives will differ following the things in the environment that might satisfy the drive. The purpose of the division, then, between the drives' aim and its eventuated expression, is to view human behavior *sans* reason; the drives are meant to pull back the curtain on what some philosophers call action theory. The object that satisfies the aim is inconsequential; it is not really chosen by an agent for its own sake but rather is a means for the unconscious need to express the active drive. The purported purpose of Nietzsche's moral psychology is to reveal the true motives that underpin the reasons that supposedly subtend our decisions.

The idea that drives and drives alone explain all that there is behind purposive behavior is well-supported in Nietzsche's *oeuvre.* I point to a representative passage from *Gay Science* 354, "The Problem of Consciousness":

> The whole of life would be possible without its seeing itself as it were in a mirror: as in fact even at present the far greater part of our life still goes on without this mirroring, and even our thinking, feeling, volitional life as well, however painful this statement may sound to an older philosopher." The conclusion that Nietzsche reaches however from his brief analysis opens up a difficult question that I will address in the subsequent sections. What then is the purpose of consciousness generally, when it is in the main superfluous?

However, this way of thinking about drives as revealing the true purposes behind decisions, raises some thorny problems regarding free will. For if drives induce an agent's behavior such that said behavior is an expression of a drive *simpliciter*, and drives are unconscious, then it would seem at first glance that we cannot act otherwise. This consequence of drive theory is important to flesh out in full as it does connect to how the scholarship has interpreted GM II 16.

Some scholars, like Brian Leiter, have embraced the full consequences of this line of thought. Leiter holds a type-fact position regarding

Nietzsche's moral psychology. The type-fact theory argues that human beings belong to fixed and immutable psycho-physiological types, which determine and, if understood correctly, explain individuals' cognitive faculties, actions, and behavior.[15] "Each person, (Leiter declares), has a fixed psycho-physical constitution, which defines him as a particular type of person."[16]

What determines one's type-facts is not always clear for Leiter as he sometimes oscillates between a more rigid somatic construal and a more fluid, drive position. This ambivalence is clearly seen in the following quote: "Call the relevant psycho-physical facts here type facts. Type-facts, for Nietzsche are either physiological facts about the person or facts about the person's unconscious drives or affects."[17] In any case, there are two types according to Leiter's interpretation. There are weak types who are impotent, reactive, prone to nursing grudges, and intriguingly, desire to create values that serve their *interests,* and then there are strong types who are active, exuberant, healthy, and express their values outwardly. Also, and in converse fashion to the weak type, the strong construct values which come to serve their *instincts.*[18]

It is important to emphasize that the above type-facts are immutable, at least according to the early Leiter. Type-facts are physiological and psychological traits that constitute a person, placing him in one of the two categories (weak/strong) noted above. These type-facts may then be used to predict the moral and theoretical beliefs of so-called persons with some degree of accuracy. "A 'person' (Leiter proclaims and his inverted commas) is the arena in which the struggle of drives (type-facts) is played out; how they play out determines what he believes, what he values, what he becomes."[19]

According to Leiter's later position, type-facts are alterable but cannot be changed by the person who 'has' them because a person remains (as with the earlier position) simply the unconscious expression of type-facts.

[15] Brian Leiter, *Nietzsche on Morality*, 91.

[16] Brian Leiter, "The Paradox of Fatalism and Self-Creation in Nietzsche," in *Willing and Nothingness: Schopenhauer as Nietzsche's Educator*, ed. Christopher Janaway (Oxford: Clarendon, 1998), 219.

[17] Brian Leiter, *Moral Psychology with Nietzsche*, Oxford University Press, 2019, 3.

[18] Brian Leiter, *Nietzsche on Morality*, (New York: Routledge, 2002), 8.

[19] Leiter, *Nietzsche on Morality*, 100.

If one's type-facts do change, then this alteration is caused by culture, perhaps by turning genes on or off. What remains true in both Leiterian accounts is the causal inefficacy of the individual. As Leiter puts it in his recent book, *Moral Psychology with Nietzsche*, "Nietzsche holds that heritable type-facts are central determinants of personality and morally significant behaviors, a claim well-supported by extensive empirical findings in behavioral genetics."[20] More notable in Leiter's later work, is his attempt to demonstrate that Nietzsche's nineteenth-century musings on the relationship between physiology and conscious action are consistent with the results of Libet's experiments which purportedly show that free will is an illusion by demonstrating that action readiness potential occurs before conscious deliberation.[21]

Katsafanas, in contrast, defends a weak reading of causation vis-à-vis the relationship between drives and conscious thoughts. For Katsafanas, Nietzsche takes issue with the Kant/Lockean model of motivational theory which holds that reflective deliberation can cause one to alter one's motivation in two ways: First, "self-conscious reflection enables us to distance ourselves from our motives thereby making these motives cease to dominate us … and second there is a claim about normativity once we have suspended a motive we consider the motive, weigh it, ask if it is really a reason to act."[22] According to Katsafanas, Nietzsche does not reject the power of self-conscious reflection in contrast to Leiter's interpretation. Deliberation helps us to choose which action to pursue. More perspicuously stated, deliberation allows us to choose amongst a number of alternatives we deem best when it comes to satisfying some drive. But what is disabled from the Kantian/Lockean model is our ability to suspend our motivations for these choices; the choices we make are filtered or controlled through a particular drive. As Katsafanas provocatively puts

[20] Brian Leiter, *Moral Psychology With Nietzsche*, (New York: Oxford University Press, 2019), 9.

[21] See Leiter's discussion of Daniel Wegner's *The Illusion of Conscious Will* (Cambridge Mass: MIT Press, 2002) on 141–142 of *Moral Psychology With Nietz*sche along with Leiter's discussion of "Libet experiments" which test RP (Readiness Potential) in Leiter's earlier paper, "Nietzsche's Theory of the Will", *Philosopher's Imprint*, Vol. 7 No. 7, 2007 1–15, 13.

[22] Paul Katsafanas, "Nietzsche's Philosophical Psychology'. In K. Gemes and J. Richardson (eds.), The Oxford Handbook of Nietzsche (Oxford: Oxford University Press. 2013), 752.

it: "This is the problem that Nietzsche's drive psychology raises: choice may control action, but agents do not control choice."[23]

Putting the philological debate between Katsafanas and Leiter to one side, if drives are expressions of definite fixed aims (e.g. the hunger drive does not manifest itself as the sex drive as Richardson puts it although this does not preclude one from sexualizing food), then it becomes unclear what work drives perform in fleshing out human behavior. Return to Alfano's example above. In each of the iterations of Alfano's sex act examples it is clear there is a subject engaged in them who reflects and has reasons for how the drive is expressed. The person engages in sex with one person today perhaps because he is attracted to her, performs a different sex act with the same person tomorrow because the act is new or exciting and masturbates thinking of that person because she is not available or perhaps, she has no interest in having sex with him because he is a lousy lay! What is clear is that a complete understanding of each action remains obscure until we can answer each, paraphrasing Anscombe, with a why.

For Anscombe, A acts intentionally only if, in a certain sense the question, 'Why?' applies to A's action. The why question under investigation cannot be understood in an evidential or causal manner but rather as reason-giving. To act in a reason-giving way is to perform an action under a description.[24] However, for Leiter, one's type-facts explain the person's choices *en toto*: we reduce reason-giving answers to causal ones for each object the drive pursues. Ethical intuitions are nothing more than confessions of an individual's physiological symptomatology; they are indicative of what a person will do, but neither they, nor the person who holds them, is causally efficacious.[25]

---

[23] Paul Katsafanas, "Nietzsche's Philosophical Psychology'. In K. Gemes and J. Richardson (eds.), The Oxford Handbook of Nietzsche (Oxford: Oxford University Press. 2013), 752.

[24] G.E.M Anscombe *Intentions Anscombe, Elizabeth, Intention, (Ithaca, NY: Cornell University Press, 1957) secs. 5–8.*

[25] There are many important works in the secondary literature that emphasize the biological and physiological aspects of Nietzsche's philosophy. See Gregory Moore's *Nietzsche, Biology, Metaphor*, (Cambridge University Press, 2002). Daniel Ahern's *Nietzsche as Cultural Physician*, (Pennsylvania State University Press, 1995). Richard S.G. Brown's two articles, "Nihilism: "Thus Speaks Physiology" in *Nietzsche and the Rhetoric of Nihilism: Essays on Interpretation, Language and Politics* edited by Tom Darby, Bela Egyed and Ben Jones (Ottawa: Carleton University Press, 1989), 133–144. "Nietzsche: That Profound Physiologist", in *Nietzsche and Science* Eds (Gregory Moore and Thomas Brobjer, (Aldershot: Ashgate Press, 2004) 51–71. Wayne Klein's *Nietzsche and the Promise of Philosophy* (Albany, NY: State University of New York Press, 1997). In what follows, I will choose to examine Brian Leiter's "type-fact" position for its lucidity and comprehensiveness.

However, providing a satisfactory reductive causal answer to 'Why' questions pertaining to intentionality are notoriously problematic and uninformative.[26] Indeed, even Leiter's marshaling forth of Libet tests to demonstrate the inefficacy of the will shows a breathtaking naiveté on his part, given the rich literature criticizing the myriad problems with these experiments. Moreover, as Mele explains, there are issues pertaining to the methods of the experimental procedure itself to conceptual ambiguities regarding what the test in fact, proves. Leiter fails to address these concerns.[27]

For Katsafanas, in contrast, both conscious deliberation and drives are required in order to give a full account regarding the Anscombe condition above. Katsafanas argues that Nietzsche promotes a kind of constitutivism regarding agency. Constitutivism is a novel position of action theory that grounds normative facts about what actions are valuable or what reasons there are to commit them and then shows that a subject that follows these standards is more of an agent than a subject who does not.[28] In this way, it stands against a standard decision theory model where one first provides an ontology of the human being and then, from this ground, demonstrates whether an action is valuable just in case it is consonant with whatever we take the human to essentially be. For example, the traditional view of decision theory holds that agency is about optimizing choices according to some metric that defines what an agent is (e.g. the Utility Principle) and then explaining the agent's actions relative to the metric provided.

On the other hand, constitutivists claim that aims generate normative reasons to satisfy those aims. They also claim that action itself has a

---

[26] This is an objection Robert Brandom makes to all forms of genealogical inquiry in his work: "Reason, Genealogy and the Hermeneutics of Magnanimity." The Howison Lectures in Philosophy delivered at the University of California, Berkeley, March 13, 2013. For a transcript, see: www.pitt.edu/~brandom/downloads/RGHM%20%2012-11-21%20a.doc. I respond to Brandom in Brian Lightbody "Hermeneutics vs. Genealogy: Brandom's Cloak or Nietzsche's Quilt" *The European Legacy*, Vol. 25 Issue 6, 2020, 635–652 Vol 2.

[27] See for example: Alfred Mele, *Effective Intentions* (Oxford University Press, 2009) Chapter Five 'Intentional Actions Alleged Illusion of Conscious Will" for a plethora of critical concerns directed at the experimental design of Libet tests.

[28] For a lucid summary of constitutivism see Luca Ferrero, "Constitutivism and the Inescapability of Agency" *Oxford Studies in Metaethics*, 2009, 303–333.

constitutive aim, that is, that every token action A aims at some goal, where having this aim is part of what constitutes A's being an action (and thereby returning us to Anscombe's why condition). We can provide a reason for performing some action because we think it better satisfies the goal to be achieved than some other. The key move made by the constitutivist is to show that agential actions have some aspect A, which not only makes the action, an action, but also makes it good. Bad actions are then identified by demonstrating that the act in question does not have the specified aspect (A). By showing that the action does not have that feature, then any action which lacks this feature entails that the agent is less of an agent than someone who committed the 'good' act, since it is action that constitutes agency.[29] The quality that Katsafanas's argument rests on is that agents are committed to aiming at maximal power. This is what makes an action good, and correspondingly those agents who maximize their power as opposed to those who do not are more robustly agential.

Furthermore, according to Katsafanas, in performing any action A, one aims at (commits to) endorsing A given the full information about A's etiology.[30] For Nietzsche all actions are underwritten by will to power. This reading retains the substantive view noted in Chap. 2. However if this is the case then we are lead to affirm that "Merely in virtue of acting, we become committed to approving of will to power… the only way we can act is to endorse will to power"[31] And furthermore "if you have an aim of which you approve," you cannot "justifiably decline to fulfill it maximally"[32] So, in acting, we commit to maximal power. Katsafanas would seem to replace Frankfurt's construal of freedom as the alignment between first and second-order desires with that of an alignment between the impulse and aim of the drive and the deliberation required to achieve it.[33]

[29] Paul Katsafanas, *Agency and the Foundations of Ethics: Nietzsche's Constitutivism:* Oxford University Press, 2013, 39.

[30] Paul Katasafanas, *Agency and the Foundations of Ethics: Nietzsche's Constitutivism* Oxford University Press, 2013, 204.

[31] Katsafanas, *Agency and the Foundations of Ethics*, 207.

[32] Katsafanas, *Agency and the Foundations of Ethics*, 208.

[33] Harry Frankfurt, "Freedom of the Will and The Concept of a Person," *Journal of Philosophy* 68.1 (1971).5–20.

Even if we put aside whether maximizing power is in fact the constitutive aim for all actions it is difficult to see how drives as vehicles of will to power are necessary. Although written 4 years earlier than Alfano's work, Stern's words remain instructive:

> Drives, recall, are the things that propel animals to behave quasi-rationally, quasi-purposively and quasi-expediently. But the salient feature of the animal, unlike the human, is that the non-'quasi-'versions are lacking: the human building a home, unlike the bee, does, prima facie, have consciousness, reason, instruction, a plan, prior models and so on. Given prima facie consciousness et al., where do the drives come in? That, precisely, is what we want to know. Reminding ourselves of the biological context of these terms solves nothing. Indeed, it brings the problem into focus.[34]

Consider Stern's example of building a home—a instinctual act for some species of animals, like birds, and now view the act through the lens of Leiter's type-fact theory. Actions according to Leiter eventuate for the weak just in case said actions serve their interests whereas in contrast actions manifested by the strong are those that serve their instincts. How do we explain the building or even purchasing of a home under a type-fact reading? To interpret these actions as either weak or strong is too crude of a framework to understand the builder's intentions behind the action. One might be able to use Leiter's model to purchase some additional understanding of why the builder designed the house she did, but that understanding would need to be contextualized within a larger narrational context that would need to be explained in terms of a reason-given framework. Yet it is this reason-giving framework that Leiter's position attempts to account for.

I now return to Alfano's example of pursuing one sexual partner over some other and relate it to Katsafanas's position. According to Katsafanas, such an act, to be considered constitutive of agency, would need to (1) maximally satisfy will to power; and moreover, (2) is mapped onto a specific drive (the etiological requirement noted above). Certainly, one might claim that sexual pursuit and subsequent attainment of someone

[34] Stern, "Against Nietzsche's Theory of Drives," 126.

who is "out of my league" might be an example of fulfilling Katsafanas's feature for constitutive agency. But, here again, that interpretation cannot be divorced from the necessarily encultured narrative as to what "out of my league means." My contention is not to argue against Katsafanas's brilliant account of constitutive agency, but rather to sharpen the problem I discussed above: when we view drives in terms of their animalistic foundations, we want to know how drives can translate from the animal case to the agential.

I contend that drive theory, in its present form as understood in the literature, cannot be employed in any meaningful way if the aims of drives are dependent on socialization. The reason for my assertion is that it would seem that we reach the following dilemma: (1) either jettison drive theory entirely because we cannot clearly demarcate (per Stern) what is socialized behavior from what is instinct, (which would entail Katsafanas's constitutivism being de-platformed as the etiology requirement clearly requires drives) or (2) instead reframe drives as implicitly consciously infused terms like intention, or interest. Yet in choosing this option, we neutralize the supposed profundity and fecundity of Nietzsche's philosophical psychology.

What is perhaps most interesting about this dilemma is that Nietzsche clearly understood its implications. Returning once again to 354 of the *Gay Science* reveals the full scope of the problem of consciousness, a passage that Stern also directs our attention to in highlighting the issues with utilizing drive theory to render an account of anything that might resemble a profound illuminating theory of philosophical psychology. But that passage is a poisoned pill of sorts. It buttresses Stern's criticism, namely, that drives perform little if any work when it comes to distal intentions (e.g. building a house), but then, as one considers the full scope of the passage, it simultaneously vitiates Stern's point, at the same time.

Turning to the 'supportive' passage in question, Nietzsche writes, "The problem of consciousness (more precisely becoming conscious of something) confronts us only when we begin to comprehend how we could dispense with it; and now physiology and the history of animals place us at the beginning of such comprehension." (GS 354). The point here, I take it, is that once consciousness comes onto the scene of human development, it becomes difficult to either explain it or explain it away as a natural evolutionary development. So that part of the section lends reinforcement to Stern's analysis. But the final details of GS 354 quickly destabilize it because Nietzsche then provides a reductionist account for the emergence of consciousness after all. He writes, "Consciousness is really only a net of communication between human beings it is only as such that it had to develop; a solitary human being who lived like a beast of prey would not have needed it." (GS 354). On the surface it appears that this passage opens the door for Nietzsche's own speculative hypothesis regarding the beginnings of consciousness in GM: II 3–5. That reading, which I will examine in much more detail in Chap. 4, is consistent with Leiter's type-fact theory. However, as discussed, there are significant problems with Leiter's position not least of those identified by Stern. We are then at an impasse: we either accept a hard reductionism position on drives a la Leiter with the problems this engenders (i.e. Anscombian 'why' questions pertaining to intentionality) or adopt a soft-determinism, following Katsafanas, that appears, in the last analysis, to be explanatorily idle. My solution to this problem posits that the above construal is a classic false dilemma: the horns of the disjunct may be exclusive but are not exhaustive. The solution is to imagine drives as implexes. I return to this position below.

Characteristic 3: Drives are Urges

This leads us to the third aspect: propulsion. Drives urge their bearers to initiate a series of steps to complete some action over some other. The idea here is that a subject performs some action because they are compelled either *simpliciter;* deliberation is causally neutral, or a drive manipulates them to do so. There is of course, a plethora of positions between these two claims and indeed even possible positions outside of them. However, in both accounts here (speaking of Leiter and Katsafanas), what is clear is that the drive motivates action. From there, some suggest that the drive alone is responsible for action while others take a more nuanced approach suggesting, in the case of Katsafanas, (as noted above) that drives influence choice and not the other way around. Once a drive is activated, like the sex drive, we have the choice as to how to express and satisfy the drive, but we do not have the power to stand back and cancel out the drive through an act of deliberative intention. Drives, minimally, then, seem to have some causal influence over a subject's action and initiate a call to action independently of deliberation.

This leads to a second puzzlement that Stern draws the reader's attention to: if drives are the ultimate engine of human action or at least one crucial component of the psychological powertrain, then there arise questions pertaining to the motivational structure of actions. Precisely what causes us to engage in the actions we do? Is it the drive *simpliciter*, or a combination of the drive and deliberation? If the former, then how do we understand deliberation? Is reflection then merely epiphenomenal? How can we render a coherent account of what appears on the surface to be rationally planned, detached, coldly calculating intention leading to action?

To help in this matter, Stern reminds the reader that Nietzsche's intended purpose of drive theory is to challenge, at least at times, the Socratic picture of moral psychology. Stern spells this out in the following, where he is discussing Socrates' predicament after his trial in the *Apology*. The discussion is a summary of Socrates's deliberation in the *Phaedo*. On Socrates' account of the relationship between what he thought and what he did, the following seems to be true or so holds Stern:

> i) Socrates could have chosen to do different things; ii) Socrates correctly weighed up his options and iii) acted according to which option he thought was right; iv) having acted, Socrates' motivations are plain for him to see and to be made available to others such that v) he can be judged morally based on what he chose to do.[35]

Although Stern does not quote the passage in question (*Phaedo* 99a), it is instructive to spend some space outlining Socrates' moral psychology. As Socrates mentions in *the Phaedo*, the true causes for his being in the jail cell awaiting his fate instead of fleeing to some other city-state, such as Thessaly, are not his flesh, bones and sinews that is, his body. If someone were to say that Socrates is in the jail cell because of where his body is, we

[35] Stern, "Against Nietzsche's Theory of Drives", 122.

would think the person mad or that he hasn't understood the question. The real reasons Socrates sits in the jail cell are explained by none other than Socrates himself: "the real causes, which are, that the Athenians decided that it was best to condemn me, and therefore I have decided that it was best for me to sit here and that it is right for me to stay and undergo whatever penalty they order." (*Phaedo* 99a)

It is at this juncture, however, that Stern reminds us that Nietzsche's drive theory is supposed to counteract this Socratic picture, which comprises a host of elements united into a logical and rational explanation that forms a narrative that we, as readers, can readily understand. We can enter into what Sellars calls the space of reasons and reflect on whether Socrates's action to stay is justified or not. In coming to form our judgment, we would consider the following: First, there is deliberation: Should I leave or stay? Next, there is a measurement of each alternative: what is the best course of action for me to do all things considered? There is alignment between measured reasoning and duty, and then finally, we have the formation of the intention to stay put. As readers of *the Phaedo*, we can understand and justify (or condemn) Socrates's decision because we can reason along with him and compare the weights Socrates assigns to the pros and cons of his eventual decisions and then compare them to what we think the right thing to do might be. But notice something else. If we were tasked with providing but one answer to Socrates's question in the *Phaedo*: What is the real cause for me sitting in this jail cell? It would not be deliberation as Stern thinks it is, (though deliberation is an integral component of the answer). It is Socrates's *intention* to stay.

Consider that one may intend to pursue action without engaging in deliberation. For example, Alfred Mele in his now classic article, "Self-Control and Second Order Desires" evinces that there are at least two different kinds of intentional actions: deliberative intentions which are grounded on a Davidsonian understanding of action theory where I commit the action just in case it conforms to an all things considered judgment, and executive actions which, usually in English, take the form of "shall."[36] To emphasize the difference between the latter kind of action

[36] Alfred Mele Akrasia, "Self-Control, and Second-Order Desires", *Noûs* Vol. 26, No. 3 (Sep., 1992), 281–302.

and the former consider Churchill's famous speech to rally Britain at the beginning of World War II: "We shall go onto the end. We shall defend our island no matter what the cost may be. We shall never surrender."

But if this is the very picture of psychology Nietzsche is challenging, where agents implement intentions of either the deliberative or executive kind, then it is incumbent on him and his defenders to explain, coherently, "(a) what sorts of things 'drives' are; (b) how many, and how much, we know about them; and (c) what the relationship is between the battle of the drives, which really accounts for actions, and the conscious deliberations that, on the Socratic picture, seem to account for choices?"[37] None of these questions, so Stern thinks, are answered. Yet there is something else that is just as important as these three critical questions Stern raises: How does a drive explain the formation of an executive intention like that of the Churchill example given above? Can we reduce or at least map intentions onto drives? On this question, Nietzsche's model is in no way preferable to what appears on the surface to be an intuitive, parsimonious and well-supported, (empirically speaking), common-sense model of moral psychology where intentions are causally efficacious full stop.

Now Nietzsche does provide answers to this question, but he is delinquent when it comes to delivering a *consistent* solution. Again, quoting Stern, "Nietzsche gives explicitly inconsistent answers regarding each of these three key points. Not that he fails to answer them: he does answer them, just in different, incompatible ways. Often—and this important point is easy to miss—he goes beyond merely stating inconsistent positions: he actually gives arguments in favor of the various contradictory positions."[38] Like Stern, I am unsure whether one can provide an accurate accounting of drive theory when one takes at face value the many places where Nietzsche discusses drives. But unlike Stern, I argue that the first step in providing anything like a coherent rendering of Nietzsche's philosophical psychology must begin with understanding what Nietzsche's Internalization Hypothesis describes.

[37] Stern, 123.

[38] Stern, 123.

Characteristic 4: The Drives are Related to Affects

Given what has been said thus far about drives, there is a significant and intimate connection between drives and affects. Take the hunger drive as an example. The hunger drive causes me to seek out the appropriate object to satisfy my craving. It is expressed with a fixed aim, but the thing may not be determined: I may have a hankering for a burger or a pizza, each would satisfy my drive. However, I am indifferent as to which option my partner chooses to order for delivery.

Moreover, hunger is biologically rooted, and there is a definite inclination or urge on the mental side of the equation that pushes me to fulfill the drive. This is where the hunger drive becomes connected to affect: the urge of the drive is accompanied by a negative valence, especially when I am famished. I experience an unpleasant feeling. In addition, the drive, when unsatisfied for too long, may produce other feelings like irritability. The word "hangry" captures this sentiment well. Also, my negative feelings may stimulate my drive toward hostility. Such feelings format by embodied experience of my surroundings. As Nietzsche claims on many occasions, affect color all things: "There is only a perspective seeing, only a perspective knowing and the more *affects* we allow to speak about one thing, the more eyes, different eyes, we can use to observe one thing, the more complete will our concept of thins our objectivity be." (GM III: 12) Consider 187 BGE where Nietzsche declares that, "In short, moralities are also merely a *sign language of the affects.*" The perspectival language of GM III: 12 is also echoed earlier in GM 1 10, "One should remember that even supposing that the affect of contempt, of looking down from a superior height, falsifies the image of what it despises it will at any rate still be a much less serious falsification than that perpetrated on its opponent … by the submerged hatred, the vengefulness of the impotent." (GM 1 10) Similar perspectival interpretations of the affects are given in GS 7, 139, 152 and 301.

However, there is another aspect of affect that brings it closer to some of the characteristics we noted above: affects have a pro and con. They induce inclinations or aversions. Nietzsche highlights this notion not just in GM III: 12 but most clearly in BGE 19: "Third, the will is a complex of sensation and thinking but above all an affect, and specifically the affect of command. That which is freedom of the will is essentially the affect of superiority in relation to him who must obey… A man who wills commands something within himself that renders obedience."[39]

But if affect both colors and evaluates the things in the world (the fifth aspect of drive theory) *and* induces an inclination toward those very things it wishes to manifest (or conversely, an aversion to those objects it seeks to avoid), what is the difference between affect and drive? Do they designate the same object? Is there a meaningful distinction to be had, or is Nietzsche's use of drive and affect merely a pleonasm?

This pleonastic concern is highlighted in the secondary literature. Lanier Anderson suggests that "many readers take Nietzsche's frequent talk of drives and affects as pleonastic such that 'affect' does not add anything to drives."[40] In some scholarly works, drive, and affect are not distinguished and are used interchangeably. For example, in Peter Poellner's *Nietzsche and Metaphysics,* under the entry index "affect" it states, "see drive, desire." Poellner uses these terms interchangeably in his work. To wit, he writes, "The mode in which the striving for the experience of power manifests itself is designated by Nietzsche as 'drives' or affects."[41]

Moreover, in Poellner's later article "Affect, Value and Objectivity" he uses affect to cover ground that drives might also map. Notice that in the following introduction, just how much territory affects circumscribe: "In the discussion that follows, I shall focus primarily on emotions, but it will be convenient to retain Nietzsche's broad usage of 'affect' for any *mental episode* which constitutively involves a *pro- or con-attitude* (or as I shall say, a favouring or disfavouring) with a distinctive phenomenology—some experience of *attraction or repulsion.* 'Affects' in this sense may include, for example, a feeling of shame, an occurrent desire for

[39] Also see "Every ideal presupposes love and hatred, admiration and contempt. Either the positive emotion is the primum mobile or the negative emotion. For example, in all ressentiment ideals hatred and contempt are the primum mobile." (KGW VIII.2.10.9).

[40] Lanier R Anderson, "What is a Nietzschean Self?" In Christopher Janaway and Simon Robertson (eds) *Nietzsche, Naturalism and Normativity*, (Cambridge: Cambridge University Press, 2012), 205–235, 216.

[41] Peter Poellner, *Nietzsche and Metaphysics*, (Oxford University Press: 1995), 174.

something absent, as well as a bodily sensation experienced unqualifiedly as painful or pleasant."[42]

Christopher Janaway is the first scholar to my understanding, that fully recognizes the potential problems in conflating affects with drives. He mentions that, "We may wonder whether drives and affects are even properly distinguishable kinds."[43] But Janaway then offers a very helpful explanation that highlights the connection between the two and their respective differences. As Janaway remarks: "A drive is relatively stable to activate behavior of some kind, while an affect, put roughly is what it feels like when a drive is active within oneself." In contrast, "An affect would then be a positive or negative feeling that occurs in response to a particular drive in its striving…"[44]

Katsafanas most fully works out Janaway's idea. In the words of Katsafanas: "Drives are dispositions that induce affective orientations."[45] For Katsafanas, Schopenhauer's conception of affect and drive is analogous to Nietzsche's. Katsafanas provides a transparent yet rich explanation when viewing Schopenhauer's psychological description of romantic love. Suppose a person wishes to express his feeling of love for his partner and intends to plan an elaborate date to impress her. The person is fully aware of what he is doing and chooses which venue to take his date to. His deliberation, reflection, and planning excite him, further motivating this very deliberation. But the true cause of the excitement that attends his deliberations is an unconscious drive for reproduction. Under Katsafanas's model, planning is not epiphenomenal but is induced by an unconscious drive that excites the would-be Romeo to discover the best

[42] Peter Poellner "Affect, Value, and Objectivity", in *Nietzsche and Morality* Edited by Brian Leiter and Neil Sinhabu, (Oxford University Press, 2007) 227–262, 229. Poellner goes on to write: "Nietzsche's claims that (i) all evaluation at the ground level involves 'affects', including prominently emotions, and that (ii) evaluative experience strikes us pre-reflectively as perceptual, point towards a construal of (some) 'affects' as apparent perceptions of value." (235).

[43] Christopher Janaway, "Genealogy and Naturalism" *Nietzsche on Freedom and Autonomy*" edited by Ken Gemes, Simon May (Oxford University Press), 2009 51–69, 55.

[44] Christopher Janaway, *Beyond Selflessness*, 214.

[45] Paul Katsafanas, "Nietzsche's Philosophical Psychology'. In K. Gemes and J. Richardson (eds.), The Oxford Handbook of Nietzsche (Oxford: Oxford University Press), 726–55 Paul Katsafanas, *The Nietzschean Self: Moral Psychology, Agency, and the Unconscious*, (Oxford: Oxford University Press), 94.

means of satisfying some desire, even though the true roots behind the desire are unknown to him.

On the mental side, we get a better understanding of Katsafanas's suggestion in terms of understanding how drives recruit affections to aid with a drive's satisfaction. However, there are two lacunae that need to be addressed when examining Katsafanas's elucidation specifically. The first is that it is unclear exactly how this harnessing of the affect by the drive occurred, etiologically speaking. The animal base of emotions and the capacity of drives to harness said emotions remains unclear. Secondly, it is still ambiguous just what an affect is on the somatic side. Indeed, Fowles raises an incisive question in this regard:

> This suggestion has much to recommend it but it does make Poellner's concern all the more pressing. If drives are dispositions that generate affective orientations the explanatory efficacy of the concept of a drive is in no small part dependent on the understanding of affect we take Nietzsche to be employing. This places affects at the heart of Nietzsche's often celebrated moral psychology but leaves us needing to say more about what they are supposed to be."[46]

I return to Fowles's own somatic solution to this deep puzzle in Chap. 5.

Characteristic 5: Drives Evaluate

I now turn to the last component: drives take up an evaluation of the world. They evaluate some object or action as good and direct the subject, which serves as the drive's bearer, as it were, to acquire or eventuate the aim of the drive.[47] This last aspect of drives is the most tendentious of all the claims made above, for the assertion is not just that drives see the world from their perspective but evaluate this perspective as good; that is something worthy of pursuit. The problem, then, is really fourfold. (1) Under a strong reading, drives are representational: they cognize the world into separate things; (2) they then provide an evaluation whether

[46] Christopher Fowles "The Heart of the Flesh, 114.

[47] Mattia Riccardi "Virtuous Homunculism", 23.

(good or bad) regarding those very things; (3) they are somehow able to harness the body (and emotions) to pursue or avoid said evaluated objects; and (4) Drives form a hierarchy and exist in relationships of commanding and obedience. This last aspect is often not well-explained in the secondary literature, but it is important to think carefully about it. Suppose drives are, in the words of Katsafanas, the basic explanatory token of Nietzsche's psychology such that drives explain all actions of the subject. In that case, one must answer how drives harness the subject's various somatic systems: the lymphatic, the endocrine, the nervous, and perhaps, most centrally the muscular and skeletal.[48] These last systems are particularly poignant given the discussion regarding the Socratic model above. In directing the individual who, as we noticed, is simply a container of primeval drives, how are these drives capable of tapping into these systems?

One answer would suggest that drives are emergent phenomena of a more fundamental biological architecture belonging to physiological processes and systems. In this way, they would be explainable in terms that is consistent with physicalism, of whether a strict monist or moderate variety. Depending on the type of physicalism adopted, drives are reducible, whether ontologically or translatively to "the sort of stuff described by physics and chemistry."[49]

Although it is tempting to reduce drives to more elemental, physical components, reductionism, as a strategy of simplification, in general, is often unsatisfactory. Accordingly, I will offer an alternative solution that relies on Dennett's intentional theoretic model (see below). Having said that, and putting the question of a drive's reducibility to one side for now, a resolution to the kind of problems the evaluative claim engenders requires us to understand just why the aspect is so problematic. The real

---

[48] One of the issues with drives is the inability of the theory to make any sense of psychological causation. They appear in the words of Riccardi: "At first sight, Nietzschean–and of course, Freudian–drives are likely to appear as obsolete remnants of 19th century-theorizing." Mattia Riccardi, *Nietzsche's Philosophical Psychology*, Oxford University Press, 2021, 67.

[49] See John Dupre, "How to be Naturalistic Without Being Simplistic in the Study of Human Nature," in *Naturalism and Normativity*, edited by Mario De Carlo and David MacArthur (New York: Columbia University Press, 2010), 289. Also see chapter four of Brian Lightbody, *The Problem of Naturalism: Analytic Perspectives, Continental Virtues* (Lanham: MD, Lexington Press, 2013) Chapter 4.

issue, I think, is that the evaluative claim holds that drives are capable of agential deliberation. They understand what is relevant to their satisfaction and what is not. They impel (and compel) the subject who has said drives to pursue the object in question, much like a subject directing her body to pursue some action that the subject deems worthwhile. And if that's right, then there doesn't seem to be much of a difference between drives *simpliciter* and the person who, apparently, is nothing more than their arrangement.

The evaluative claim may appear not all that dissimilar to the aim thesis made above, so it is essential to clarify the differences between these two further, though, as we will discover, the two are connected. The aim of the drive is equivalent to the motivational force of the drive and not to the specific goal pursued. The aim aspect states that drives have fixed pursuits rooted in our biology that may be redirected but do not lose their initial purpose. To consider the element of aims above, we can say that the wolf *aims* for the sheep without thereby claiming that the wolf is aware that it is targeting a sheep for its next meal and explicitly or even tacitly evaluates the sheep as good.

To analyze the aim claim in more detail, consider the wolf example again. There is a pragmatic advantage in ascribing qualities of mind like intentions or aims to the wolf rather than attempting to reduce the wolf's pursuit of its prey to more basic biological interpretations in a crude reductive naturalistic way. Consider, for a moment, what would be needed to reduce the aim of the wolf to a physical account. First, we need to explain how the wolf's ocular retinas transmit electrical signals to its visual cortex, which then displays images that the lupine brain then processes. Next, we need to explain how particular images, turn on evolutionarily pathways triggering the wolf's nervous system. Finally, we would need to show how these signals activate the wolf's muscular/skeletal system to engage in pursuit. Obviously, some of the features of this explanation are going to be more difficult to explain than others are.

I now turn to examine the aim of the wolf under Daniel Dennett's intentional stance ascription. Dennett's model will be a critical framework employed by Riccardi, and myself, to resolve the homunculi problem, so it is vital to treat the paradigm in detail. Under this model, it makes sense to think of the wolf's aim as an intentional stance. This model is incredibly fertile as it offers ways to naturalize phenomena, which, minimally construed here would imply not relying on agential language to explain various features of mind (e.g. deliberation, consciousness, reflection etc.), without falling prey to a brute and unhelpful reductionism. Here is how it works. We are licensed in using intentions to describe the wolf's behavior. In doing so we can take the appropriate measures to protect our sheep, supposing we are a shepherd, by having guard dogs to protect the flock. However, it is crucial to recognize that this "intentional stance" we assign to the wolf, does not leave the matter settled there. We are not guilty of anthropomorphic projection because the perspective is neutral: it is a bridging mechanism that attempts to fill in, step by step, the gap between folk psychology and "bare adders and subtractors."[50] As Dennett proclaims, "This very neutrality regarding the internal details permits intentional systems theory to play its role as a middle-level specifier of subsystem competencies (sub-personal agents, in effect) in advance of detailed knowledge of how they in turn, are implemented. Eventually, we arrive at intentional systems that are simple enough to describe without further help from the intentional stance".[51] This approach is one that Riccardi seemingly adopts. However, as I will show, he is an insincere intentionalist—drives are still too premeditated to meet the minimal threshold Dennett stipulates here as a middle-level specifier. They would need to be replaced by something less reflective and reflexive.

The aim aspect focuses on the inflexibility of drives; we do not expect the hunger drive of the wolf to turn into pacification, where it lays down with the sheep. The aim character of drives, as in the case of the wolf chasing after sheep, can be understood dispositionally or even deflationarily. However, the evaluative claim has a greater epistemic and ontological commitment than this. It measures an object based on what it takes to be valuable for its expression. The question is whether Dennett's intentional systems model, which seems to succeed in naturalizing the aims of

[50] Daniel Dennett, Intentional Systems Theory, Microsoft Word - dennett_ready_for_CE _2_.doc (tufts.edu), 20.

[51] Dennett, "Intentional Systems Theory", Microsoft Word - dennett_ready_for_CE _2_.doc (tufts.edu), 20.

the wolf in the above example, works on the evaluative component of drives. To answer this question, we will need to look more closely at the aspect itself.

To draw out the main features of this aspect it is incumbent to examine some of the most cited passages in Nietzsche's *oeuvre* where the aspect seems to be supported. I begin with GS 333

> For the longest time, conscious thought was considered thought itself. Only now does it the truth dawn on us that by far the greatest part of our spirit's activity remains unconscious and unfelt. But I suppose that these instincts which are here contending against one another understand very well how to make themselves felt by, and how to hurt *one another*...Conscious thinking especially that of the philosopher, is the least vigorous and therefore also the relatively mildest and calmest form of thinking: and thus precisely philosophers are most apt to be led astray about the nature of knowledge. (GS 333)

This passage presents instincts as a different kind of thinking, indeed, as a more robust, invigorating, and primordial kind. The passage in question evinces two points: The first point is that instincts are a kind of thinking which I take to mean that instincts are representational. They are reflective. They are capable of monitoring their stated aim.[52] If Nietzsche's theory of mind is a species of HOT (Higher-Order Theory of consciousness) where a subject possesses consciousness if and only if he can take a mental state as an object of cognition (S feels pain and knows that he is in pain) then instincts can take up their own aims. They have the capacity to recognize what these aims are. Nietzsche elsewhere writes, "The drive toward "something good" thus involves some kind of 'valuation.'" (KSA 11, 167).

The second and more troubling point to consider is that these same instincts are in a constant state of *agon* with each other and understand "how to be felt by and hurt one another." I take this passage to mean that drives are not just reflective in that they know they have aims but

[52] Rex Welshon, *Nietzsche's Dynamic Metapsychology: This Uncanny Animal*, (New York: Palgrave 2014), 138.

reflexive. Reflexivity is sometimes associated not just with conscious awareness as with reflection but self-conscious awareness. Rex Welshon explains the difference: "In reflexive conscious states, the self is disclosed as a relatum of conscious states and as the owner of other conscious psychological states."[53] Drives, then, are not just simply aware of the objects that would satisfy their aims, but also understand that they are vehicles with this very aim. Also, they comprehend that there are other drives and that these drives have ambitions of their own. If that's not enough for drives to be considered reflexive, consider that they comprehend how they might influence the aims of these other drives in order to benefit from that very influence. Grouping these features together, I will call drives, "drive-conscious."

In most passages, these two attributes of drives, what I call the evaluative and drive-consciousness, respectively are united within the same extract. For example, Nietzsche writes in BGE 19:

> For our body is only a social structure composed of many souls—to his sensations of pleasure as commander. L'effet, c'est moi: what happens here is what happens in every well-constructed and happy common wealth: the ruling class identifies itself with the successes of the commonwealth. In all willing, it is absolutely a question of commanding and obeying, on the basis, as I have said already, of a social structure composed of many "souls."

Another section to consider where Nietzsche fuses the evaluative and agonic components of drives is found in section 7 of *Beyond Good and Evil*:

> But anyone who considers the basic drives of man…will find that all of them have done philosophy at some time-and that every single one of them would like only too well to represent just itself as the ultimate purpose of existence and the legitimate master of all of the other drives. For every drive wants to be master-and it attempts to philosophize in that spirit. (BGE 7)

Again, this passage runs together the above two points I draw the reader's attention to: (1) the desire to bring about some state of affairs; and (2) that

---

[53] Welshon, *Nietzsche's Dynamic Metapsychology*, 138.

every instinct has a yearning for mastery of the other instincts with the intention to use these drives for its purposes which, as was explained above, is to satisfy its aim. A final passage that again melds these two points can be found in section 481 of *Will to Power (*Nietzsche's *Nachlass*): "Every drive is a kind of lust to rule; each one has its perspective that it would like to compel all the other drives to accept as a norm."

Interpreting the implications of these passages following a natural reading, the agonic dimension of drives suggests that drives understand not only that their aims are in contention with the aims of other instincts, but there is also 'understanding' of how to make their aims salient to these other drives. Furthermore, a particular drive, say the sex drive, also comprehends that whatever drives it tries to master by taking up a perspective on them are doing the same thing to it. There is then the capacity for second-order thinking, which I call reflexive or drive-conscious thinking: the drive does not just represent some object to itself and thinks it is 'good' inducing the subject to pursue the object but is able to "drive read"—it understands there are other drives and 'knows' the aims of these drives as well.

In examining this aspect above regarding drives as expressions of will to power, it is hard not to think that Nietzsche has anthropomorphized the world; at bottom, all things are comprised of little subjects or "underwills." This symbolic interpretation then diffuses to other aspects of Nietzsche's philosophy, to his zoology and then to his moral psychology. Consider what Nietzsche writes in relation to the animal: "Every animal therefore *la bete philosophe* too–instinctively strives for an optimum of favorable conditions under which it can expend all its strength and achieve its maximal feeling of power; every animal abhors, just as instinctively and with the subtlety of discernment that is 'higher than all reason', every kind of intrusion or hindrance that obstructs or could obstruct this path to the optimum." (GM III 7).

I shall call these two problems the evaluative and the agonic. The agonic is subtended on the evaluative since drives require the capacity to take up an evaluation before they can take up a contentious perspective toward other drives. With this explanation in hand, I now turn to the homunculi fallacy. Focusing first on the evaluative aspect proper, the notion that drives are like little homunculi—agents with their own views and desires—is deeply disconcerting because drives are meant to naturalize subjectivity writ large. Recall that the biological character of drives, presupposes that the purpose of employing drives in the first place is to provide a naturalized explanatory model for consciousness. Secondly, if drives are like little agents, it is unclear how drives connect to their biological foundation. As Richardson explains, "Indeed, he (Nietzsche) readily attributes 'perspectives' to all of these drives. So despite his attacks on our mental model, it is hard not to suspect that he falls back on it in thinking of wills and drives."[54] A variety of solutions has been proposed to tackle, what shall become known, as the homunculus problem.

My purpose in this last section is to articulate the problem in broad brush strokes before turning to several solutions proposed in the secondary literature. My project is not meant to criticize these solutions in full, in fact, doing so would be next to impossible because some scholars like Welshon's, and Riccardi's respective accounts, for example, are articulated and defended in monograph size works. No, my issue is to point to an undertheorized yet necessary component of drive theory, which is the etiology pertaining to the internalization of drives themselves. I demonstrate that the Internalization Hypothesis may hold the key to offering a way out of the problem. The path to working out a successful solution to the homunculi problem, entails attempting to naturalize the features of drives into simpler components a la Dennett. In this manner, I am a sincere intentional systems analyst in contrast to Riccardi, who I deem insincere.

Before examining the solutions commentators have put forward to deal with this problem, it is essential to understand why scholars in the secondary literature have found Nietzsche's homunculism embarrassing and indeed, what all the blushing is about. Therefore, I begin by painting what the problem is in very broad brush strokes before articulating several different solutions that I categorize into three broad groups. The first is the embodied defense, of which there are two interpretations (Janaway's

[54] See Mattia Riccardi's *Nietzsche's Philosophical Psychology* Oxford University Press, 2021) pp. 49–50.

and Katsafanas's). The second is Richardson's recessive reading, and third is what I call the insincere intentional theoretic stance proposed explicitly by Riccardi and implicitly by Welshon.[55] Before looking at each proposed solution, I explicate the problem drawing on Riccardi's helpful diagnosis.

---

[55] There is another reading which I will not examine: the normative interpretation proposed by Clark and Dudrick. I will not engage with this reading for two reasons. One, my goal is to take Nietzsche's thesis in *Beyond Good and Evil* section 230 and GM II 16 more particularly seriously in that both passages suggest that Nietzsche is attempting to translate "man back into nature." The normative reading, as I understand it, instead, attributes rationality to drives themselves in order to account for their ranking within the 'soul.' The idea of rank here according to Clark and Dudrick is irreducible to causal etiology. As Clark and Dudrick mention: "One drive has a higher rank than another not in virtue of causal efficaciousness, its ability to win cases of conflicts, but in virtue of being recognized as having a right to win in such cases." Maudemarie Clark and David Dudrick. *The Soul of Nietzsche's Beyond Good and Evil.* Cambridge: Cambridge University Press, 2012) 150. They invoke Sellars' distinction between the realm of causes and that of reasons to buttress their argument. See Wilfrid Sellars, Science, Perception and Reality (London: Routledge and Kegan Paul), 169. "In characterizing an episode or a state as that of knowing, we are not giving an empirical description of that episode or state; we are placing it in the logical space of reasons, of justifying and being able to justify what it says."

However and this leads me to my second reason for rejecting a more fulsome discussion of this view point, I find Riccardi's criticism of this model to be particularly devastating. As he demonstrates, their project is incoherent. He writes:

> In my view, these difficulties stem from a deeper problem at the heart of C&D's normative reading and ultimately deriving from their oscillation between the naturalistic model of the mind defended by Dennett and the anti-naturalistic one underlying the Sellarsian framework. On the one hand, the followers of Sellars who argue that psychological descriptions cannot be further analyzed into causal ones typically deny that they can be applied at the subpersonal level. In other words, they propose that the normative-causal distinction be straightforwardly aligned with the personal-subpersonal distinction. This crucial feature of the standard Sellarsian story, however, is clearly rejected by C&D, for they want to ascribe normative features to the subpersonal drives. On the other hand—and precisely to find support for the idea that agent-like features can also be found at the subpersonal level—they fall back on Dennett's understanding of the personal- subpersonal distinction. However, though Dennett does argue that personal-level predicates can also be meaningfully applied to a person's parts, he allows descriptions so couched to be further analyzed into causal ones. Thus, at least in principle, there is for Dennett no limit to the further decomposition of the mind's functions all the way down to elementary processes manageable of causal description. There is no place for irreducible normativity in this picture, nor for any strict compartmentalization between 'space of reasons' and 'space of causes.' (Mattia Riccardi, *Nietzsche's Philosophical Psychology*, 58). My interpretation is an attempt to flesh out what a sincere intentionalist system theoretic model would look like.

Section II: The Homunculus Fallacy

In writing about the homunculi problem, Janaway states, "He (Nietzsche) came to the idea of an inner active tendency towards increase and competition between parts of an organism, which had to be viewed as will like or soul like in the sense that they are in some sense striving in competition with one another."[56] John Richardson in *Nietzsche's New Darwinism* argues that Nietzsche's notion of will to power, in many of his works, "leaves Nietzsche with no other alternative but to a mental vitalism, reading mind into all things."[57]

Although not explicitly stated, Janaway's and Richardson's joint consternation pertains to how drives, and significantly will to power, leads Nietzsche to the inescapable position of attributing mind to all things. But why is such an attribution problematic? Riccardi sheds light on this problem by indicating that if these descriptions of Nietzsche's philosophy are accurate, he commits the homunculus fallacy, of which there are two versions. The first one I will discuss, Riccardi calls the explanatory fallacy. The problem here is that the so-called explanation for the emergence of mind from non-mental physical systems is not an explanation at all. For consider that the capacity to represent an internal state to oneself is one of the characteristics of consciousness. Yet drives, which are sub-personal units, also possess exactly the same ability to the same degree. Thus, the same feature that drives were brought in to explain remain a mystery. This is but one aspect of the homunculus fallacy. Riccardi sums up the position well. "The problem here is that any account of this form is simply explanatorily idle, for it presupposes the very capacity it is supposed to elucidate."[58]

The second version of the fallacy Riccardi calls the mereological fallacy. This fallacy is committed when we attribute qualities to sub-conscious, sub-personal units, namely drives, that can only be applied to the whole embodied subject.[59] A good example of such a fallacy is in thinking that

[56] Janaway, *Beyond Selflessness*, 160.

[57] Richardson, *Nietzsche's New Darwinism*, 6.

[58] Riccardi "Virtuous Homunculi", 24.

[59] Riccardi, *Nietzsche's Philosophical Psychology*, 49.

pain may be reduced in its entirety to more basic biological units, A-delta fibers, C-fibers, and so forth. However, as Dennett notes, such a reduction is an example of a mereological fallacy because to make sense of pain, we must ascribe it to the person or creature who has it; not to the process that transmits it.

One solution to this problem is simply to argue that drives do not denote sub-personal units at all but may only be applicable to the subject person. This line of defense is taken up by Katsafanas and, in a sense, by Janaway. I will examine these positions in more detail below.

There is a third problem that Riccardi fails to mention, though. I suspect that Janaway's and Richardson's embarrassment has to do with the fact that Nietzsche's reliance on will to power (and drives) as the bedrock for his philosophical psychology represent a significant failure of his overall task namely, "to translate man back into nature." (BGE 230) As Nietzsche mentions, the entire project of the *Genealogy* can reasonably be viewed as an attempt to explain how the "breeding of man," defined as an animal with the right to make promises, came about. (GM II 1) Such a task is a process. Therefore, what needs to be done is to take the first, albeit tentative steps, in demonstrating how to get to the adders and subtractors Dennett speaks of if one's aim is to naturalize our psychological transformation. However, suppose drives, *qua* representational mental units, are the basic explanatory tokens of our philosophical psychology. In that case, it is hard to see how a naturalized investigation into the very process can get started.

In any case, turning to the solutions of "saving him (Nietzsche) and us from all embarrassment" as Janaway puts it, proposed by scholars, I begin with Janaway's own quarantine position.[60] In his *Beyond Selflessness,* Janaway limits the scope of drives to deal with, what I called the agonic problem. He turns to what he calls a "power analysis." It can be profitably used, so thinks Janaway, provided that we constrain the scope of the analysis.[61] To curb the scope of analysis would entail investigating what drives civilized human beings possess and how different cultures have promoted values that reflect the interests and/or instincts of those who wield power

[60] Christopher Janaway, *Beyond Selflessness*, 160.

[61] Christopher Janaway, *Beyond Selflessness*, 163–164.

within the culture in question. Another way of putting this is to say that we take up the drive theory and limit its analysis to the socialized human being. This approach may be successful, but it comes at substantial cost because it denaturalizes drives in a way. After all, we uproot them from their biological underpinnings.

In contrast to Janaway, Richardson returns to the Arche of drives themselves, namely will to power. In *Nietzsche's New Darwinism*, he suggests a recessive view of will to power that denies it the robust power-ontology as the singular cosmological force responsible for "setting drives and organisms against one another in advance of the process of selection."[62] Richardson notes that, "…such a "cosmic" teleology is deeply at odds with other positions Nietzsche takes. By undercutting selection, it leaves him no other way to ground will-to-power teleology than mentally."[63]

Richardson claims the German philosopher takes up a recessive view of drive theory in his more sober moments. This recessive view offers Nietzsche an opportunity to naturalize his psychology. "In better moments he treats drives as designed by selection. They are so designed simply qua drives, in that organisms are crucially rendered fit by being equipped with plastic dispositions (drives), physical set ups with causal tendencies that are plastic toward certain ends."[64] Richardson is advocating a position where genes and their phenotypical expressions give rise to bodily processes, giving rise to drives. Drives are physically platformed yet plastic enough to respond to environmental pressures.

Turning to the feature of plasticity itself is a significantly important aspect of natural selection theory. Since genes and, indeed, entire biological structures can be co-opted or exapted by natural selection, Richardson argues that drives too, if they are to be explained via natural selection models, must also be capable of this exaptation. Perhaps the best analog to this process of drive plasticity is the phenomenon of convergent evolution. Convergent evolution is when organisms develop the same biological characteristics even though their ancestors are only distantly related. A prominent example of such a process is the evolution of the eye. Birds

[62] Richardson, *Nietzsche's New Darwinism*, 51.
[63] Richardson, *Nietzsche's New Darwinism*, 51
[64] Richardson, *Nietzsche's New Darwinism*, 53.

are not directly linked to mammals regarding their phylogeny, but they too have developed a keen sense of sight independently of mammalian clades.

Richardson sums up this view by noting: "The drives that have best served reproductive success and that dominate drive economy of most organisms are drives whose goals involve some control, either over other organisms, or over other drives in the same organism. It's not really the pleasure of the outcome but the power or control it takes, that shows us what selection actually favors in drives."[65] This position acknowledges the evaluative and agonic issues I discussed above. Drives are dispositions that aim toward some salient feature of the environment. Yet 'aim' should not be understood mentalistically because drives are ultimately culled by natural selection (Richardson uses goal in Dennett's sense as an intentional fill-in bridge to a simpler adder and subtractor). In that sense, the drives are not reflective because they aim for something only if it is congruent with genetic reproductive success. The 'understanding' of their aim is not genuinely self-aware.

We can eliminate Nietzsche's notion of drive-reading concerning the agonic claim in a similar fashion. Drives seize control of other drives in the same organism because they advance reproductive success. The seizing of the drive is not due to a prior *telos* that the drive represents to itself, rather, said seizing is functional through and through. Consider Nietzsche's example of bodily systems to flesh this out. Each organ has its own purpose or goal to achieve. But all are united in a complex web of "chains of nutrition" that permit those same organs to work together, creating the promise-making animal with the capacity to exhibit more complex and complete means of domination over other organisms and, indeed, the world itself.

Although promising, the problem with Richardson's construal of drives, though, is that it represents a refraction of Janaway's. Where Janaway's solution cleaved to the encultured individual therefore forgetting the biological rootedness of drives, Richardson's problem is that he does not provide a convincing explanation or reduction of the mental dimension of drives to the biological or indeed the zoological. As I argue

[65] Richardson, *Nietzsche's New Darwinism*, 42

in previous work, an account that would seek to naturalize will to power must provide an explanation that elucidates the conscious willingness, on behalf of some subjects, who recognize that all other drives are merely means for the striving of domination.[66] Richardson's mechanical interpretation of drives does not adequately account for this reflexive nature of will to power itself where subjects strive to acquire and maintain power at all cost. Having said that, the most charitable way to read Richardson's reconstruction of drive theory is to view it as the tail end of a process of intentional systems theoretic account. Richardson is demonstrating what the pen-ultimate mechanical view of drives must look like before getting to Dennett's most basic adders and subtractors. Thus, my account is consistent with Richardson's after all in that my theory is upstream from his.

There is a second problem with Richardson' position, however. This problem undermines Richardson's attempt to address the central question of the *Genealogy*: "To breed an animal with the right to make promises–is not this the paradoxical task that nature has set itself in the case of man? Is it not the real problem regarding man?" (GM II 1) This is the fundamental issue of the *Genealogy* because it is only in exploring how the promise-making animal came about that we stand any chance of knowing ourselves (GM Preface 1) Richardson's approach to Natural Selection, however, cannot answer this essential question because it is too passive: it does not cohere with Nietzsche's views of how human beings came to internalize drives nor does is it consistent with recent developments of co-emergent evolution. Putting this last point in clearer terms, natural selection, for Richardson acts as a sieve: genes and their phenotypical and drive expressions are the actual engines of change in the world. All Natural Selection promotes is those genes that may proliferate in an environment. However, Selection may also work in a top-down fashion. Neil Campbell has noted that environmental pressures can cause specific genes to turn on and off.[67] According to the ecological niche in which the animal finds

[66] See Brian Lightbody *Nietzsche's Will to Power Naturalized Translating the Human into Nature and Nature into the Human* (Lanham Maryland: Lexington Books, 2017) 100.

[67] Neil Campbell, *Biology*. Menlo Park California, Benjamin and Cummings, 1991. Also see George F. R. Ellis, "On the Nature of Emergent Reality" *in The Reemergence of Emergence: The Emergentist Hypothesis from Science to Religion*, edited by Philip Clayton and Paul Davies, Oxford University Press, 2006), 79–109.

itself, its base pairs of DNA, adapt to those selective pressures. Moreover, the study of epigenetics has also shown how non-genetic features play a significant role in gene replication and inheritance.[68] Richardson's reductive "one-factor" analysis of drives as analogous to genes is too coarse to explain the fecundity and profundity of animal and human evolution.

I now apply the above insight to Nietzsche. Assuming we take the Internalization Hypothesis at face value—it is clear that the evolution of our species was fomented by a series of "mental acts" (i.e. representational states). The first warrior-artists desired to breed a particular type of animal and therefore developed technologies to help initiate this process. Yet Richardson does not note the importance of internalization in any considerable detail. I think this failure is because he views the Internalization Hypothesis as promoting an outdated, false theory of Lamarckism. Thus, Richardson reasons he must find another solution to do Nietzsche's work of breeding particular drives.[69] As I will show in Chap. 4, there is another way to read the internalization process such that it remains coherent with Darwinism. The upshot of my critique is meant to show that one cannot quickly expunge all mental aspects from a strictly mechanical reading as Richardson attempts to do. Rather than ignoring the Internalization Hypothesis or relegating it to the periphery, one must give it a central role if, that is, the goal of elucidating drives remains at the topmost of mind.

A similar critique can be launched at Katsafanas's tackling of the homunculus problem (even though, like Janaway, he offers an embodied defense of drives to circumvent the homunculus challenge). Katsafanas is able to side-step the mereological diagnosis of the homunculus problem because he claims, "we can deny that drives, considered in isolation, can reason, evaluate, and interpret, while maintaining that embodied drives—drives considered as part of a whole organism—can reason, evaluate, and

[68] Enrique d'Harcourt Rowold, Lara Schulzea, Sandra Van der Auwera, Hans Jörgen Grabea "Paternal transmission of early life traumatization through epigenetics: Do fathers play a role?" *Medical Hypotheses* Volume 109, November 2017, Pages 59–64. Youngeun Choi and Susan E. Mango, "Hunting for Darwin's gemmules and Lamarck's fluid: Transgenerational signaling and histone methylation" Biochimica et *Biophysica Acta (BBA)—Gene Regulatory Mechanisms* Volume 1839, Issue 12, December 2014, Pages 1440–1453.

[69] "Indeed, Nietzsche's Larmarckian tendencies—which we've noted before—erode the boundary between these two kinds of selection (natural and social)." Richardson, *Nietzsche's New Darwinism*, 192.

interpret"[70] To flesh this out, Katsafanas argues that the hunger drive does not and cannot represent its aim, namely the acquiring of food to itself. Instead, it makes a particular object salient for the embodied subject who experiences hunger. Nevertheless, returning to Stern, the use of salient is grossly underdetermined in Katsafanas's account. It can simply mean making one aware of particular foods in one's environment or have a more robust intentional connotation. In looking at the former, though, if what Katsafanas means by salient is akin to using italics to highlight some word for the reader's attention, he has in no way elucidated the evaluative or agonic elements of drive noted above. As Stern gives notice of this problem, "'Making salient', though, can also be an intentional action, just as much, say, as 'giving orders' (which he takes to be problematic)...Certainly, then, we are owed, on Katsafanas's terms, a better account of 'making salient' which doesn't turn drives into the homunculi he wants to avoid."[71]

Section III: Returning to Dennett's Intentional Systems Theoretic

I now wish to turn to Riccardi's solution to the homunculus problem he helped clarify and diagnose above. His position is fully fleshed out in his most recent work *Nietzsche's Philosophical Psychology*. His argument is framed per Dennett's intentional systems stance where taking up agential language is allowed provided that said terminology applies to a sub-personal unit and does not use qualities that apply only to persons (e.g. self-consciousness). For Riccardi, we can move along the bridge Dennett provides by treating drives as dispositions that induce affective responses. The target, for Dennett's model, it should be noted, though, is not drives *per se* but their agonic ranking. This concern presents problems for Riccardi's account, as we will see later.

---

[70] Paul Katsafanas, "Nietzsche's Philosophical Psychology", 2013 744 and *The Nietzschean Self*, 101. Katsafanas writes: "We have already seen that drives do not just blindly impel an agent to act. Rather drives operate by influencing the agent's perception and reflective thought, generating affective orientations."

[71] Stern, "Against Nietzsche's Theory of Drives", 122.

Riccardi uses Hume's deflationary view of power and repurposes it to assist in better understanding drives. Hume suggests that a superior way to think about power other than recognition and authority is to think about it dispositionally. For example, a person Hume calls a "master" has power over others, a servant, to carry out some tasks. The means of this kind of power, so holds, Hume may be established either in terms of force or agreement, but the goal of understanding this kind of power, as Hume makes clear, is to trace the relationship of domination to its causal forces.[72] This task is easier said than done, however. As even Riccardi admits, "The way this power is displayed can be made sense of in standard causal terms, though the account will arguably be much more complex than in textbook cases, such as the collision of two billiard balls."[73] That is an understatement! Thus, while Hume's framework is suggestive, he has not provided the means to establish the causal relationship that both he and (Riccardi) so desperately seek. Recognition by the servant of his master's interests is clearly required in order for the model to do any explanatory work. We haven't moved our explanation along the causal/representational dial at all.

A better way to put Riccardi's insight into motion is by turning to Steven Lukes. In his classic *Power: An Explanatory Framework*, Lukes identifies what he calls "three faces of power." The first describes domination as, "A has power over B to the extent that he can get B to do something that B would not otherwise do."[74] This understanding of power requires an acknowledgment on behalf of B that it is A who has power over him. The power could be seen as legitimate by B or could be construed as coercive. To see an example of legitimate recognition, imagine that B is an employee and is asked by A to clean the washroom. Cleaning the washroom is something B would otherwise not do, but B does it because he wants to receive a pay cheque. This notion of power clearly requires us to think about B and A as self-conscious agents with features

[72] David Hume *A Treatise of Human Nature.* Edited by L. A. Selby-Bigge. 2nd ed. Oxford: Clarendon Press. I.1 v: 12.

[73] Riccardi, *Nietzsche's Philosophical Psychology*, 60.

[74] Robert Dahl quoted from *Power a Radical View Second Edition* by Steven Lukes (London: Palgrave, 2005).

of freewill, deliberation, and the like. The other two descriptions of power, however, are more germane for our purposes.

(2) A has power over B if A can prevent B from presenting B's preferences to the fore (within an organization).[75] Power is exercised under the model "because an organization is the mobilization of bias."[76] This notion of power suggests that B might be dominated somehow because B does not understand how his interests are either curtailed or attenuated because of the very organizational setting in which he finds himself. To flesh this out, consider the following example. B is the sole representative for a group (students) on a university senate. The senate is the highest form of governance at this institution in that, it decides curriculum, budget, and so on. Policies are passed so long as the majority of senators assent to a proposed motion. B can both vote and present motions, as a member, but he is only one senator representing the largest group at the university, namely students. Other factions, faculty, administrators, and so forth, have many more members on senate. They have the means, as recognized by the governmental policies of the institution, to present their motions, which represent their interests in a meaningful way.

Furthermore, motions are brought forward in accordance with *Robert's Rules of Order*. *Robert's Rules* requires that before a motion can be voted on, it must be seconded. Yet B cannot get anyone to second his motions. Therefore, the *de jure* representative of students cannot get the senate to vote directly on what he takes to be pressing student interests and concerns. B's interests, which, given this example, are the *de facto* majority of students' interests, are prevented from being addressed in any meaningful way. Insofar as B buys into the system, dutifully attends senate meetings, votes on motions and so forth, he is prevented from addressing the concerns of students directly and is complicit in allowing the disenfranchisement of student voices to continue.

This way of thinking about power assists with understanding Riccardi's point. If we substitute "senate" for "bodily organization" or even "societal organization" then we can put flesh on how something other than recognition and interest and the like explains how some drives do not have the

[75] Lukes *Power A Radical View*, 20.

[76] Lukes, *Power A Radical View*, 20.

power for expression while others do. Consider Riccardi's example of the criminal type in *Twilight of the Idols* sec. 45. There Nietzsche argues that his (the criminal's) liveliest drives fuse with depressive affects because of society: civilization is so organized that hostile drives are severely punished. Thus, the impulse the criminal experiences to commit murder or other acts of violence is met with an affective counterforce; through past punishment, he knows that expressing the aims of such drives will bring about more pain than pleasure.[77] As a result, he becomes in the words of Nietzsche, anemic because his own feelings turn against his instincts. "The criminal type, Nietzsche evinces…is the type of the strong human being under unfavourable conditions, a strong human made sick." (TI 45)

Now Riccardi explains this phenomenon by positing that some drives are expressed more often than others because of their ability to command resources. These resources, principally, are affective capacities. Here Riccardi borrows from Gemes who lays the groundwork for a dispositional understanding of drives.[78]

> Conflicting drives dispose one towards different patterns of behavior. Which drive will eventually succeed in orienting the whole agent towards its own aim is (at least in part) a matter of each drive's impact on one's affective life. More precisely, for a drive to become and remain dominant it needs to succeed in consistently causing (or recruiting) affects through which they can issue commands to the other drives.[79]

Conversely, suppose a drive cannot recruit the right affective orientation, for example, harming someone will be met with far more pain than pleasure, say. In that case, those drives will fail, weaken, and disappear entirely; the criminal type becomes pallid. From a philological standpoint, the proposal has much to recommend it. Consider for a moment what

[77] Riccardi, "Virtuous Homunculi", 37.

[78] "Thus consider an individual who sees a moderately large animal in his or her proximity. The drive to nourishment might prompt the individual to interact with that animal as if it were a potential source of food; so, for instance, under the influence of that drive perceptual capacities would be trained to help figure the quickest route toward that animal." Riccardi's utilizes Geme's recruitment model of drives and extends its capacities to emotions. Ken Gemes, "Freud and Nietzsche on Sublimation." *Journal of Nietzsche Studies* 38 (1): 38–59, 2009, 51.

[79] Mattia Riccardi, "Virtuous Homunucli", 37.

Nietzsche writes in *Daybreak* sec. 109, where Nietzsche discusses how one may lessen the impulsive power of a drive. "I find no more than six essentially different methods of combating the vehemence of a drive. First, one can avoid opportunities for gratification of the drive, and through long and ever longer periods of non-gratification weaken it and make it wither away." (D 109) We can now claim that a drive withers away because it fails to gather affective resources.

This construal by Riccardi, where drive hierarchy is established in concomitance with the drive's ability to command affective resources, presents more problems than it solves, though. I list the main issues below:

(1) If affects both determine which drives are expressed and which will "wither away" then drives are not the real engines behind action. The true motivational force behind actions would be emotions. The relationship between drives and affects needs to be fleshed out in more detail. This question leads to the second problem.
(2) How does a drive recruit an affect? This problem becomes more pressing when one considers the substantial neuroscientific research which locates the limbic system (the hypothalamus, thalamus, amygdala, and hippocampus) as the most important components of the body in manifesting emotion. A second system integral to the generation of emotions includes the automatic Nervous System.[80] There are several others as well. Given that these systems are the indisputable somatic platform of emotional mental states because they produce chemicals like dopamine and serotonin in the former and adrenaline in the latter, we want to know how exactly a drive *qua* mental state recruits these chemical compounds? Indeed, Riccardi's difficulty in providing a causal account to answer this question becomes strikingly apparent. Observe what he writes on the hierarchical relationship of drives: "Each of us harbours numerous drives disposing us towards conflicting patterns of behaviour. According to Nietzsche which drives manages to orient the entire individual is a

[80] For a recent work that summarizes the physiology of emotions see Lisa Feldman Barret, *How Emotions are Made: The Secret Life of the Brain* (New York: Mariner Books, 2018). Chapter 4 The Origin of Feeling, 56–84.

matter of the hierarchical arrangement among them. A higher-ranked drive can activate the organism's cognitive and affect resources more easily than a lower ranked drive."[81] However, if we recall, the ranking of drives, under Riccardi's model, is the result of a drive's ability to recruit affects. But it is precisely the idea of recruitment that remains mysterious: how does the hierarchical arrangement begin? Riccardi's account is circular. This circularity leads to problem 3.

(3) If we wish to follow Dennett's model Avant letter, isn't it better to do away with drives entirely and instead focus on how affects are the true motivational source of action? If, in principle, we can reduce affects to their chemical components, then when we appeal to drives to explain how affects are causally produced, are we not using a more complex and obscure downstream element, namely drives, to describe a more straightforward, upstream unit in affect?

What is perhaps more perplexing is that Riccardi intimates that he understands these problems. He notes that "At first sight, Nietzschean and of course, Freudian drives are likely to appear as obsolete remnants of 19th century theorizing."[82] Rather curiously and in a last-ditch effort to save drives from the inevitable conclusion, namely that they are either epiphenomenal and therefore, explanatorily idle, or something else entirely (as I argue), Riccardi appeals to Panksepp's Affective Neuroscience model (hereafter AN).

In order to close off this reading, I now turn to Panksepp's neuroscientific seeking systems theory. I examine this model in some detail in order to demonstrate the superiority of my interpretation which is to view drives as symbolic implexes.

Panksepp carved out seven primary-process emotional command systems in humans and mammals. These include (SEEKING/expectancy, RAGE/anger, FEAR/anxiety, LUST, CARE/Nuturing, PANIC/sadness, and PLAY/social/joy).[83] While I do not have time to explore Panksepp's

[81] Riccardi, *Nietzsche's Philosophical Psychology*, 67.

[82] Riccardi, *Nietzsche's Philosophical Psychology*, 67.

[83] Panksepp, J. (1998). *Affective Neuroscience: The Foundations of Human and Animal Emotions*. New York, NY: Oxford University Press.

model in detail here, the purpose of these systems is to ground the affective character of mammalian behavior as well as the corresponding assimilative, inquisitive, and appropriative actions observed in animals on a neurophysiological platform.[84] More specifically, these systems are primary in that they are grounded in the subcortex (as one of Panksepp's experiments purports to show that rats that had their cortex surgically removed still displayed at least some of these basic emotions).[85]

Riccardi and Rex Welshon have used Panksepp's understanding of these systems to lend neuroscientific justification to Nietzsche's drive theory. Welshon, for example, claims that these systems are "entirely congruent with Nietzsche's claims about the causal efficacy of drives."[86] While Riccardi states that, "The parallels between this picture (Panksepp's) and Nietzsche's drives -cum-affects psychology are obvious enough."[87] However, there are some severe problems in equivocating these two. The issues become apparent when examining the choice of words Welshon and Riccardi use when comparing drives to Panskepp's affective neuroscience. Let me explain.

Notice that both use analogical language to describe the relationship between Panksepp's sub-cortical systems and drives. Drives and systems are "congruent" or "parallel" but not, it is vital to note, identical. It is easy to explain why. Panksepp's AN framework describes systems involving many components. They are not singular units *a la* drives. These systems, qua systems, aim is to ground primarily complex behavioral traits like play or inquisitiveness as properties that emerge from more straightforward biological arrangements, including affective states.

When viewed as systems, however, it becomes clear just how incongruent they are with drive theory. Consider Riccardi's dispositional drive

---

[84] Panksepp, J. (2011). Cross-species affective neuroscience decoding of the primal affective experiences of humans and related animals. PLoS ONE 6:e21236. https://doi.org/10.1371/journal.pone.0021236.

[85] Panksepp, J., Normansell, L., Cox, J., and Siviy, S. (1994). "Effects of neonatal decortication on the social play of juvenile rats." *Physiol. Behav.* 56, 429–443. https://doi.org/10.1016/0031-9384(94)90285-2.

[86] Rex Welshon, *Nietzsche's Dynamic Metapsychology: This Uncanny Animal*, 121.

[87] Riccardi, *Nietzsche's Philosophical Psychology*, 68.

framework. Drives induce affects. The ability or lack thereof of a drive to recruit affective resources determines its rank in the drive hierarchy *qua* individual. Individuals, moreover, are just a collection of drives. In addition, it was noted that the lack of expression of a drive signals its death knell; drives that are not expressed weaken and wither away. But, for Panksepp, the system under consideration contains mental states like affects along with the physical components responsible for their generation. They, therefore, cannot induce affects because affects, to use a Hegelian term, are sublated within the system itself. Rather than thinking they are congruent with drives it is more accurate to claim they are replacements for them. Indeed, this is the very view that Panksepp adopts. Panksepp's systems represent the architecture supporting conscious drives (and even feelings) in so far as the latter are emergent properties from these systems. Cezary Żechowski provides a succinct summary of this relationship:

> The drive and emotion activity of the brain is underpinned, in Panksepp's opinion, by primary emotional processes, which are instinctive and constitute a form of evolutionary "memory". Mammals need this memory to survive in the environment." Primary processes are associated with *subcortical centers* located in the lower parts of the brain, mainly in its medial part. Primary emotional processes include: sensory affects (emotions triggered by sensory stimuli—the feeling of pleasure or disgust), homoeostatic affects (resulting from interoceptive stimulation—hunger, thirst, etc.) and emotional affects (emotions and motivations experienced when acting, so-called Emotions-in-Action).[88]

Notice that although one may argue, as Riccardi and Welshon do, that drives run parallel to Panksepp's "seeking systems," there is a major disanalogy which neither scholar reveals. Where the former are the basic building blocks of human psychology [at least for Nietzsche], the seeking

[88] Cezary Zechowski, "Theory of drives and emotions—from Sigmund Freud to Jaak Panksepp *Psychiatry. Pol.* 2017; 51(6): 1181–1189 1184–1185. "Tertiary processes include cognitive functions, thoughts and planning as well as reflection, regulation of emotions, and "free will", called Intention-in-Action by Panksepp and mentalization by Fonagy." (1185) These functions of which drives also share some features emerge from other parts of the brain according to Panksepp.

systems that Panksepps refers to are a constellation of physical components of the brain. Drives are not the fundamental "adders and subtractors" a sincere intentionalist systems theorist is looking for. They are explainable to more basic elements.

However, there is another, more obvious incongruence. Panksepp's systems denote architectural inheritances that are millions of years old. One of the salient features of his research, as he has noted on numerous occasions, is to identify affective systems in animals that correspond to the same sub-cortical systems in humans.[89] If animals experience the same basic emotions as we do and these emotions are scaffolded by the same evolutionary pathways and sub-cortical brain systems, then any drugs that work to alleviate panic feelings in animals (what Panksepp calls the gateway to depression) should work on us.[90] If this emotional equivalence holds, then novel and dangerous experiments that cannot be conducted on humans for ethical reasons can be performed on animals. Humans reap the rewards of said experimental research while reducing the risk to human test subjects.

The above aspect of Panksepp's affective neuroscientific theory leads to a deeper problem for drives however: there is no room for the Internalization Hypothesis. IH, on a natural reading of drive theory, claims that what we were once semi-animals whose drives (read here AN systems) turned inward. These instincts subsequently became subverted, altered, and redirected—they expanded, taking on new aims and developing more capacious techniques of evaluation. Furthermore, they took on the capacity to evaluate and dominate other systems—an essential claim, the agonic claim as I have called it, which is nonexistent in Panksepp's theory. They became something different and much more than the systems Panksepp's describes. Once again, only a true exploration of drive theory that is colored and informed by IH can resolve this deep issue.

---

[89] See Panksepp, J. B., and Huber, R. (2004). Ethological analyses of crayfish behavior: a new invertebrate system for measuring the rewarding properties of psychostimulants. *Behav. Brain Res.* 153, 171–180. https://doi.org/10.1016/j.bbr.2003.11.014.

[90] Panksepp, J., and Yovell, Y. (2014). Preclinical modeling of primal emotional affects (Seeking, Panic and Play): gateways to the development of new treatments for depression. *Psychopathology* 47, 383–393. https://doi.org/10.1159/000366208.

It is fitting at this juncture to remind ourselves of a question raised by Stern: in explaining human action, where do drives fit in? Secondly, how can we provide a coherent framework of drives given Nietzsche's many different and sometimes contradictory things he says about them? Two solutions are required to get Nietzsche out of these respective philosophical and philological impasses. Turning to the philological, first, instead of ignoring passages, one should privilege some passages over others. As I argue in Chap. 2, the key to understanding Nietzsche's philosophical psychology is the Internalization Hypothesis. The sudden violent incorporation of what were once animal instincts set our forebears on the path of humanity, or so Nietzsche argues. Any interpretation of drive theory in the literature that does not put pride of place on I.H. is delinquent vis-à-vis offering a cogent and substantive drive theory. My purpose in the next chapter will be to set drive theory on the right track as it were. I begin by analyzing drive theory in terms of GM II 16.

Second, we need to employ the Separation Thesis to drive theory. If the Separation Thesis is simply a manner of operationalizing will to power and drive theory is will to power just circumscribed to the psychological (e.g. Janaway) and perhaps the zoological (e.g. Richardson) then by separating the symbolic from the mechanical may allow us to refrain from blushing when discussing will to power as a global explanation for all things. In concrete terms, this entails recognizing that drives are implexes; they are the intersection of two more fundamental and older physiological processes: cognition and affect. In the next chapter, I provide a new interpretation of the Internalization Hypothesis that demonstrates how we can pry apart the representational quality of drives from their biological, mechanical element. In the subsequent chapters, I provide a genealogical investigation into these two skeins: the cognitive thread on the one hand and the affective on the other.

References Used in this Chapter

Ahern, Daniel. *Nietzsche as Cultural Physician*. Pennsylvania: Pennsylvania University State Press, 1995

Alfano, Mark. *Nietzsche's Moral Psychology.* Cambridge University Press, 2019

Anderson, Lanier R. "What is a Nietzschean Self?" In Christopher Janaway and Simon Robertson (eds) *Nietzsche, Naturalism and Normativity*, Cambridge: Cambrdige University Press, 2012, 205–235.

Barret, Lisa Feldman *How Emotions are Made: The Secret Life of the Brain* (New York: Mariner Books, 2018

Brandom Robert. "Reason, Genealogy and the Hermeneutics of Magnanimity." The Howison Lectures in Philosophy delivered at the University of California, Berkeley, March 13, 2013. For a transcript, see: www.pitt.edu/~brandom/downloads/RGHM%20%2012-11-21%20a.doc.

Brown, Richard, S.G. "Nihilism: "Thus Speaks Physiology" in *Nietzsche and the Rhetoric of Nihilism: Essays on Interpretation, Language and Politics*. ed(s)., Tom Darby, Bela Egyed and Ben Jones. Ottawa: Carleton University Press, 1989.

Brown, Richard, S.G. "Nietzsche: That Profound Physiologist." *Nietzsche and Science* Eds Gregory Moore and Thomas Brobjer, Aldershot: Ashgate Press, 2004.

Campbell, Neil. *Biology*. Menlo Park California, Benjamin and Cummings, 1991

Choi, Youngeun and Mango, Susan. "Hunting for Darwin's gemmules and Lamarck's fluid: Transgenerational signaling and histone methylation" *Biochimica et Biophysica Acta (BBA)—Gene Regulatory Mechanisms* Volume 1839, Issue 12, December 2014, Pages 1440–1453.

Clark, Maudmarie and Dudrick, David. *The Soul of Nietzsche's Beyond Good and Evil.* Cambridge: Cambridge University Press, 2012

Dupre, John. "How to be Naturalistic Without Being Simplistic in the Study of Human Nature," in *Naturalism and Normativity*, edited by Mario De Carlo and David MacArthur (New York: Columbia University Press, 2010

Dennett, Daniel. "Intentional Systems Theory". Microsoft Word - dennett_ready_for_CE _2_.doc (tufts.edu)

Ellis, George. "On the Nature of Emergent Reality" in *The Reemergence of Emergence: The Emergentist Hypothesis from Science to Religion*, edited by Philip Clayton and Paul Davies, Oxford University Press, 2006)

Ferrero, Luca. "Constitutivism and the Inescapability of Agency" *Oxford Studies in Metaethics*, 2009, 4, 303–333.

Fowles, Christopher. "The Heart of the Flesh: Nietzsche on Affects and the Interpretation of the Body" *Journal of the History of Philosophy* 58 (1) 113–139, 2020.

Frankfurt, Harry. "Freedom of the Will and The Concept of a Person," *Journal of Philosophy* 68.1 1971

Gemes, Ken. "Freud and Nietzsche on Sublimation." *Journal of Nietzsche Studies* 38 (1): 38–59, 2009.

Hume, David. 1978. *A Treatise of Human Nature*. Edited by L. A. Selby-Bigge. 2nd ed. Oxford: Clarendon Press.

Janaway, Christopher, *Nietzsche on Freedom and Autonomy* edited by Ken Gemes, Simon May Oxford University Press, 2009 51–69.

Janaway, Christopher. *Beyond Selflessness: Reading Nietzsche's Genealogy* (Oxford: Oxford University Press, 2007

Katsafanas, Paul. "Nietzsche's Philosophical Psychology'. In K. Gemes and J. Richardson (eds.), *The Oxford Handbook of Nietzsche* (Oxford: Oxford University Press), 2013a, 726–55

Katsafanas, Paul *The Nietzschean Self: Moral Psychology, Agency, and the Unconscious.* Oxford: Oxford University Press, 2016.

Katsafanas, Paul. *Agency and the Foundations of Ethics: Nietzsche's Constitutivism.* Oxford University Press, 2013b.

Klein, Wayne. Nietzsche and the Promise of Philosophy. Albany, NY: State University of New York Press, 1997.

Leiter, Brian. "The Paradox of Fatalism and Self-Creation in Nietzsche," in *Willing and Nothingness: Schopenhauer as Nietzsche's Educator*, ed. Christopher Janaway (Oxford: Clarendon, 1998), 219.

Leiter, Brian. 2002. *Nietzsche on Morality*. New York: Routledge

Leiter, Brian. "Nietzsche's Theory of the Will", *Philosopher's Imprint*, Vol. 7 No. 7, 2007 1–15.

Leiter, Brian *Moral Psychology with Nietzsche*, Oxford University Press, 2019

Lightbody, Brian. "Can We Truly Love That Which is Fleeting? The Problem of Time in Marcuse's Eros and Civilization." *Florida Philosophical Review* (1) 25–42 2010.

Lightbody, Brian. *The Problem of Naturalism: Analytic Perspectives, Continental Virtues* (Lexington Press, 2013)

Lightbody, Brian. *Nietzsche's Will to Power Naturalized Translating the Human into Nature and Nature into the Human* (Lanham Maryland: Lexington Books, 2017)

Lightbody, Brian. "Hermeneutics vs. Genealogy: Brandom's Cloak or Nietzsche's Quilt" The *European Legacy,* Vol. 25 Issue 6, 2020, 635–652 Vol 2.

Lukes, Steven. *Power a Radical View* Second Edition London: Palgrave, 2005.

Mele, Alfred. "Akrasia, "Self-Control, and Second-Order Desires", *Noûs* Vol. 26, No. 3 (Sep., 1992), 281–302.

Mele, Alfred. *Effective Intentions* Oxford University Press, 2009.

Moore, Gregory. *Nietzsche, Biology, Metaphor*. Cambridge, UK: Cambridge University Press, 2002.

Panksepp, J. (1998). *Affective Neuroscience: The Foundations of Human and Animal Emotions*. New York, NY: Oxford University Press.

Panksepp, J. (2011). Cross-species affective neuroscience decoding of the primal affective experiences of humans and related animals. *PLoS ONE* 6:e21236. doi: https://doi.org/10.1371/journal.pone.0021236

Panksepp, J., Normansell, L., Cox, J., and Siviy, S. (1994). "Effects of neonatal decortication on the social play of juvenile rats." *Physiol. Behav*. 56, 429–443. doi: https://doi.org/10.1016/0031-9384(94)90285-2

Panksepp, J. B., and Huber, R. (2004). Ethological analyses of crayfish behavior: a new invertebrate system for measuring the rewarding properties of psychostimulants. *Behav. Brain Res*. 153, 171–180. doi: https://doi.org/10.1016/j.bbr.2003.11.014

Panksepp, J., and Yovell, Y. (2014). Preclinical modeling of primal emotional affects (Seeking, Panic and Play): gateways to the development of new treatments for depression. *Psychopathology* 47, 383–393.

Poellner, Peter. *Nietzsche and Metaphysics*, Oxford University Press, 1995.

Poellner, Peter. "Affect, Value, and Objectivity", in *Nietzsche and Morality* Edited by Brian Leiter and Neil Sinhabu, Oxford University Press, 2007 227–262, 229

Riccardi, Mattia. "Virtuous Homunculi: Nietzsche on the Order of Drives", *Inquiry an International Journal of Philosophy*, 61 (1) 21–41 (2018)

Riccardi, Mattia, *Nietzsche Philosophical Psychology*, Oxford University Press, 2021.

Richardson, John. *Nietzsche's New Darwinism*. Oxford: Oxford University Press, 2004.

Rowold, Enrique, Schulzea, Laura,Van der Auwera, Sandra and Hans Jörgen Grabea "Paternal transmission of early life traumatization through epigenetics: Do fathers play a role?" *Medical Hypotheses*, Volume 109, November 2017, Pages 59–64.

Sellars, Wilfred. "Empiricism and the Philosophy of Mind." In *Science, Perception and Reality*. New York: The Humanities Press, 1963

Stern, Tom. Against Nietzsche's Theory of Drives *Journal of the American Philosophical Association* Vol 1. Issue 1 Spring (2015) 121–140, 12.

Tse, Peter, Ulric. "Symbolic Thought and the Evolution of Human Morality." *Moral Psychology: The Evolution of Morality: Adaptations and Innateness* Vol. 1 Ed. Walter Sinnott-Armstrong. MIT Press, 2008, 269–297, 269–271.

Wegner, Daniel. *The Illusion of Conscious Will* (Cambridge Mass: MIT Press, 2002).

Welshon, Rex. *Nietzsche's Dynamic Metapsychology: This Uncanny Animal* New York: Palgrave 2014.

Williams, Linda. *Nietzsche's Mirror, The World as Will to Power*. Lexington MD: Rowman and Littlefield, 2000.

Zechowski, Cezary, "Theory of drives and emotions—from Sigmund Freud to Jaak Panksepp *Psychiatry. Pol.* 2017; 51(6): 1181–1189

4

The Internalization Hypothesis: A New Reading

In the previous chapter, I advocated for an implexic view of drives. In contrast, the standard view of drive theory takes drives to be the basic explanatory token of Nietzsche's philosophical psychology. In brief, my argument is that drives are symbolic in that they serve as the intersection of cognitive and affective systems. They are a representational interpretation, a narrative we tell ourselves to explain more primal and ancient psychical architecture. Such a viewpoint is in keeping with implexic genealogy. An implexic genealogy proceeds by employing the Separation Thesis in an effort to trace the strands that make up a phenomenon. In this case, we can use this methodological tool to sketch the more fundamental elements within the systems noted above. For example, the affective component, too, will be comprised of two units: a stable, somatic part and a narrational element. It is conceivable that we can continue tracing each of these strands using the same procedure of separating the more stable element from the fluid features to arrive at simpler and more primeval elements. We then take these elements and tell stories about their intersection and *voila*, we have a genealogical analysis.

With the above framework in mind, my goal in this chapter is to lay the groundwork for a naturalized account for the first stage of 'psychical

B. Lightbody, *A Genealogical Analysis of Nietzschean Drive Theory*,
https://doi.org/10.1007/978-3-031-27148-9_4

encasing' which the Internalization Hypothesis marks. Looking first at the ingestion of hostile instincts, we can examine internalization as an event that displays two characteristics: (1) docility on the affective side and (2) the development and enhancement of consciousness for which Nietzsche provides the following helpful, functional definition ("thinking, inferring, reckoning, coordinating cause and effect" GM II 16) along the cognitive dimension. These cognitive abilities are not simply created *ex nihilo* (as is often suggested in the secondary literature) but are fostered and amplified. I will argue in Chap. 5 that these attributes, both affective and cognitive, in conjunction with the trauma suffered by captured tribal peoples by states like that of Rome and other political empires, led to the development of a particular kind of individuating process—a subjectivizing development.

Subjectivization is a Foucauldian term that denotes how subjectivity becomes organized. In one of his last interviews, the French philosopher defines the term as follow: "I will call the process of subjectivization the procedure by which one obtains the constitution of a subject or more precisely of a subjectivity which of course is only one of the given possibilities of organization of self-consciousness."[1] Those "semi-animals" in Nietzsche's hyperbolic language discussed in GM II 16 undergo a radical process of traumatic self-reorganization and this is what internalization denotes, or so I argue. The final step of the argument, which I detail in Chap. 6, is to demonstrate that traumatic subjectivization is an ongoing process. To illustrate this, I compare two very different forms of Christian subjectivization namely those of Tertullian and Augustine.

To expand my thesis, I argue that docility and the development of higher order theories of consciousness, particularly the capacity and tendency to turn what Colin McGinn calls "selective cognition" on oneself, are greatly amplified with the emergence of city-states like Rome and, possibly, ancient Sumer. McGinn defines selective cognition as follows: "By this I mean the ability of thought to concern a single object in abstraction from surrounding objects: to pick one object out and focus

[1] Michel Foucault, "The Return of Morality" 242–254 in *Politics, Philosophy, Culture Interviews and Other Writings*, 1977–1984, 253.

on that object to the exclusion of others."[2] The object in question becomes the self or, more accurately put, one's bodily integrity. These cognitive powers and tendencies are advanced and promoted in part through the practice of culling the most aggressive slaves in city states. On the mechanical side, I argue that the twin processes of artificial and unconscious selection are the causal drivers responsible for the elevation of the formatting and augmentation of these two aspects (e.g. the cognitive and affective). In the next chapter, I continue to explore the causes behind the formatting of cognition and affectivity.

With the summation of the goals of this chapter in mind, I begin critically. I start by outlining the problematic nature of sections 16 and 17 of the second essay *of the Genealogy*, before turning to two solutions: The Lamarckian and the Postian. The first solution, which is more in keeping with a natural reading of the second essay as a whole, and is the dominant reading in the secondary literature, suggests that Nietzsche's account for the "internalization of man" was one subtended on Lamarck's inheritability thesis. While this proposed interpretation of these sections tracks well with a documentarian mode of the genealogical method and the claims made by Nietzsche in essay 2 specifically, the proposal is a poisoned-pill of sorts. For if Nietzsche underpins his genealogy of memory, bad conscience, and guilt on a false scientific theory, then it vitiates the entire *Genealogy* as a whole. My argument, in brief, is that the psychological mechanism of internalization misleads more than it enlightens. One can better explain the output of this relatively sudden process Nietzsche calls "the transformation of man" by undertaking the problem implexically: examining drives as the intersection of simpler components (e.g. cognitive faculties and affective dispositions). One can then show how new technologies formatted the particular somatic systems responsible for these capacities.

It may seem strange to go to such lengths to dismantle the standard reading of GM II 16 in the secondary literature, but it is vital to my project. The interpretation is so deeply entrenched in the literature that, even

[2] Colin Mcginn, *Prehension: The Hand and the Emergence of Humanity* (Cambridge, MA: MIT Press, 2015), 76.

when a countervailing reading of GM II, such as Morrison's (see below), is proffered, it is difficult to see one's way out of the internalizing framework.

This now brings me to the second part of my solution which is philological in spirit. It proposes an entirely novel reading of sections 16 and 17. More specifically, the interpretation holds that chronologically speaking, GM II 19 and 20 describe an earlier period of humanity's pre-history than GM II 16 and 17; thus, the standard reading is entirely off the mark. The problem of Lamarckism is defused. This interpretation has the added advantage of making GM II's account cohere with the anthropologists of Nietzsche's day, many of whom he read, the most significant being Albert Post. This explanation, proposed by Iain Morrison, has much to recommend it, and I will adopt features of Morrison's interpretation in providing my own solution to the problem. Nevertheless, there are two issues with this interpretation. After outlining the problematic features of both views, I turn to my own solution.

Section I: Was Nietzsche a Lamarckian?[3]

The Internalization Hypothesis provides an account of how semi-animals were transformed into human agents. When one combines, section 5 of GM II with 16, scholars have assumed that what Nietzsche is talking about is how traumatic memory is intergenerationally transmitted to offspring *via* a Lamarckian mechanism of inheritance. But the question, "Was Nietzsche a Lamarckian?" poses severe problems for the *Genealogy* if answered affirmatively. For, if Nietzsche underpins his genealogy of memory, bad conscience, and guilt on a false scientific theory, then it vitiates the *Genealogy* as a whole. Thus, those Nietzscheans who hold that Nietzsche is a Lamarckian of one stripe or another, most notably Richard Schacht, swallow a poisoned pill of sorts.

Before tackling the question whether GM II 16 is undergirded by a Lamarckian theory, I wish to zoom out a bit and examine whether there

[3] Much of this chapter constitutes a reworking of an earlier article. See Brian Lightbody "Artificial and Unconscious Selection in Nietzsche's Genealogy: Expectorating the Poisoned Pill of the Lamarckian Reading." *Genealogy*, 34.3 June, 2019, 1–23.

are other passages in Nietzsche's *oeuvre* which demonstrate an allegiance to the French botanist. In accordance with that aim, I examine two recent articles discussing Nietzsche's Lamarckism: one pro the other con. In support of Lamarck's influence on Nietzsche is Richard Schacht's paper "Nietzsche and Lamarckism." Against a Lamarckian interpretation of Nietzsche's philosophy in general, as well as the passages Schacht employs to confirm Nietzsche's Lamarckism, in particular, is Maudmarie Clark's "Nietzsche Was No Lamarckian."[4] After examining the arguments of these scholars, I then zero in to examine GM II in greater detail.

There is some debate within the secondary literature regarding Nietzsche's indebtedness or lack thereof to Lamarck.[5] There are two problems in interpreting Nietzsche as a Lamarckian. Firstly, there is only one passage in Nietzsche's published work where Lamarck is explicitly mentioned (section 99 of *The Gay Science*). There are, in addition, only two references in unpublished notes within the KSA (68 NF-1885, 34 [73]).[6] Secondly and more disconcerting, Nietzsche provides little clarity where Lamarck is mentioned directly. This is a point I do not wish to belabor as

[4] Schacht, Richard. 2013. "Nietzsche and Lamarckism", *Journal of Nietzsche Studies* 44: 264–281, 2013. Maudmarie Clark, "Nietzsche was No Lamarckian", *Journal of Nietzsche Studies* 44: 282–296, 2013.

[5] The debate regarding Lamarck's influence on Nietzsche begins with Walter Kaufmann. See his note (footnote 18 to section 264 of *Beyond Good and Evil.* Kaufmann writes, "Here, as elsewhere, Nietzsche gives expression to his Lamarckian belief in the hereditary of acquired characteristics, shared by Samuel Butler and Bernard Shaw but anathema to Nazi racists and almost universally rejected by geneticists". 404

[6] NF-1880,8[68 and NF-1885,34[73] äckel: die Disposition, die Descendenz-Theorie und die unitarische Philosophie anzunehmen, bilde den besten Maaßstab für den Grad der geistigen Superiorität unter den Menschen: er nennt die Engländer und die Deutschen: er läßt die Franzosen weg Lamarck und Comte! (According to him, the disposition to accept the theory of descent and unitary philosophy formed the best measure of the degree of spiritual superiority among men: he calls the English and the Germans; he lets the French go away Lamarck and Comte!) NF-1885,34[73] Dies ist der große Umschwung. Lamarck und Hegel—Darwin ist nur eine Nachwirkung. Die Denkweise Heraklit's und Empedokles' ist wieder erstanden. Auch Kant hat die contradictio in adjecto "reiner Geist" nicht überwunden: wir aber. (This is the big turnaround. Lamarck and Hegel—Darwin is just an aftereffect. The mindset of Heraclitus and Empedocles has risen again. Kant, too, has not overcome the contradictio in adjecto "pure spirit": we, however). These passages, are at best neutral; they demonstrate neither Nietzsche's approval nor disapproval of Lamarck.

Clark, in my opinion, definitively showed the complexity of section 99 where Nietzsche directly references Lamarck by name.[7] Like her, I think the section is too convoluted to be used as an interpretive touchstone.[8] Thus, the best means of proving Nietzsche's Lamarckian heritage, therefore, is to adopt an indirect method. Before analyzing those passages Schacht presses into service to prove his case, the first issue to be clear about is of course what Lamarckism is and, if Nietzsche is a Lamarckian, is he faithful *tout court* to the Frenchman or a heretic of some sort?

Starting with Schacht's notion of Lamarckism, he writes the following:

> I am referring to the idea that it is possible for characteristics acquired by individual creatures of some type (through intensive application, however prompted) to be biologically transmitted in some degree to their progeny—a process that, if repeated over a number of generations, can result in significant changes in the descendant tokens of the type, and may, therefore, be the explanation of the development of many traits that are now to be observed.[9]

Is this Lamarckism or some bastardized version thereof? To answer this question, it is incumbent to examine Lamarck's work. Perhaps the best summary of the French botanist's principles of evolution is given by Lamarck himself in the article "On The Influence of Circumstances on The Actions and Habits of Animals, and That of the Actions and Habits of Living Bodies, as Causes Which Modify Their Organization".[10] Lamarck, thankfully, summarizes the main principles of his theory in this clearly written article. I quote all three in full below.

> 3d. That every new want necessitating new actions to satisfy it requires, from the animal which experiences it, more frequent employment of some of its parts of which it made less use before. Thereby are developed and enlarged considerably the new parts which the wants have insensibly created in it by the efforts of its 'interior sentiment'. This is the question, as I

[7] Clark, "Nietzsche was no Lamarckian", 284.

[8] See Clark, "However, contrary to what Schacht suggests here, GS 99 does not mention or imply any concern with Lamarck's idea of "how developmental change can come about. 284.

[9] Schacht, "Nietzsche and Lamarckism", 265.

[10] Jean Baptiste Pierre Antoine Lamarck, "On the Influence of Circumstances on the Actions and Habits of Animals, and that of the Actions and Habits of Living Bodies, as Causes Which Modify Their Organization". *The American Naturalist* 22, 1888, 960–972.

> will presently prove by known facts. To arrive at a knowledge of the true causes of so many diverse forms and so many different habits, of which known animals offer us examples, it is necessary to consider that the infinitely diversified circumstances, but slowly changing, which the animals of each race are continually encountering, produce for each of them new wants and necessarily changes in their habits.[11]

What is interesting in this passage is Lamarck's notion that new wants spring from within the animal itself. Thus, to use Lamarck's giraffe example, the want of eating leaves situated on high treetops led to the more frequent employment of the giraffe's ancestor stretching its neck to reach these leaves. Presumably, the desire of eating such leaves, perhaps because they were tastier than the leaves on lower branches, led to the gradual development and lengthening of the giraffe's neck.[12] The chief principle, however, contained in this passage is one, unfortunately, that Schacht neglects to mention; interior sentiment or want is the true driver of organism evolution. Modifications of an organism are produced because the animal has new desires. However, the passages that Schacht utilizes in the *Genealogy* show that something else produces wants in the human being, namely, those "blond beasts of prey," who laid their "terrible claws upon a populace." (GM: II 17) It was these warrior-artists—as Nietzsche calls them—that laid the tracks for the formation of the modern human. (GM: II 17). Indeed, as Schacht puts it,

> It is essential to Nietzsche's account here that the phenomenon of 'bad conscience' must have originated in an abrupt transformation of the conditions of existence of a human population, and that this must have been imposed upon that population by another group, which 'went on working until this raw material of people and semi-animals [bis in solcher rohstoff von Volk und halbthier] was at last not only thoroughly kneaded and pliant but also formed [geformt]'. (GM II:17)[13]

[11] (Lamarck, 967–968).

[12] Abdul Ahad, 2011. "Evolution Without Lamarck's Theory and its Use in the Darwinian Theories of Evolution." *International Journal for Bio Re-Source and Stress Management* 2: 363–368 See Section 2 for an informative yet succinct overview of the principal animals Lamarck used to prove his theory of acquired trait inheritance.

[13] Schacht, 277.

The human being's wants are, at least initially, exogenous and not endogenous to it; they are fabricated by other creatures with specific goals in mind.

The next principle is what Lamarck refers to as the First Law. He writes,

> In every animal which has not passed the time of its development, the frequent and sustained employment of an organ gradually strengthens it, develops and enlarges it, and gives it power proportional to the duration of its use; whilst the constant disuse of a like organ weakens it, insensibly deteriorates it, progressively reduces its functions, and finally causes it to disappear.[14]

The continued use of an organ further develops, enhances, and most importantly enlarges that organ. These three traits Lamarck grouped together, calling them the "complexifying force" of life. Yet this principle is one that is not mentioned by Schacht. The standard reading of GM II 16 suggests that what Nietzsche is attempting to show is how our animal instincts are restricted due to the straitjacket of civilization. Yet these drives are not sloughed off only to be peeled away as the First Law would suggest (assuming, of course, that we read the "evolution of drives" as being materially equivalent with organ development which is perhaps another interpretative problem in using Lamarck to underwrite Nietzsche's account); they instead turn inward. "I regard the bad conscience"—Nietzsche writes in essay 2 section 16 of *The Genealogy*, a section I return to later—"as the serious illness that man was bound to contract under the stress of the most fundamental change he ever experienced—that change which occurred when he found himself finally enclosed within the walls of society and peace" (GM II 16) However, on the other hand, if Nietzsche is a Lamarckian, then we should see a corresponding increase in the size of our brain and a corresponding enlargement regarding the power and scope of our mental faculties. Moreover, although Nietzsche does, of course, acknowledge humanity's increasing technological mastery over the world, there is, however, ample proof to suggest that reason *en toto* (consciousness, reflection, memory, rationality,

[14] Lamarck, 968.

etc.) never developed fully.[15] "Man like every living being thinks continually without knowing it; the thinking that rises to consciousness is only the smallest part of all this—the most superficial and worst part". (*Gay Science*, Book V sec. 354)[16] Some wants increase our desire for self-flagellation, broadly construed, but this want is one produced by those warrior-artists, those blonde beasts of prey responsible for the creation of both civilization and subjects. They do not come from internal sentiment as Lamarck suggests.

What Lamarck calls the Second Law is the principle typically identified as truly Lamarckian.

> All that nature acquires or loses in individuals by the influence of circumstances to which the race has been exposed for a long time, and in consequence by the influence of the predominate employment of such organ, or by the influence of disuse of such part, she preserves by generation, among new individuals which spring from it, providing the acquired changes be common to both sexes, or to those which have produced new individuals.[17]

It is this passage that supposedly reveals Nietzsche's purported Lamarckism, according to Schacht. What needs to be examined is if the preparatory ground for later normative and conative developments such as memory, conscience, bad conscience, promise-making, and guilt can be formulated in terms of cultural inheritance. If they cannot, and Nietzsche holds to the Second Law, he may yet not be a full-fledged Lamarckian. Darwin, it is important to note, "directly accepted Lamarck's theory of 'inheritance of acquired characters' in the 'Origin of Species' (in 1859) in the chapter 'Laws of variation', under the sub-heading 'the effect of use and

[15] "In this new world they no longer possessed their former guides, their regulating, unconscious infallible drives: they were reduced to thinking, inferring, reckoning, co-ordinating cause and effect, these unfortunate creatures; they were reduced to their 'consciousness' their weakest and most fallible organ!" (Nietzsche, GM II 16).

[16] The Body, Zarathustra declares "is a great intelligence, a multiplicity with one sense, a war and a peace, a herd and a herdsman". Consciousness, by contrast, is called the little reason by Nietzsche. (Nietzsche 1975), Part 1 IV "On the Despisers of the Body.

[17] Lamarck, 967.

disuse".[18] One may adopt Lamarck's Second Law while rejecting, what ostensibly appears to be equally important, principles peculiar to the French botanist.

Thus, the question "Was Nietzschean a Lamarckian" is ill-phrased. Nietzsche rejects at least one aspect of Lamarck's thesis, namely, complexification. However, more importantly, Nietzsche is at pains to show, at least according to the traditional reading of drives in the scholarship, that our wants do not spring from interior sentiment at all but they are artifices of sorts; they consist of primal emotions that are blocked from their natural forms of expression. They are twisted alchemical mixtures of affect and interpretation. A more precise question is, "Does Nietzsche adopt Lamarck's Second Law (hereafter the Inheritability Thesis), i.e., that characteristics acquired by an organism during its life-cycle can be transmitted biologically to its offspring?" In what follows, I show that artificial and unconscious selection can do the same work as Lamarck's Second Law. Utilizing the notion of animal husbandry, construed rather broadly, has significant advantages over the Inheritably Thesis; the major advantage is that it is likely to be true. However, there are also two interpretative advantages. Firstly, "human husbandry" is a better fit with Nietzsche's well-known remarks on breeding (*Zuchten*) that appear throughout his *oeuvre*. Secondly, in utilizing artificial and unconscious selection as lenses through which to view key passages of *the Genealogy*, a novel understanding of the real purpose regarding the erection of walls and torture in early empires can be gleaned.

Section II: The Time-Crunch Problem: Evidence for the Inheritably Thesis in *On The Genealogy of Morals*?

By far the strongest evidence for Nietzsche's supposed Lamarckism, constrained as it now is to mean a minimalist construal of the Second Law, can be found in the passages quoted perceptively by Schacht from the

[18] Ahad, "Evolution without Lamarck's Theory and its Use in the Darwinian Theories of Evolution", 363.

second essay of the *Genealogy*. *Prima facie*, it is incredibly difficult to interpret these passages as suggesting that the development/enhancement of certain features of humanity such as memory, consciousness, and the bad conscience is the product of some non-biological, that is, cultural mechanism. They appear, rather, as characteristics acquired directly by some organism and then passed down to subsequent generations. These traits, then, are employed as scaffolds, bred-up (*heranzuzüchten*) to use Nietzsche's terminology to support more complex concepts or practices. In addition, these three acquired traits are presented as necessary components to produce Nietzsche's new, more intricate, and thoroughly normative creature "man," now defined as the only animal who has the right to make promises. Nietzsche declares the project as such in the first line of GM II: 1: "To breed an animal with the right to make promises –is not this the paradoxical task that nature has set itself in the case of man? Is it not the real problem regarding man?" (GM II: 1)

What makes these passages all the more critical (and convincing as evidence in support of Nietzsche's Lamarckism) is when they are placed within the larger framework of *The Genealogy* as a whole. The purpose of *The Genealogy*, at least when read through the lens of the documentary model, is to provide a naturalistic account for the development of morality *per se* and subsequent proliferation of moralities. This account, moreover, is one that does not invoke nor appeal to the supernatural (whether construed as the Christian God or any other deity). What we are dealing with, then, is an "animal" who grows a conscience—a moral "organ," as it were—that acts, at times, against the animal's natural, selfish instincts.[19] By viewing Lamarckism with this background in mind, specific questions come into sharper relief. The first and foremost of these is "How did this moral organ come into existence?" There is an indefinite number of possible solutions to this question, but I wish to examine three leading contenders. The first answer is in keeping with a strict natural selection reading which, by and large, would assert that the neural and conative structures responsible for altruism, to take but one example of morality, were already in place prior to the evolution of the human species. Such structures were then culturally and religiously reinterpreted in accordance

[19] See especially Nietzsche's account of "Good and Evil" in Sections 1–3 of GM I.

with the peculiarities and requirements of the geographic region in which humans found themselves. One rather robust version of this Neo-Darwinian account of morality is the position taken up by Michael Ruse. Ruse attempts to perform an end-run around Hume's is/ought distinction by arguing that our genetic make-up, as confirmed by the empirical sciences (an "is" discourse), is not something we can shake-off. He writes, "To be blunt, my Darwinism says that substantive morality is a kind of illusion, put in place by our genes, in order to make us good social cooperators. Thus, we are ethical because we feel that acting ethically is the right thing to do."[20] Feelings of wanting to help others are simply expressions of some as yet to be identified gene or genes. When we act ethically, we do so not because of a Kantian intention, Aristotelian virtue, or Utilitarian equation, but because some ethical gene "kicks in." The upshot of Ruse's biologism is that one cannot help but be altruistic broadly construed if one possesses the "ethical" gene(s).

This model is obviously one that Nietzsche cannot accept and not just because it relies on Mendelian genetics, a conception of biology that comes to prominence long after Nietzsche's death. No, the principal reason Nietzsche cannot account for altruism, guilt, or any other moral feeling in terms of natural selection is that natural selection requires millions of years of selective pressures being applied to our early non-human ancestors. Nietzsche, however, is under a "time-crunch"; he wants to show that the seemingly distinctive features of human nature such as bad conscience, guilt, and agency are the products of a sudden, violent, and rapid process—civilization.

However, the best evidence at our disposal suggests that civilizations (defined as communities with walls and tax collection) began roughly 5000+ years ago. Indeed, even if we expand civilization to mean the human Domus, we only tack on another 5000 or so years. This "time-crunch" as I am calling it means that Nietzsche requires a mechanism (whether he knows it or not) that can account for the radical kind of organismal evolution we humans went through in the proverbial blink of an eye when compared to a process like that of natural selection.

[20] Michael Ruse, "The Biological Sciences Can Act as a Ground for Ethics" *in Contemporary Debates in the Philosophy of Biology*, (New York: Wiley-Blackwell), 2010 Chapter Seventeen, 309.

Nietzsche's question that opens up his inquiry to this evolutionary process, "How can one create a memory for the human animal?", becomes all the more perplexing and challenging when viewed within the larger framework of time noted above (See GM II 1). Two other contenders that may account for such a rapid change and, thus, solve the time-crunch problem are Lamarck's Inheritability Thesis and the twin selective mechanisms of artificial and unconscious selection.

It is the unarticulated temporal background, as noted above, that informs Schacht's position. It is the time-crunch problem that presents Schacht with one desperate solution, namely, Lamarckism. It is the time-crunch problem that leaves Clark, as we shall come to discover, with so little to say.

In what follows, I show why Schacht is convinced that Nietzsche is a Lamarckian. I examine those passages in *The Genealogy*, which he and (other scholars) believe avow Nietzsche's Lamarckian leanings. In the section that follows, I demonstrate that the very same passages that Schacht presses into service in support of Lamarckism are consistent with Darwinian theories of selection of the non-natural kind. I further buttress Darwin's views by explaining the genetic underpinnings of these mechanisms demonstrating, in effect, that Darwin has hit upon the right mechanism, to explain rapid, phenotypic changes in organisms, although he would be clueless that an animal's genotype engenders phenotypic expressions. Analogously, I believe that Nietzsche too hits upon the right drivers for rapid organismal change, namely walls and "torture", but misinterprets these forces and ironically commits the same fallacy of presentism he chastises the English Utilitarians for perpetrating. Thus, just as the Utilitarians conflate the drama of an event, in this case punishment, with procedures of that same event, Nietzsche makes the same mistake in thinking that ancient forms of torture were meant to "deter." The more likely scenario is that torture was a culling device in the early Domus and that such bodily practices became infused with the narrative of deterrence much, much later.

I now quote the passages taken from essay 2 of *The Genealogy* that demonstrate Nietzsche's Lamarckism, at least according to Schacht. I examine these passages (along with Schacht's commentary) in order to show that, on the surface, there is much to recommend an interpretation of GM:II along the lines of Lamarck's Inheritability Thesis.

> The task of breeding up [heranzuzüchten] an animal that may [darf] promise […] requires as a condition and preparation the more immediate task of first making man to a certain degree necessary, uniform, like among like, regular, and consequently calculable [die nähere Aufgabe in sich, den Menschen zuerst bis zu einem gewissen Grade nothwendig, einförmig, gleich unter Gleichen, regelmässig und folglich berechenbar zu machen].[21]

Schacht interprets Nietzsche as suggesting that the uniformity of human beings was produced via a combination of torture and new physical surroundings (e.g. walls surrounding early communities) which restricted the mobility of our early ancestors. According to Schacht, then,

> A part of it (the explanation of our new found 'essence') would appear to be the idea that the application of 'fearful means' of 'torture' over a very long period of time eventually altered the character of the dispositions we start out with. So, Nietzsche famously writes, 'With the aid of such images and procedures, one finally remembers five or six 'I will not's' […]—and it was indeed with the aid of this kind of memory that one at last came 'to reason'! Ah, reason, seriousness, mastery over the affects, the whole somber thing called reflection, all these prerogatives and showpieces of man: how dearly they have been bought! How much blood and cruelty lie at the bottom of all 'good things'![22] (GM II:3)

A combination of purely non-discursive elements (torture, images of those being tortured, and physical enclosures) was used to traumatize early humans over numerous generations until, miraculously, a generation inherited (via Lamarck's second law), five or six of the prohibitions created by the first Ur community comprising what Nietzsche calls warrior-artists. (GM II, 17)

It should be noted that the overt Lamarckian interpretation of this passage is one that is not just unique to Schacht; it is also upheld by John

[21] Schacht, 274.

[22] Schacht, 275.

Richardson. In regard to GMII 3, Richardson argues, "Consider his famous account in GM ii of how a 'memory' was 'burned into' pre-civilized humans: this memory is fixed not by selection of those who can remember, but by the acquisition of pain associations that are inheritable".[23] Richardson cites other passages from Nietzsche's work (most notably GS 143 and BGE 213) that support a Lamarckian reading.[24] All this leaves Richardson to conclude that, Nietzsche " carries much further a Lamarckism that Darwin also accepts, but uses much less."[25]

The effect of these restrictive conditions created something new, "man," the sick animal. The drives for hunting, adventure, and war in our early ancestors were never extirpated but exapted. They remained ever present, ever growing, but, because these drives were now prevented from expressing themselves naturally, outwardly, they turned inward carving out the features we typically associate with subjectivity, such as a robust capacity to remember, consciousness, agency, and later guilt. Nietzsche's explanation for what he calls the "internalization of man" serves both as proof for his conjecture and as a general psychological law: "All instincts that do not discharge themselves outwardly turn inward—this is what I call the internalization of man; thus, it was that man first developed what was later called his 'soul'" or so this reading affirms. (GM: II, 16)

Section III: The Standard Reading of GM II 16 and the Covert Lamarckians

The above reading of GM II 16 by Schacht and Richardson assumes that Nietzsche subtends his account of the creation of subjectivity by invoking Lamarckism. There are other scholars, however, who take up the standard reading yet do not profess Nietzsche's indebtedness to Lamarck. I call this group the covert Lamarckians. For example, Daniel Conway, in his deeply insightful and illuminating commentary on the *Genealogy*,

[23] John Richardson, *Nietzsche's New Darwinism*, (Oxford: Oxford University Press, 2004), 18.

[24] Richardson, 17.

[25] Richardson, 17.

emphasizes the importance of the above section as the cornerstone of Nietzsche's explanation for the formation of guilt and, really, all psychological realities. Conway argues that Nietzsche presents five claims to the reader for further consideration. These five claims are as follows:

(1) Human psychology is simply a complicated instance of animal psychology;
(2) The basic processes of animal psychology are best understood as articulations of unconscious drives and instincts;
(3) It would be possible for a species to survive, and adapt to the enforced introjection of its native instinct;
(4) A naturalistic account can be provided of how this enforced introjection might have taken place;
(5) Culture or civilization is not a permanent fixture of the human condition, but a developmental stage that human beings might yet outgrow.[26]

This reading, as a whole, supports Schacht's contention. Notice that closer inspection of claims 2, 3, and 4, require a Lamarckian reading. To proffer an explanation where the enforced introjection of an animal's native instincts (via torture and enclosure) to account for the development of human psychology is to provide a purely naturalistic, non-cultural narrative. These two features reformat the prior animal psychology of humans into its more sophisticated form today, but there remains a vestige of the original primeval ancestry because "culture and civilization is not a permanent fixture of the human condition" but, by implication, torture and enclosure are permanent.

Brian Leiter's interpretation of these passages would also serve as evidence for a Lamarckian reading. In commenting on "the technique of mnemonics" in GM: II, 3, to create the preparatory groundwork for the capacity of promise-making, namely, memory, Leiter notes,

[26] Daniel Conway, Nietzsche's *On the Genealogy of Morals*, Lanham Maryland: Rowan and Littlefield, 2008, 80.

> "What bears emphasizing here is that we are discussing a phenomenon of pre-history: we are discussing what the animal man had to be like before regular civilized intercourse with his fellows (the advantages of society) would even be possible. That means, of course, that the phenomenon we are discussing—the development of conscience and, in particular, bad conscience—predates the events discussed in the First Essay of the Genealogy."[27] (My italics)

From the above passages, it would appear that Conway and Leiter are unprofessed Lamarckians, as the only other mechanism to account for the radical formatting of humans (like the cultural transmission of practices) is simply non-existent at this stage of pre-human history.[28]

Moreover, and just to be absolutely clear to his readers what he means by "soul", in case one might suspect an interpretative overreach of the above passage, Nietzsche seems to double down on his Lamarckian explanation regarding the acquirement of mental characteristics via inherited trauma. He continues, "The entire inner world, originally as thin as if it were stretched between two membranes, expanded and extended itself, acquired depth, breadth and height in the same measure as outward discharge was inhibited"(GM II, 16). Notice that Nietzsche's explanation for the creation of agency or "soul" as the capacity to reason, plan, denying impulses and forming intentions, is a process that is best understood causally; the relationship between agency and the completely mechanical, physical reigning in of desires is best expressed as a ratio. There is a direct equivalence between the means and measures of torture along with the restriction of movement and one's depth and breadth of agential formation. This process of internalization, which continued unabated for, presumably, many generations, eventually led to the social illness of humankind, the bad conscience.

---

[27] Brian Leiter, *Nietzsche's Genealogy of Morals* London: Routledge, 2002, 229.

[28] David Owen, in his *Nietzsche's Genealogy of Morality,* also affirms the standard reading where GM II 16 describes some period of our collective animal pre-history. He writes: "This accounts for the initial form of bad conscience, bad conscience at its origins, in which it is the expression of cruelty towards the animal instincts of man, a taking pleasure in the ascetic punishment of the animal instincts, of man as an animal." David Owen, *Nietzsche's Genealogy of Morality, (*McGill-Queens University Press, 2007), 105.

Descriptions such as these, along with Nietzsche's very clearly stated goal of explaining the mnemonics of memory and later consciousness, raises a significant problem for Clark's overall solution which is to provide an enculturated, socialized interpretation of the above phenomena in contrast to Schacht's interpretative schema.[29] However, how, one might ask, can these creatures who are so flighty, so impulsive, so without an understanding of self and, most importantly, with such an impoverished capacity to remember form the rudiments of any social fabric resembling customs and traditions?

Indeed, so biting is this question that Clark does not even attempt to provide an alternative interpretation of these passages. Below is the total response she gives to the plethora of primary source evidence Schacht extracts from *The Genealogy* in support of his thesis. Her response is a mere four sentences.

> I end with a short comment on GM. Schacht reads all sorts of passages from GM as revealing Nietzsche's Lamarckianism. But he devotes his account of the book to presenting its familiar story, especially concerning the origins of promising, conscience, and bad conscience. What he doesn't do is to argue for his account of these, for example, that what Nietzsche calls 'conscience' actually develops historically before 'bad conscience', or for his assumption that features of GM's story make sense only given the assumption of Lamarckianism.[30]

[29] Katsafanas' interpretation of GM II 16, brief as it is, is also susceptible to this critique. As he notes: "Once a **person** becomes a **member of society**, these drives can no longer be allowed to discharge freely. Nevertheless, Nietzsche claims that drives have a definite quantity of force, and this force cannot be straightforwardly eliminated, but only restrained or redirected. For a reason that we will examine in a moment, Nietzsche uses the term "internalization" to refer to the restraint and redirection of these drives." (My bolding) Paul Katsafanas, *The Nietzschean Self: Moral Psychology, Agency and the Unconscious,* (New York: Oxford University Press, 2016), 57. Notice that this interpretation assumes the individuals denoted in GM II 16 are persons (in contrast to the standard reading) and that at some point in history become "members of a society." While I agree that the individuals Nietzsche describes in GM II 16 are persons, Katsafanas's exploration of this passage (which is only 3 pages in length) is significantly underdetermined—he does not explain how GM II 16 connects with such sections as GM II 1–3 and 17. My account, which is fully articulated in Chap. 5, fills in many gaps of this, shall we say, "enculturated" interpretation.

[30] Clark 2013, 294.

It is true that Schacht neither provides respective accounts of promising, bad conscience or conscience nor and, just as importantly, the etiological order and subsequent causal coordination of these developments. The reason for this lacuna, in my judgment, is twofold: (1) the historical and psychological coordination between said concepts is contentious in the secondary literature; and (2) an explanation of each idea, along with an historical account regarding its development and an explanation of the historical relationship between all three notions, requires, clearly, a stand-alone book and not an article.[31] What is clear, nevertheless, is that Nietzsche sought to explain the preliminary groundwork for the possibility of such notions and, that, viewing the passages in question through a Schachtian-Lamarckism lens, within the framework of the time-crunch problem (and in the absence of some competing theory), it is difficult to interpret Nietzsche's account of psychological trait inheritance as one that is merely culturally acquired. Even so, I present Schacht's evidence in a stronger light, by focusing on the foundational requirements of the three concepts/feelings, namely, memory.

Nietzsche's account regarding the formation of culture-serving memory as the necessary precursor of promise-making, bad conscience, and the like begins in section 3 of the second essay. There Nietzsche writes,

> The worse man's memory (*Gedächtniss*) has been, the more fearful has been the appearance of his customs; the severity of the penal code portrays perhaps the clearest example of the significant measure of the degree of effort needed to overcome forgetfulness (*Vergesslichkeit*) and to impose a few primitive demands of social existence as present realities upon these slaves of momentary (*Augenblicks-Sklaven*) affect and desire". (GM II, 3) (Nietzsche's italics)

In the next paragraphs, Nietzsche goes on to list a number of horrific, and most importantly deathly forms of torture. The common attribute that all the tortures Nietzsche visits here in section 3 feature the demise of the

[31] In saying that, Richard Schacht does provide a comprehensive account of the relationship between bad conscience and guilt in his earlier essay. See Richard Schacht "Morality and Menschen." In *Nietzsche's On the Genealogy of Morals: Critical Essays, E.D.* Richard Schacht, (Berkeley: University of California Press, 1994) 427–449.

supplicant creature. The fact that these tortures end in the death of their sufferer is an important point that seems to be glossed over in the secondary literature, but it is one to which I return. When we combine this fragment with the passage just above it, where it is implied that the results of the procedures of primeval torture are somehow infused within modern humans, a picture of Lamarckian inheritance comes into sharper focus. In GM II, 3, Nietzsche declares, "One might even say that wherever on earth solemnity, seriousness, mystery, and gloomy coloring still distinguish the life of man and a people, something of the terror that formerly attended all promises, pledges, and vows on earth is still effective. The past, the longest, deepest and sternest past, breathes upon us and rise up in us whenever we become 'serious'" (GM II 3)

It is trying to read these passages as anything but an avowal of torture being utilized to improve the memory of humans on a phylogenetic scale. The harrowing and distressful feelings we, as modern humans, are all too familiar with were first engendered because of the painful practices our ancestors experienced. These practices tether ancient feelings associated with torture such as weight, pressure, and physical discomfiture, to new, complex valuations found in advanced societies such as piety, reverence, or indeed any action that requires a measure of seriousness.

Torture, combined with enclosure, produces both the distinctive, powerful, and seminal type of memory human beings now enjoy along with the first remnants of what religious types, such as shamans, would call a "soul."

> All instincts that do not discharge themselves outwardly (*Aussen*) turn inward—this is what I call the internalization (*Verinnerlichung*) of man; thus, it was that man first developed what was later called his 'soul' (*Seele*). The entire inner world, originally as thin as if it were stretched between two membranes, expanded and extended itself, acquired depth, (*Tiefe*) breadth, (Breite), and height (Höhe), in the same measure as outward discharge, was inhibited". (GM II 16)

When one takes the full measure of the passages above, they appear so obviously Lamarckian that it is challenging to view the thoughts and feelings Nietzsche claims we experience as simply the product of cultural transmission. Why, for example, is it that the unspeakable terror of the past where promises were tied to life and death is infused in our current concepts and actions where the stakes of keeping or breaking promises are not nearly so as high? Secondly, the ancient, bodily practices of torture and physical punishment Nietzsche describes are established to create a hearty capacity of memory in early humans. Furthermore, a fecund and formidable capacity of recall must be the *sine qua non* for the establishment of a culture, however broadly construed. One cannot recite the songs, stories, beliefs, and practices of a culture, no matter how simply construed, without the aid of memory. Is there, then, an alternative narrative of which to avail ourselves? To answer this question, we must first pay closer attention to the standard interpretation of the list of punishments Nietzsche provides in the section.

The standard interpretation suggests that the nine "punishments" Nietzsche lists denote entirely "mechanical" forms of torture (in that they work on the body not on the mind) devised and employed to prevent early humans from escaping primeval enwalled communities.[32] After cataloging a number of particularly gruesome punishments, Nietzsche declares, "With the aid of such images and procedures, one finally remembers five or six 'I will not's, in regard to which one had given one's promise so as to participate in the advantages of society—and it was indeed with the aid of this kind of memory that one at last came 'to reason'!" (GM II 3) However, there is a key element in the list of tortures that was missed: each torture results in the death of the victim! Consider the list of old German punishments Nietzsche compiles (as analogical forms of torture used in the earliest civilizations) to indicate the fearful means required to instill a few "I will nots" in the very first human settlements.

> Stoning (the sagas already have millstones drop on the head of guilty), breaking on the wheel (the most characteristic invention and specialty of

[32] As noted above, Daniel Conway in his *On the Genealogy of Morals: A Reader's guide* presents the standard chronological interpretation of the Genealogy where essay 2 comes before essay one and essay three comes last. Brian Leiter in *Nietzsche on Morality* and David Owen in *Nietzsche's Genealogy of Morality* also argue for the standard account. Iain Morrisson, however, in "Ascetic Slaves: Rereading Nietzsche's *on the Genealogy of Morals*", *Journal of Nietzsche Studies* 45: 2014, 230–257 argues for a very different chronology. For Morrison, essay one comes last while the third essay is contemporaneous with the last few sections of essay 2.

> the German genius in the realm of punishment!), piercing with stakes, tearing apart or trampling by horses ('quartering'), boiling of the criminal in oil or wine (still employed in the 14th and 15th centuries), the popular flaying alive ('cutting straps'), cutting flesh from the chest and also the practice of smearing the wrongdoer with honey and leaving him the blazing sun for the flies". (GM II 3)

If the above gruesome punishments are meant to correct the behavior of an early malefactor, then the person so tortured must remain alive to receive the benefit of punishment. All of the so-called punishments (some of which were first recorded in the Middle Ages but were utilized much earlier), however, conclude with the killing of their victim. Nietzsche is guilty of the very same fallacy of historical presentism he levels against the English Utilitarians. Just as he condemns them for thinking that the idea of punishment remains the same from historical epoch to historical epoch, namely, as a means of deterrence, so too Nietzsche argues that deterrence was the main purpose of all those bizarre tortures he describes in section 3. This is wrong. Examine for a moment Nietzsche's account through the lens of Pavlovian behaviorism and ask, "Can deathly methods of torture create a conditional behavioral response in its victims when those victims are terminated by that very adverse stimulus they should come to fear?" The clear answer to this question is no because the animal dies from the very negative stimulus it is meant to dread. A causal connection between the thought, "I should not break laws because doing so will lead to my death," cannot be formed. Indeed, at this stage of civilization, the idea is literally unthinkable because Nietzsche wants to make clear that it was these very procedures of torture that produced a persistent, yet unconscious state of unease, the bad conscience which, over the centuries, became the instinctive, yet subterranean touchstone for religious and moral reinterpretation. Torture or, more precisely, the kinds of torture Nietzsche mentions cannot act as "flight deterrents" in early human communities.

One might respond by claiming that those who saw others punished refrained from committing similar acts for fear of meeting the same fate. While such an inference makes sense once the establishment of a robust kind of memory is firmly in place, it cannot explain the sort of creature depicted by Nietzsche in the first several sections of essay 2 (or so the standard view would have it). It is hard to describe the beings so formatted as anything other than flighty creatures with little in the way of rational reflection, planning activity, or control over their emotions or desires. What we are dealing with, Nietzsche thinks, again assuming a very natural literal interpretation of the passage, is a creature not much, if at all, beyond the "animal." Indeed, in a prior section, Nietzsche remarks just how cruel the first states were in their need to format early humans into something we would recognize today. Nietzsche writes, "The oldest state, thus, appeared as a fearful tyranny, as an oppressive and remorseless machine, and went on working until this raw material of people and semi-animals was at last only thoroughly kneaded and pliant but also formed." (GM II 17) One may infer that, if someone is tortured and subsequently killed for violating some law, then I too will suffer the fate should I commit a similar act. However, how would such creatures with little capacity to remember, a limited (if any) faculty to draw causal conclusions, completely devoid of the capacity for long-term planning, and *sans* the notion of self-identity, make such an inference? The simple answer is that they could not and, therefore, such practices were not meant for them. For whom were they designed?

The deathly tortures Nietzsche describes in vivid detail were meant for those who felt compelled to flee the "pens" of domestication. It was for those creatures who could not stand to allow their instincts for adventure, war, and hunting to become internalized. Those creatures who were more docile, by nature were predisposed to stay within in the early confines of civilization. Torture only served to eliminate those who were too wild to be tamed. Our early domesticators chose to work with those who could be broken in. Most of our ancestors who could not be tamed, so this interpretation holds, were killed before they had a chance to breed.

Interestingly, there is a corollary between the domestication of proto-human beings and the domestication of sheep. Anthropologist James C. Scott, himself a sheep farmer, notes:

> I have always been personally offended when sheep are used as a synonym for cowardly behavior and lack of individuality. We have, for the past 8000

> years, been selecting among sheep for tractability, slaughtering first the aggressive ones who broke out of the corral. How dare we, then, turn around and slander a species for some combination of normal herd behavior and precisely those characteristics we selected for?[33]

In keeping with the standard reading of this passage which suggests that Nietzsche is discussing some scene from our collective human pre-history, it is clear that this same process of corralling and culling particularly adventurous early humans (those who climbed the walls of early civilization) is exactly analogous to Nietzsche's explanation regarding the formation of memory and consciousness, the pre-conditions for more complex, reflexive relationships such as ethics. Torture neither acted as a deterrent nor instilled a general sense of terror as a result of horrific images, at least not initially, when it came to producing fearful, obedient less forgetful creatures in the first societies.

If this reading is correct, then Nietzsche is just as guilty of the historical presentism fallacy he diagnoses in section 12 of the essay II as the English Utilitarians against whom he rails. Paraphrasing his critique of the English Utilitarians who confuse the sequence of bodily procedures with the drama of punishment, Nietzsche too has naïvely sought out the purpose of torture as either a form of fear inducement and/or deterrence and then "guilelessly placed this purpose at the beginning of the causa fiendi of torture." (GM: II, 12) Nietzsche is guilty, yet again, we might say, following Richardson, of "blurr[ing] or ignor[ing] the difference between genetic and cultural inheritance."[34]

Torture, at least initially, was a just a gratuitous means of exercising the real purpose of said procedures, namely, death. Torture did not enhance our ancestors' ability to remember, at least not initially. It did serve to create particular memories (especially cause-and-effect relationships, I would argue) once a more responsive, robust capacity to remember was present. A faculty of memory that we would recognize, a "culture-serving memory" I shall call it—which would entail the capacity to absorb and then subsequently follow, laws, practices, and traditions and adhere to

[33] James C. Scott, *Against the Grain: A History of the Earliest States*, (New Haven: Yale University Press), 2017, 80.

[34] Richardson, *Nietzsche's New Darwinism*, 18.

cause-and-effect relationships conducive for survival—was formed, then, on a genetic basis and not because of biologically inherited trauma. Assuming Nietzsche is right, namely, that our ancestors were incredibly impulsive creatures with little ability to retain disciplinary lessons, possessing a fuller capability of retention than one's conspecific (to borrow a term from the animal testing literature) must have been a genetic mutation that had tremendous selective advantages in the early Domus. Humans who could remember five or six "thou shalt nots" would have a higher survival rate than those who could not, since what is tacked onto these pronouncements would have been painful tortures leading to death. These creatures would then pass on the genes that served to underwrite a robust memory as a phenotypic capacity. Furthermore, this interpretation does not vitiate the main thrust of Nietzsche's thesis, namely, the importance of torture in forming the bad conscience. The bad conscience is an internalization of desires and feelings that typically had an outward expression. However, cultural-serving memory served as the pre-condition for the effectiveness of torture; torture was not a causal instrument in the formation of culture-serving memory *per se* but became essential in the formation of memories and epistemic relations we, as contemporary humans, would recognize, once the capacity developed more fully. The internalization of the human being began much later than Nietzsche anticipated. The capacity to remember (in a robust sense of this term) has to be first firmly ingrained in early humans, and only gradually and much later in history did deathly tortures become vastly overdetermined serving first to cull, then to please, then, much later, to deter and only more recently to correct

I now turn to another well-known passage from essay one section 11 (and a passage quoted by Schacht) to prove his case for Nietzsche's Lamarckianism.

> The meaning of all culture [*der Sinn aller Cultur*]—at least in the first place and with respect to its original function, is 'breeding the predatory animal 'Mensch' into a tame and civilized animal, a domestic animal [*aus dem raubthiere 'Mensch' ein zahmes und civilisirtes thier, ein Hausthier her-*

> *auszuzüchten*]—is a correct treatment of the development of human psychology but in a way that Nietzsche did not anticipate".[35]

The drives for adventure, war hunting, and the like manifested themselves in distinct individuals. These specific drives were blocked from expression not because they were internalized but because they were bled out as a result of culling of these very individuals. Cruelty to oneself was and is a genetic predisposition that grew to feverish pitches as more and more adventurous types were eliminated from the genetic pool and more individuals with the desired genetic traits took their place. Tameness was not initially something produced through internalization but simply genetically selected for.

Indeed, there is evidence within *the Genealogy* that supports a straightforward Darwinian reading. In section 16 of essay 2, Nietzsche compares the creation of the bad conscience to that of the transition from sea-going creatures to land animals.

> The situation that faced sea animals when they were compelled to become land animals or perish was the same as that which faced these semi-animals, well adapted to the wilderness, war, to prowling, to adventure; suddenly all their instincts were disvalued and 'suspended'. From now on, they had to walk on their feet and 'bear themselves', whereas hitherto they had been borne of water: a dreadful heaviness lay upon them".(GM II 16)

This passage could not be more anymore Darwinian; Nietzsche acknowledges the environment to be the cause of evolutionary adaptation and not the interior wants of the animal as Lamarck would have it. The animal is forced either to adapt to new environmental pressures or to die. The twist the *Genealogy* introduces, at least according to my reading, is that our adaptation was not natural but artificial and unconscious, a point that Nietzsche again upholds. "He who is by nature master," Nietzsche evinces, "comes like fate … they appear like lightning appears, too terrible, too sudden, too convincing, too 'different' even to be hated.

[35] Schacht, 273.

Their work is an instinctive creation and imposition of forms; they are the most involuntary, unconscious artists." (GM II 17)

In the next section, I explore how warranted Nietzsche's claims truly are. I demonstrate that he is more justified than he knows. I show that domestication was a rather sudden affair and that early humans were domesticated along two lines of selective practice already intimated in the above section by Nietzsche himself: artificial and unconscious.

Section IV: The Justification of Nietzsche's Account

Animal husbandry is a form of selective breeding that has its roots in the Neolithic period of approximately 12,000 years ago.[36] Our early ancestors selected animals for mating according to traits that humans found to be beneficial (e.g. fecundity, large offspring, greater frequency of gestation, healthier offspring, etc.). What is more, such selection can take place without any knowledge of the relationship between genes being transferred and their phenotypic expression. Natives of the American Plains, for example, were nomadic peoples and utilized dogs to drag supplies across great distances. As such, physical traits of dogs such as their size and strength were highly valued. Buffalo Bird Woman, a nineteenth-century Native of the North Plains, describes a traditional practice of how these traits may be manifested in litters. "As we wanted only big dogs, and those of the first litter never grew large, we always killed them, sparing not even one. From the second litter, we kept three or four of the puppies with large heads, wide faces, and big legs, for we knew that they would be big dogs; the rest we killed."[37] Artificial selection can produce significant phenotypic differences when one compares the original organism and its descendants in only a few generations removed. There would have been a strong motivation to multiply and enhance the positive

[36] Scott, *Against the Grain*, 5–7.

[37] Joshua Abram Kerscmar, "Wolves at Heart: How Dog Evolution Shaped Whites' Perceptions of Indians in North America." *Environmental History* 21: 516–540, 2016.

physical traits of some of the first domesticated animals of the late Neolithic period (e.g. dogs, goats, and sheep).[38]

In turning to the rulers of early states our 'domesticators', if Nietzsche's account, understood within the framework of the standard view is even remotely true, would have paid particular attention to the traits they wished to enhance along with the conditions under which such traits were produced. Maximizing these conditions would have been of fundamental importance for our domesticators. What specific traits were our captors "those blonde beasts of prey" seeking as we too were brought under the microscope of domestication? The answer is once again not mysterious: tameness, because tameness is the chief trait sought by all domesticators, even though such a trait, as applied to the husbandry of animals, is only selected for unconsciously. Let me explain.

Darwin argued that, in the course of artificial selection, two paths are carved: the valuable traits (as defined by the domesticator) which are consciously selected for and the unconsciously selective traits that follow these former ones.[39] Chief among these latter attributes was tameness because the domesticated animal, now taken from its wild environment, found its previously cherished characteristics (such as aggressiveness and alertness), which helped it survive before its enclosure in the early human Domus, to be non-favorable. New characteristics like docility, early socialization, and submissiveness in animals are now evolutionarily preferred in early civilization as these traits help animals to survive and reproduce. These characteristics, which appear in conjunction with the consciously selected for traits favored by breeders noted above, have a higher degree of fitness and, thus, the genotypes capable of producing these phenotypic tendencies are passed on.

---

[38] Scott, *Against the Grain*, 77.

[39] "In the present time, eminent breeders try by methodical selection, with a distinct object in view, to make a new strain or sub-breed, superior to anything existing in the country. But, for our purpose, a kind of selection, which may be called unconscious, and which results from everyone trying to possess and breed from the best individual animals, is more important". Charles Darwin, *On the Origin of Species by Means of Natural Selection*, 1st ed. (London: John Murray 1859), 34.

The famous silver fox experiment conducted by Dmitry Belyaev demonstrates Darwin's thesis of unconscious selection beautifully.[40] In 1959, Belyaev set up a long-term experiment of domestication of wild foxes (*Vulpes vulpes*) in which individuals were exclusively selected for tameness. Today, almost 50 generations later, nearly 100% of the experimental population actively seeks contact with humans.[41] They exhibit typical dog-like behavior (e.g. seeking eye-contact with humans, paying attention to facial expressions, and tail-wagging) which is directly related to neuroendocrine and ontogenetic modifications.[42] Similar behavior is found in domiciled sheep, dogs, and pigs. As James Scott notes,

> Indeed, the part of the brain most affected in domesticates is the limbic system which is responsible for activating hormones and nervous system reactions to threats of external stimuli. The shrinkage of the limbic system across all domesticated animal species from pigs to goats, to weavels to dogs, as well as commonsenls like rats, pigeons, and sparrows, is associated with raising the threshold that would trigger aggression, flight, and fear.[43]

Animals artificially selected for their reproductive characteristics also exhibited unconscious selection for traits such as reduced brain size and, therefore, impoverished alertness when compared to their wild cousins, because they were no longer affected by the selective pressures obtained in natural environments.[44]

How might we apply these facts to Nietzsche's story in the *Genealogy*? I wish to provide a skeletal examination drawing on my mechanical solution above before putting historical flesh on the framework itself. Thus, I ask the reader to bear with me for a moment. Two points are essential in this regard. One is that there would have been those humans who would have climbed the walls of ancient civilizations, only to be struck down, tortured, and killed. As discussed, torture was not meant

---

[40] Claudio Bidau, "Domestication through the Centuries: Darwin's Ideas and Dmitry Belyaev's Long-Term Experiment in Silver Foxes". *Gayana* 73: 2009, 55–72.

[41] Bidau, 65.

[42] Bidau, 65.

[43] Scott, *Against the Grain*, 81.

[44] Bidau, 59.

as a deterrent. It was not a punishment, but likely, as Nietzsche argues in essay 2 when discussing the Twelve Tables of Rome and the cutting of shares, a source of malevolent pleasure ("*de faire le mal pour le plaisir de le faire*") that had the added benefit of killing the malefactors in some horrible manner (GM II 5). The genes which caused this group of incorrigibles to be more adventurous, risk-taking, and aggressive were not selected for. The second point relates to those humans who, instead, were genetically predisposed to obey and, therefore, would have populated more rapidly. These genes would have been passed down to subsequent generations and those creatures with the most obsequious behavior would have been bred. This process, of course, does not entail that the drives that were turned inward were rooted out entirely (nor that the process of killing the most aggressive human beings was always successful), but that other drives promoting social cohesion, obeyance, genuflection, and so on became more dominant in the population. As a particular society continued to grow, fewer of Nietzsche's much heralded "strong types" would have survived the pressures of civilization, at least as conceived in the West, and would have found or experienced novel ways to die before procreating.

I argue that selective pressures on sheep and other domesticants were the same for us. Those who were not predisposed to accept their new masters actively sought ways to escape from civilization and, when caught, they were killed but not expeditiously. Instead, they were subjected to gruesome and horrendous torture. The inhabitants who remained were more docile than their aggressive counterparts and, like the silver foxes in the experiment noted above, were interbred, creating, over just a few generations, a substantively more submissive populace. These individuals would then be more receptive to the much later discourse and practices of the priestly type who, acting as shepherds for their new-found cow-eyed herd, would have directed the emotional predispositions (and perhaps on a deeper level the very drives) of their flock artificially selected for, in new ways. The cultural transmission of ideas would then have stepped in to advance further these life-denying behaviors (just as Nietzsche explains and predicted) once the genetic predispositions for submissiveness, culture-serving memory, and consciousness were formed. Docility, as a product of a genetic drive, was exapted by the priestly type who put the inherently plastic dispositions of this drive toward new ends.[45]

The argument that I advance, then, is that aggressive or non-conducive drives for civilization itself, such as adventure, war, hunting, and the like manifested themselves in some individuals and not others. Those pre-modern humans who had these drives were considered anathema to civilization and were tortured and killed for entertainment by the rulers of the first "Ur community."

However, the entertainment—"for without cruelty there is not festival" (GM II 6)—of the warrior-artists also produced another unconscious benefit, at least from their point of view: the genetic code of these individuals was not selected because they were not bred. Such belligerent instincts, noted above, were held, in the opinion of the first rulers of civilization, to be impediments to successful breeding, and they were therefore blocked from expression not because they were internalized but because they were bled out (literally) as a result of the painful practices of unconscious culling (torture) adopted by said rulers. Cruelty to oneself was and is a genetic predisposition that grew to feverish pitches as more and more "adventurous" types were eliminated from the genetic pool and more individuals with the desired genetic traits took their place. Tameness, then, the capacity to accept the new fetters of civilization was not initially something produced through internalization but genetically selected for.

In contradistinction, the I.H. performs no explanatory work in terms of elucidating the behavior of the weak; the actual driver behind obsequious, genuflection before power is to be explained via the genes said individual inherited. Nietzsche too, it would seem is guilty of attributing a false cause in the *Genealogy*, and thus much like his explanation for

[45] Richardson, *Nietzsche's New Darwinism*, 53. Plasticity is an important aspect of natural selection theory, so Richardson argues. Thus, drives may be reshaped and adapted to new ends. Richardson writes in this regard: "This account may also explain why certain drives may flourish while others wither away (see *Daybreak*, 114 and *Beyond Good and Evil*, 274). Since the environment, broadly construed, can turn genes on and off and, therefore, the drives that supervene on them, teachings of the ascetic caste, then, that were promoted to, and practiced by members of a religious or spiritual flock, would also present themselves as selective pressures." Richardson, *Nietzsche's New Darwinism*, 53.

Cornaro's diet, in section the 'Four Great Errors' of *Twilight of the Idols*, the effects of the I.H. are the consequence and not the cause of the weak's propensity for at least in part, docility.[46]

As I demonstrated, I provided both a more consistent interpretation of the text than the standard reading as well as a more warranted one. Yet, much of what my explanation remains absurd when we compare even my improvised account with all that we know about the evolution of the human species. Take language as but one example. Our capacity to use oral language surely predated the establishment of the human domus and thus so too would the culture-serving memory that scaffolds it. If that is right and surely it is, several questions remain. Who were these blond beasts of prey? Who are these semi-animals? And finally, can we use the principal elements of my solution and connect them to a historically warranted account? In what follows, I will fuse the principal feature of this account, namely that we can account for an intensification of cognitive thinking and docility by demonstrating that captured tribal peoples, as depicted in GM II 16, would have faced selective pressures when they were transported and subsequently enslaved in ancient political states.

Section V: The Postian Solution: A New Reading of GM II 16

As already noted, GM II Section 16 of *The Genealogy* is indeed puzzling. If the passage is taken at face value, that is, as a warranted description of what proto-human beings were like before the historical emergence of city-states, then it is false. Indeed, based on what is available to twenty-first century archeologists and ethnologists, the 'account' is patently

[46] In an earlier paper, I provided an alternative reading that promotes a more robustly eliminativist account of the Internalization Hypothesis. In that paper, I argued that genes played a leading role in accounting for docility. I now think that account is incorrect and my rethinking of my earlier position is largely due to Morrison. See Brian Lightbody, "Twilight of the Genealogy or A Genealogy of Twilight? Saving Nietzsche's Internalization Hypothesis from Naïve Determinism." *Philosophical Readings*, Volume 3, Sept 2021, 183–194.

absurd.[47] However, there is a deeper problem: parts of the section would appear to be ridiculous even to nineteenth-century anthropologists. More perplexing still is that Nietzsche was well acquainted with the anthropological findings of his day. We know, for example, that he read the leading nineteenth-century anthropologists such as Lubbock, Tyler, Post, and Caspari.[48] With these facts in hand, several mystifying questions emerge: How then should we interpret the passage? Who are these semi-animals? In thinking about the scope of the Internalization Hypothesis, is the hypothesis Nietzsche's attempt, no matter how crudely conceived, to explain the emergence of humanity from an earlier animal-like state? Or is it something else entirely?

The first step in articulating the problem is to address the standard reading of the passage. According to Morrison, "the overwhelming consensus amongst scholars is that Nietzsche imagines the violent conquering and entrapment of a large, loosely bound population described in sections 16 and 17 of the Second Essay—that is to say, the events that set the stage for the internalization of aggressive instincts and the formation of bad conscience—as the foundation for all human socialization."[49] This claim is undoubtedly accurate—consider Leiter's and Conway's above readings. Indeed, Morrison lists a fair number of scholars who endorse it, but it might be helpful to highlight Risse's peculiar reading to bring the problem into sharper focus.

According to Risse's gloss, Nietzsche means to demonstrate that "people are living more or less by themselves, following their instincts for food, shelter" What is important to notice here is that Risse's interpretation holds that the semi-animals are people. Yet what sort of people? If Risse's description maps onto what is known about tribal communities in the Neolithic or even Mesolithic eras, it is hard to imagine Risse's 'people'

[47] The hunter-gatherer hypothesis is firmly established in anthropology. The position holds that human beings were organized into small tribes or even simpler packs between the middle (300000–50000 BCE) and upper paleolithic (50000–12000) BCE eras. The Mesolithic and Neolithic periods come next. It is in this last period where humans begin cultivating crops on a large scale. Importantly nothing is "sudden" about any of these developments despite Nietzsche's speculations to the contrary.

[48] Iain P. Morrison, "Nietzsche, the Anthropologists, and the Genealogy of Trauma" *Genealogy* 1–16, 1.

[49] Morrison, "Nietzsche, the Anthropologists, and the Genealogy of Trauma", 8.

living by themselves.[50] Thus, whether Nietzsche's description of these semi-animals is construed literally as a unique type of beast (Conway et al.) or even figuratively, à la Risse, there is something unreasonable about Nietzsche's explanation when it is interpreted literally prompting a more figurative, imaginary reading a la Williams and Queloz.[51] Either way, any literal reading of the passage is fraught.

There are two problems then. The first is epistemic. Nietzsche's story is unwarranted based on archeological and anthropological evidence. The second is philological. I will demonstrate that in order to address the epistemic, we need to address the philological problem first. To accomplish that goal, we must return to Morrison's helpful paper, which situates Nietzsche's views amongst the anthropologists of his day. By scrutinizing the nineteenth-century context of Nietzsche's anthropological sources, we better understand what Nietzsche is advancing in section GM II 16.

In the late 1870s, a good decade before he wrote the *Genealogy*, Nietzsche read the works of English anthropologists John Lubbock and Edward Tylor in German translation. By the early 1880s, Nietzsche was acquainted with the works of Albert Post and Otto Caspari, two leading German anthropologists influenced by Lubbock and Tylor. As Thatcher as shown, the work by these and other writers (attempting to document humanity's pre-history with, albeit incredibly crude tools), had a profound impact on Nietzsche's philosophical ideas. In particular, they proved highly influential vis-à-vis *The Genealogy's* content and overall psychological typology (noble types vs. slave types).[52]

However, Nietzsche's conception of early pre-state tribal communities is most indebted to Post, at least according to Morrison. As Morrison evinces, Nietzsche adopts Post's story of community progression: from egalitarian, nomadic, hunter-gatherer societies to pastoral tribal societies organized along kinship lines, to agrarian political states.[53] Although Nietzsche stresses one component that promoted tribal unification,

---

[50] Mathias Risse, "The Second Treatise in On the Genealogy of Morality: Nietzsche on the Origin of the Bad Conscience," *European Journal of Philosophy* 9: 2001, 55–81, 57.

[51] Although neither Williams nor Queloz treats GM II 16 directly, they both would surely think that it is further evidence for an imaginary reading of *The Genealogy.*

[52] David Thatcher, "Nietzsche's Debt to Lubbock." *Journal of the History of Ideas* 44, 1983, 293–309.

[53] Morrison, "Nietzsche, The Anthropologists and the Genealogy of Trauma", 9–11.

namely paying homage to the gods in GM II 19 in the form of animal and human sacrifices, one must turn to Post to get a more fulsome understanding of the rituals surrounding the payment of spiritual debt, the true tie that binds. By turning to Post, Nietzsche's construction of early tribal political organization as depicted in GM II 19 comes into view.

Post explains the development from nomadic hunting gathering communities to pastoral tribal units as societies that developed settled forms of peace cooperatives—"the *Gaugenossenschaft* or peasant community, and the *Hausgemeinschaft* or house community."[54] In fleshing out what this peace cooperative entailed, we need to contrast it with Nietzsche's and Post's story of state organization. State organization, for Post and Nietzsche, begins with the enslavement of other tribes. According to Post, the introduction of slaves into a community leads to further social stratification eventually giving rise to the notion of an elite caste, the nobility.[55] In sections GM II 16 and 17 Nietzsche argues that the enslaving of one ethnic group by another leads to hierarchical organization and layering within the original community. As the tribal community grows in number and becomes better organized, it further incorporates other groups (GM II 19). We now have a snow balling effect where such tribes form raiding parties capturing members, (predominately females capable of child-bearing) from other communities. As Morrison summarizes, "It is surely from these kinds of considerations that Nietzsche draws his conception of a small band of conquerors in sections 16 and 17."[56]

Pre-state communities are structured along two different organizing principles. "The simplest is the *Friedensgenossenschaft* is, at least initially, egalitarian and communistic in its attitudes towards property (movable and immovable)."[57] Clan associations, in contrast, are organized around blood relationships (*Blutverwandtschaftlichen*).[58] Thus, according to Morrison, sections 16 and 17 come after—assuming Nietzsche is attempting to present a somewhat accurate pre-history of human social

[54] Morrison, 10.
[55] Morrison, 10.
[56] Morrison, 11.
[57] Morrison, 10.
[58] Morrison, 10.

development—Nietzsche's description of early pre-history as given in section 19. As Nietzsche describes these early tribal communities in II 19, they repay their indebtedness to their ancestors, as noted, through sacrifices. According to Post, what both communities share in common is a kind of peace cooperative—members within the tribe identify with the spirit, aims, members, and culture of the group as a whole.[59] While there may be distinctions between Chiefs ("Big men") and social roles according to one's gender, the members are of the same ethnic makeup; there is not an oppressor and oppressed class as we clearly have in the early political states.[60]

Yet Nietzsche argues that memory, and socialization writ large are the products of civilization itself. Indeed, he refers to the first subjects of civilization as "semi-animals" with their interior subjectivity "as thin as if it were stretched between two membranes." (GM II 16) Moreover, Nietzsche writes in section 17 that the people [on whom the blonde beasts preyed] were like shapeless and impressionable dough: "The oldest state thus appeared as fearful tyranny, as an oppressive and remorseless machine, and went on working until this raw material of people and semi-animals was at last not only thoroughly kneaded and pliant but also formed." (GM II 17)

We have a paradox: on the one hand, Nietzsche seems to suggest that memory, socialization and subjectivity themselves are products of civilization and yet, as Morrison shows, the sources for Nietzsche's view do not mention anything like a founding act of violence for the emergence of the state. How then do we work our way through this paradox?

Morrison's solution is to take his cue from Post. According to Post, war, and its intended consequences (e.g. the taking of slaves) injects a new feature into the peace cooperative of the early tribes described by Nietzsche in section 19. Slaves are not part of the tribe and therefore are not part of the cooperative. A division now between original tribal members and outsiders gives rise to further stratification and hierarchy. Morrison then employs Nietzsche's theory of drives to solve the problem

[59] Morrison, 9–10.

[60] See Keith F. Otterbein, *How War Began,* Texas A and M University, 2004, Chapter 6: Four Pristine States and Their Warfare.

noted above: To whom does the Internalization Hypothesis apply? Morrison answers, "The drive-based psychological expressions and outlets of the conquered tribe are simply cut off and the slaves are violently forced into a pre-made system of order and function, their practices and customs completely dictated to them. The trauma of enslavement for such a group is followed, then, by a complete damning up of instinctual expression."[61]

This interpretation does, on the surface, fill in some philological holes as the anthropologists Nietzsche read seemed to believe that pre-state people were herd-like and not individuals as such.[62] However, I also agree with Morrison that we must read section 19 as coming before sections 16 and 17, historically speaking. Indeed Nietzsche himself seems to flag this in writing: "Within the original tribal community—we are speaking of *primeval times*—the living generation always recognized a juridical duty toward the earliest generations and toward the earliest, which founded the tribe" (GM II 19). In reading this section as coming before, chronologically speaking, the passages discussing the Internalization Hypothesis, we can now make sense of who these early captives of the warrior-artists were. Taking the events of GM II 19 to occur before, chronologically speaking, GM II 16, is perhaps the most beneficial aspect of Morrison's solution, and I will come back to it.

However, the mechanism that Morrison appeals to in order to make sense of this section, namely the Internalization Hypothesis, performs no real work in clarifying this process of agential development. It misleads more than it enlightens. Surely, such tribal subjects would have a language, understand what had happened to them, and could immediately infer what might happen if they disobeyed their new masters, the blonde beasts of prey and so on. It is a criticism that returns us to Stern. Stern is at pains to remind interpreters that drives perform no illuminating work in many cases and obscure the real reasons for the phenomenon in question. The same could be said here. The phenomenon we are attempting to understand is socialization or, as Katsafanas's put it, "becoming a

[61] Morrison, 12.

[62] Morrison, 11.

member of society."[63] Drives, I contend, are not required to understand the resocialization of enslaved people. Moreover, they are unhelpful in trying to comprehend this process and, moreover, obscure the real mechanism. For consider that even according to Morrison, the individuals in GM II 19 are subjects; they are full-blown moral agents capable of reasoning, learning, and forming intentions. Therefore, enslaved peoples learn either through language (or even sign language) or through classical conditioning what behavior is endorsed and what is punishable in the new city-state in which they find themselves. Individuals would see their once tribesman being tortured or killed—assuming GM II 3 is remotely accurate—due to some orders being disobeyed. They would reason that not following the directions given by their new masters entails extreme torture and, likely, death. Once more, there is nothing for drives, as traditionally understood, to explain in any of this. At most, one might say that enslaved people follow the direction of their new-found masters because their collective drive for survival is dominant. Yet such an explanation is otiose. The appeal to the tribe's "dominant drives" whatever that might mean, to explain this resocialization process is explanatory idle.

The second problem with Morrison's approach is what we discovered above: Nietzsche's reference to the original captives as "semi-animals." Yet it is these same semi-animals, so Morrison holds that have feasts, music, honors, and sacrifices? Moreover, they deem such events significant because they believe their existence is possible because of the struggle their ancestors went through who they turn into gods. Underwritten by their understanding of debt to their forebears, as primitive and underdeveloped though it may be, these practices are inconsistent with the beastly like ascriptions Nietzsche gives to such individuals in section 16. How then do we make sense of this?

The way to work through the problem is to remember the separation of explanations. Drives are implexic: they are the interstice where the biological meets the mental. If Morrison is right (and I think he is), in that sections 16–17 are really, "about the psychological implications of trauma undergone by the conquered tribe" then one must trace how that

[63] Paul Katsafanas, *The Nietzschean Self, (*Oxford University Press, 2016, 57.

trauma was practiced and inherited in terms of the Separation Thesis. And that means, clearly explaining the practices of trauma as they orbit the body.[64]

Here is what I propose. Before turning to section 17, we must look at the sea-creature parable once more, this time through a narrational (e.g. horizontal line) in keeping with implexic genealogy. Nietzsche writes, "The situation that faced sea-animals when they were compelled to become land animals or perish was the same as that which faced these semi-animals, well adapted to the wilderness, to war, to prowling, to adventure." (GM II 16) Here I submit Nietzsche is talking about those subjects who were taken captive, transported to some larger market square (state capital), and then sold into slavery. They are the ones who undergo, as Orlando Patterson notes: social death.[65] They are stripped of their ranking within their tribe, and their entire social network collapses; whatever meaning they had given to their lives and was given to them by their home tribe has been stripped off and discarded. Thus, when Nietzsche turns to examine the formation of the state in section 17, his account is not objective—he is explaining how the state *appeared*. But to whom does it seem that way? He is not capturing the view of the state from the perspective of full-fledged Roman citizens or (Summerian nobility). No, he is looking at the state through the framework of the slaves of those very communities. Their stance confirms that "the state" is an act of violence and nothing but acts of violence. Thus, a more sensible interpretation of this passage would suggest that Nietzsche is not providing an objective account of the historical development of states *per se* in GM II 17 as the standard reading holds.[66] Instead, he presents how states seem to those dispossessed of their previous social networks. "That the oldest state thus *appeared* as a fearful tyranny, as an oppressive and remorseless machine". (GM II 17)

---

[64] Morrison, 12.

[65] Orlando Patterson, *Slavery and Social Death: A Comparative Analysis* (Harvard University Press), 1982.

[66] I am here referring to Nietzsche's perspectivism claim advanced in GM III 12. I explore this claim in more detail in Chap. 5. For a treatment on how this claim has been interpreted in the secondary literature see Brian Lightbody Nietzsche, "Perspectivism, Anti-Realism: An Inconsistent Triad," *The European Legacy: Towards New Paradigms*. Vol. 15 issue 4, 2010, 425–438.

From the standpoint of the slaves, within what is now the state, they now found their dominant drives, the ones inculcated and promoted in their tribe, to be not just worthless but indeed "false": Acting on those drives would get the slave killed in the new city-state. Thus, the 'instincts' of their original tribe (striking back at an aggressor e.g.) were devalued and (had to be) "suspended."[67] Morrison is correct in suggesting that tribal peoples were resocialized when rehomed in imperial states as slaves. However, his description of how this 'retraining' occurred is grossly undetermined. The traditional interpretation of the Internalization Hypothesis is not up to the task of performing this kind of work.

When we combine Morrison's account with the one provided above, we not only see an interpretation that is more consistent with other parts of GM II but with the genealogical method as a whole. I now tack on the stable account above to demonstrate how said resocialization took place. Artificial and unconscious selective pressure would apply to these slaves in their newly found Domus. Those slaves who survive the novel demands and rigors of indentured life would have the opportunity, depending on the state, to have children. Those who could not suffer under the lash of their masters would rebel and likely be killed—their line would be discontinued. The cauldron of civilization would continue this process and select for docility—only those who could tolerate suffering, pain, and trauma would be softened, 'cooked', and made palatable for civilizing forces. Those who could not endure such brutal mistreatment and inhuman conditions would either fight or escape, with both choices leading to the same result—their immediate elimination.

Working coevally with the pressures that select for tameness as described above would be those that also select for cognitive ability. Slaves who were incapable of learning the jobs their masters required or, even more tellingly, who could not predict their master's temperaments would be killed forthwith. Those who could use their "consciousness" "their

---

[67] I am using instinct and drive symbolically here. My contention is that we can explain this "suspension" in terms of the cognitive and affective threads that, when united, form drives. Such a strategy is in keeping with the deflationary ethos of implexic genealogy. For more on this ethos which I cannot treat here see my earlier paper: Brian Lightbody, "Letting the Truth Out: Children, Naïve Truth and Deflationsim" *Kriterion: Journal of Philosophy* 34 (1) May, 2019, 1–26.

most fallible organ" which, again, Nietzsche operationalizes instrumentally as the ability to reckon, infer, calculate, and so forth, would understand the need to put away their old tribal ways (social dispositions). They would survive and, perhaps in time, flourish to have children and even property of their own, depending, of course, on the state in question. The above account I offer is admittedly painted in very broad-brush strokes. In the next chapters, I explain the mechanisms behind the resocialization of conquered tribal people by imperial states. I focus on two components: docility and the amplification of specific cognitive abilities such as pattern recognition and memory. I examine how trauma further conditioned the slaves in Nietzsche's genealogical history in the next chapter.

References

Ahad, Abdul. Evolution Without Lamarck's Theory and its Use in the Darwinian Theories of Evolution. *International Journal for Bio Re-Source and Stress Management* 2, 2011, 363–368.

Bidau, Claudio J. Domestication through the Centuries: Darwin's Ideas and Dmitry Belyaev's Long-Term Experiment in Silver Foxes. *Gayana* 73, 2009, 55–72.

Clark, Maudmarie. "Nietzsche was No Larmarckian". *Journal of Nietzsche Studies* 44, 2013, 282–296.

Conway, Daniel. *Nietzsche's On the Genealogy of Morals: A Reader's Guide.* London: Rowman and Littlefield, 2008.

Darwin, Charles. *On the Origin of Species by Means of Natural Selection*, 1st ed. London: John Murray, 1859.

Dennett, Daniel. *Darwin's Dangerous Idea*. New York: Simon and Schuster, 1994.

Foucault, Michel. "Nietzsche, Genealogy, History". In *Language, Counter-Memory, Practice Selected Essays and Interviews by Michel Foucault*. Edited by Donald F. Bouchard. Ithaca and New York: Cornell University Press, 1977.

Foucault, Michel. "The Return of Morality" *Politics, Philosophy, Culture Interviews and Other Writings, 1977–1984,* Trans. Alan Sheridan, 1988.

Kerscmar, Joshua Abram. "Wolves at Heart: How Dog Evolution Shaped Whites' Perceptions of Indians in North America." *Environmental History* 21: 516–540, 2016.

Lamarck, Jean Baptiste Pierre Antoine. "On the Influence of Circumstances on the Actions and Habits of Animals, and that of the Actions and Habits of Living Bodies, as Causes Which Modify Their Organization". *The American Naturalist* 22, 1888, 960–972.

Leiter, Brian. *Nietzsche on Morality*. New York: Routledge, 2002.

Lightbody, Brian. "Nietzsche, Perspectivism, Anti-Realism: An Inconsistent Triad." *The European Legacy: Towards New Paradigms*. Vol. 15 issue 4, 2010, 425–438.

Lightbody, Brian. *Philosophical Genealogy: An Epistemological Reconstruction of Nietzsche and Foucault's Genealogical Method*. New York: Peter Lang, vols. 1 and 2. 2010 and 2011.

Lightbody, Brian. "Letting the Truth Out: Children, Naïve Truth and Deflationsim" *Kriterion: Journal of Philosophy* 34 (1) May, 2019, 1–26.

Lightbody, Brian. "Twilight of the Genealogy or A Genealogy of Twilight? Saving Nietzsche's Internalization Hypothesis from Naïve Determinism." *Philosophical Readings*, Volume 3, Sept 2021, 183–194.

Mcginn, Colin. *Prehension: The Hand and the Emergence of Humanity*. Cambridge, MA: MIT Press, 2015.

Migotti, Mark. "Slave Morality, Socrates, and the Bushmen: A Critical Introduction to On the Genealogy of Morality, Essay 1". In *Nietzsche's On the Genealogy of Morals: Critical Essays*. Edited by Christa Davis Acampora. Lanham: Rowman and Littlefield, 2006.

Morrisson, Iain. Ascetic Slaves: Rereading Nietzsche's on the Genealogy of Morals. *Journal of Nietzsche Studies* 45, 2014, 230–257.

Morrisson, Iain P. Nietzsche, the Anthropologists, and the Genealogy of Trauma" *Genealogy* 1–16, 1, 2021.

Otterbein, Keith F. *How War Began*. Texas A and M University Press, 2004.

Owen, David. *Nietzsche's Genealogy of Morality*. Montreal: McGill-Queen's Press, 2007.

Patterson, Orlando. *Slavery and Social Death: A Comparative Study*, Harvard University Press, 1982.

Ricardson, John. *Nietzsche's New Darwinism*. Oxford: Oxford University Press, 2004.

Risse, Mathias. "The Second Treatise in On the Genealogy of Morality: Nietzsche on the Origin of the Bad Conscience". *European Journal of Philosophy* 9, 2011, 55–81

Ruse, Michael. The Biological Sciences Can Act as a Ground for Ethics. In *Contemporary Debates in the Philosophy of Biology*. New York: Wiley-Blackwell, 2010.

Schacht, Richard, "Morality and Menschen." In *Nietzsche's On the Genealogy of Morals. Berkeley* (Ed.) Richard Schacht, University of California Press, 1994.
Schacht, Richard. "Nietzsche and Lamarckism". *Journal of Nietzsche Studies* 44: 2013, 264–281.
Scott, James C. 2017. *Against the Grain: A History of the Earliest States*. New Haven: Yale University Press.
Thatcher, David. 1983. "Nietzsche's Debt to Lubbock." *Journal of the History of Ideas* 44, 1983, 293–309.

5

A Closer Look at the Internalization of Drives as Implexes: The Cognitive and Affective Strands

I sought to provide a new interpretation of the Internalization Hypothesis in the previous chapters by examining what exactly Nietzsche meant by the internalization of drives. There I proposed that drives are implexes. As applied to I.H., an implex represents the intersection of two systems: cognition and affect. Drives, then, are a symbolic interpretation of this intersection as they too have a mental and a biological side. If that is right, they remain within the scope of the Separation Thesis, which claims that there is a stable element and a fluid component for every historical phenomenon. Given this construal, the task before the genealogist is to trace these individual skeins to earlier practices and composites, rinse and repeat: these prior practices would consist of individual threads and so on. In this way, we can sincerely take up Dennett's intentional theoretic call while acknowledging that we may never get to the Holy Grail: the bare subtractors and adders that make up these many systems. Nevertheless, we are proceeding to offer a simpler explanans of a much more complex explanandum.

My position is that scholars in the secondary literature get off on the wrong foot because they take the meaning and significance of drives to be fundamental. But under my interpretation, drives are simply a symbolic

B. Lightbody, *A Genealogical Analysis of Nietzschean Drive Theory*,
https://doi.org/10.1007/978-3-031-27148-9_5

interpretation of more primal processes. Whatever the drive (e.g. sex, hunger, luxury, the philosophical, etc.), these are largely symbolic gestures of the conditioned biological systems that underwrite them. The proper way to understand drives, then, is to take them as analogs for punishment—just as torture has a stable and fluid element, so too do drives.

In keeping with the Separation Thesis, I stripped drives of their symbolic function in Chap. 4, revealing their underlying mechanisms. My investigation there focused on the mechanical side (the vertical inherited axis) of the Separation Thesis, that is to say, the stable element. I focused mainly on the biological mechanisms that enhanced obedience, such as artificial and unconscious selection practices. The logical first step of my argument is to reject the section's standard reading, which interprets the I.H. as an accurate depiction of the Pleistocene era, as Williams puts it. It is not. Instead, GM II 16 is a vignette that contextualizes what happened to enslaved people entering the market as commodities in an advanced political state such as the Roman Republic and later Empire. My argument is that the selective pressures at work on newly enslaved individuals in the Roman Empire, for example, would have been similar to the same sort of pressures on wild animals domesticated in the first early human domuses. That is, of course, assuming Nietzsche's likening of the warrior artists to domesticators is in anyway remotely accurate. My reading of I.H. is not only consistent with the Separation Thesis, but unlike the standard interpretation, it has the advantage of bringing it in line with our contemporary understanding of biology, anthropology, and archeology.

Of course, the full impact of subjects from tribal communities entering into political states, like the Roman Republic, as slaves, cannot be understood in purely mechanistic terms. Genealogy is not a brute reductionism, after all. There are other factors to consider. I now show how the technologies relating to slavery as employed by the Romans: laws, punishment, and 'enclosures' (*domiciles*), broadly construed, intensified, and accelerated two broad, pre-existing capacities. On the cognitive side, I argue that features pertaining to instrumental reasoning: pattern recognition, cause and effect thinking, selective cognition, and so on, were intensified and that on the affective side, new pressures, cultural practices, and narratives came to redirect ancient emotional pathways. These two skeins (the cognitive on the one hand and the affective on the other) serve as the genealogical tracings for the emergence of Christian subjectivity. I now turn to examine each by reexamining the Internalization Hypothesis.

Section I: A Re-reading GM II 16: The Cognitive Dimension

Before turning to the Internalization Hypothesis proper, I analyze the sea-creature analogy. In that analogy, Nietzsche argues that the path of early humans (what he calls semi-animals) was similar to the course of sea creatures who were forced to become land animals–in other words, they had to adapt to a new climate or die. Nietzsche explains:

> The situation that faced sea animals when they were compelled to become land animals or perish was the same as that which faced semi-animals, well adapted to the wilderness, to war, to prowling, to adventure: suddenly all their instincts were disvalued and "suspended." (*alle ihre Instinkte entwerthet und "ausgehängt"*). From now on they had to walk on their feet and "bear themselves" whereas hitherto they had been borne by the water: a dreadful heaviness lay upon them. They felt unable to cope with the simplest undertakings; in this new world they no longer possessed their former guides, their regulating unconscious and infallible drives (*unbewusst-sicherführenden Triebe*): they were reduced to thinking, inferring, reckoning, co-ordinating cause and effect, these unfortunate creatures; they were reduced to their consciousness their weakest and most fallible organ! (GM II 16)

From this passage, I now want to draw out several salient features that inform the reader about drive theory as an implex of cognitive and affective systems. First, you will notice that I analyzed this passage in Chap. 3 in terms of a mechanical reading. Now I examine the same extract from the cognitive dimension. But before doing so, I begin by offering a standard interpretation of this section and then demonstrate the advantages of my implexic reading.

The received view in the literature suggests that we read this passage as follows. First, pre-humans were well-served by animal instincts. These are what some scholars such as Brian Leiter have called "hostile instincts." Leiter notes: "First a fundamental human instinct for cruelty is a necessary presupposition of the account of the origin of bad conscience later in the Second Essay: bad conscience, after all, is said to arise from cruel instincts that had to be internalized."[1] Christopher Janaway agrees with Leiter's assessment. He writes: "The second treatise is structured around two central thoughts concerning cruelty and it's turning back against the self the first which nature calls an old powerful human all too human proposition might be put as follows because of an instinctive drive human beings tend to gain pleasure from inflicting suffering we might call this the pleasure in cruelty thesis."[2]

Finally, we have Lawrence Hatab. Hatab, in his Nietzsche on the *Genealogy of Morals An Introduction*, echoes the above interpretations by writing the following:

> In section 3 Nietzsche elaborates on the "long history" of cruel practices that made something like conscience possible … such a phenomenon could only come about when prepared by the struggle to establish memory in the face of active forgetfulness. This is the role played by cruel punishments and torments–Nietzsche mentions practices such as mutilation, stoning, impaling, flaying, drawing and quartering, boiling alive–which served to "burn" a memory into the victims and onlookers because "pain was the most powerful aid to mnemonics."[3]

Moreover, Nietzsche's comments on this passage in *Ecce Homo* would seem to confirm this interpretation: "Cruelty is here exposed as one of the most ancient and basic substrata of culture that simply cannot be imagined away." (E.H. *Genealogy of Morals*) While turning to the earlier work, *Beyond Good and Evil* Nietzsche defines the essence of life "essentially appropriation, injury, overpowering of what is alien and weaker;

[1] Leiter, *Nietzsche on Morality*, 231.

[2] Janaway, *Beyond Selflessness*, 125.

[3] Lawrence Hatab, *Nietzsche's On the Genealogy of Morals an Introduction* (Cambridge Introductions to Key philosophical Texts, Cambridge, Cambridge University Press, 2008).

suppression, hardness, imposition of one's own forms, incorporation and at least, at its mildest, exploitation." (BGE 259)

I now look at this same passage from my stance, which argues that the Internalization Hypothesis denotes the fusion of cognitive and affective vectors. I examine the computational thread in this section and the affective in the next. In order to see the advantages of my reading, it is incumbent to consider what Nietzsche says regarding the targets of these instincts. According to Kaufmann's translation, Nietzsche states that these drives were once infallible; they were guides related to the old environment before internalization. But Kaufmann has taken liberties in translating *sicherführenden* as infallible. A more literal translation is safe (*sichler*)-guiding (*fuhrenden*). Indeed, Clarke and Swenson's translation of the *Genealogy* puts the sentence this way: "They felt awkward doing the simplest tasks; for this new, unfamiliar world they no longer had their old leaders, the regulating drives that unconsciously guided them safely" (GM II 16) This intense focus on *sicherführenden* may seem unimportantly pedantic, but it is critical to focus on it for three reasons.

First, the term infallible is rarely deployed, at least in a literal sense in ordinary usage. When it is, it is typically applied to a doctrinal matter regarding the Pope's epistemic capacities. Conceptually, infallibility supposes that one cannot be wrong, make mistakes, or otherwise be in error. To be wrong entails that one's reasons for believing p are inadequate; they do not meet some unspecified, normative standard. In saying one is incorrect, one is judging that one's capacities have failed in some regard: whether these capacities are cognitive capacities *simpliciter* or the reasoning that often attends them. They presuppose that my idea of p, which I took be true, does not match p.

Drives, however, are, per theory, unconscious; neither the drives nor the creatures who have them represent the features of the environment in some Cartesian theater proclaiming these drives represent reality and judging that they do so with absolute certainty. Thus in describing the drives as infallible, we inject the very pernicious representationalism we seek to jettison–we are obscuring what drives are. Kaufmann's translation of the passage lends support to viewing drives as homunculi. There is, then, a lack of clarity in understanding the proper epistemic relation between drives and their environment in thinking that drives are infallible.

But there is a second difficulty. Infallibility is an epistemic status that is not usually conceptually connected to impulse. I can have infallible knowledge (though there are innumerable hypothetical defeaters for this claim) that, for example, a triangle is a plane figure whose interior angles equal 180 degrees, still, I am not pulled to pursue triangles, whether the pursuit is to imagine them or construct them. I do not find myself chasing after triangle-like objects; there is no connection between infallibility and desire. In contrast, *fuhrenden*, as interpreted as "guiding" or "leading," affirms that drives propel or, more accurately, pull the creature forward: just as a guide leads a group through a wooded trail, the drives tug the creature along a path toward some desired object.

However, the final objection to Kaufmann's translation is the most serious. Nietzsche emphatically denies the very category of infallibility, especially as it applies to what one can know about the world. When musing speculatively about the epistemic relationship between creatures and the world, he makes abundantly clear in several passages that animals do not understand the fundamental structure of the world. "Not to know but to schematize—to impose upon chaos as much regularity and form as our practical needs require. In the formation of reason, logic, the categories, it was need that was authoritative; the need to, not to know, but to subsume, to schematize, for the purpose of intelligibility and calculation."[4] Compare this passage to what Nietzsche writes in GS 111: "He for example, who did not know how to discover the 'identical' sufficiently often in regard to food or to animals hostile to him, he who was thus too slow to subsume, too cautious in subsuming, had a smaller probability of survival than he who in every case of similarity at once conjectured identity."[5]

I offer a reading superior to the standard interpretation because it addresses the three problems noted above and is more consistent with the text's original wording. An enriched alternative would be to interpret

[4] The Will to Power, WP 515. Also see KSA XIII 333–334.

[5] Nietzsche, A Nietzsche Reader, Trans. Holingdale, *The Gay Science*, section 111, 60. See also Daybreak, section 117: "A thirst, the habits of our senses have woven us into lies and deception of sensation: these are the basis of all our judgments and 'knowledge'—there is absolutely no escape, no backway or bypath into the real world! We sit within our net, we spiders, and whatever we catch in it, we can catch nothing at all except that which allows itself to be caught in precisely our net." See GM III 12.

these instincts as truth conducive; they are warranted in so far as the initial capacities belonging, as they do, to full-blown human agents (and not semi-animals) track those things that those same capacities were selected for to track.

Tracking epistemic positions are a species of broader externalist theories of knowledge. They often put the tracking condition in counterfactual terms. Consider for a moment Nozick's four requirements for knowledge:

1. P is true;
2. S believes that P;
3. If P were not true, S would not believe that P;
4. If P were true S would believe that P.[6]

The essential aspect of an externalist theory focuses on the causal infrastructure of belief formation rather than on the reasons and inferences one draws upon to justify said belief. To perhaps oversimplify, the notion of warrant is often replaced by the word justification. Where justification emphasizes the internal reasons, a subject has in judging some belief to be true, warrant places emphasis on the causal factors external to the agent that, if they exist in the proper relation, guarantees that the agent has knowledge of p.

Critically, whether the agent is aware of these causal factors is very often unimportant for determining the degree of credence for the belief in question. For example, Plantinga puts this matter this way: "Put in a nutshell, then, a belief has warrant for a person S only if that belief is produced in S by cognitive faculties functioning properly (subject to no dysfunction) in a cognitive environment that is appropriate for S's kind of cognitive faculties, according to a design plan that is successfully aimed at truth."[7]

[6] The above is Nozick's first attempt to develop a tracking theory of knowledge and does not represent his considered fully fleshed out position. See pp. 172–176 of Robert Nozick *Philosophical Explanations* (Harvard University Press), 1984. Nozick raises several problems in regard to these simple conditions and develops a much more sophisticated framework to handle them. See particular p. 179. Also see Jennifer Nagel's *Epistemology a Very Short Introduction*, (Oxford University Press, 2014), 60–72.

[7] Alvin Plantinga, *Warranted Christian Belief* (Oxford: Oxford University Press, 2000) 156.

Now Nietzsche would have no truck with some of the features of this definition, such as "design plan." However, the first two aspects are significant and consistent with Nietzsche's hypothesis. Proper function, in this case, relates not to the instinctual capacities that tribal people had before civilization but instead to culturally implanted dispositions: attitudes. These behaviors were soft-wired into individuals due to their standing in the respective tribes in which they found themselves. The setting of sea creatures, then, is analogous to Plantinga's notion of an "appropriate environment." As it applies to GM II 16 and 17, people living in tribal communities would unconsciously track those activities conducive to their health. In Nietzsche's case, that which is conducive to one's health promotes will to power, understood as the capacity to overcome obstacles in its environment. Every biological system in the person functions to service this requirement.

Specifying this idea expressed above more clearly, Nietzsche's position is not altogether different from yet another externalist theory of knowledge– Evolutionary Reliabilism (E.R.). Although there are many various stripes of E.R., they all have one thing in common: "natural selection would likely have favoured reliable cognitive processes – that is, processes that tend to produce a high proportion of true beliefs – over unreliable cognitive processes, because the former would have been more conducive to survival and reproductive success than the latter."[8] The conscious criteria for establishing true beliefs must be a necessary component because, as we have seen, drives, as implexes, have a mental side. The tribal person who is now enslaved in a strange empire must find entirely innovative processes that will reliably guide them in their new, novel environment. Unfortunately, the only systems that remain even somewhat veridical would be the bare-bones ones: thinking, reckoning, and inferring. Any other intellectual virtue that would typically direct a subject's dispositionally induced guidance systems reliably for that same subject in a tribal communal setting is now deemed false when the subject, now slave, finds himself in a foreign and dangerous city-state.

[8] Michael J. Deem, "A Flaw in the Stich–Plantinga challenge to Evolutionary Reliabilism," *Analysis* Vol 78 | Number 2 | April 2018 | pp. 216–225 217.

Whether we subscribe to Nozick's tracking theory or a kind of Evolutionary Reliabilism is not essential to note here. However, it is vital to recognize that the intellectual virtues, reliably construed, that were once truth conducive are now false and treated suspiciously by the tribal person who has them now that he finds himself enslaved in a strange new political order. As will be examined below, such a feeling of alienation and danger for newly enslaved peoples meant that, "a dreadful heaviness lay upon them." (GM II 16).

We now turn to Nietzsche's formulation of the Internalization Hypothesis proper. The thesis has it that because the impulsive energy of these drives was blocked, so too was their hostile expression. The consequence of this blockage resulted in these drives having to go elsewhere, internally, in order to be satisfied. Since these avenues had nowhere else to go because of the strict rules of early civilization and the subsequent punishments that enforced them, they produced subjectivity *ex nihlo*: "The entire inner world, originally as thin as if it were stretched between two membranes, expanded and extended itself, acquired depth, breadth and height, in the same measure as outward discharge was inhibited. More specifically the animal soul (which is nothing more than a collection of hostile drives) turned against itself, taking sides against itself" (GM II 16)

When parsing this passage, there are three points to keep in mind: (1) Nietzsche suggests that drives that are obstructed from expression seek new channels to discharge (*Entladen*) their impulsive energy; (2) Once the drives are subverted, they combat one another within the admittedly thin container of the animal soul; (3) This agonic struggle between competing drives causes the inner world or subjectivity to form. I have purposely described the drives as having intentional tendencies because I now want to show how intention and expression come apart *via* the Separation Thesis. The tension between drives within the soul, "which is as thin if stretched between two membranes," expands over time to become the robust sense of agency we experience today, or so a traditional reading of this passage suggests.

In examining the first point, I take issue with Kaufmann's (and Clarke and Swenson's) translation of *Entladen* and later *Entladengung* as "discharge." A more natural interpretation would be off-loading or, indeed, draining. My reason for preferring draining or off-loading to discharge is, first, using discharge makes for some awkward, redundant phrasing. Consider the sentence: "The entire inner world … acquired depth, breadth and height, in the same measure as outward discharge was inhibited." Is there such a thing as inner discharge? (*gegen sich selbst Partei nehmenden*). Secondly, the use of draining retains the fluid analogy of will to power: will to power is much like Heraclitus's river of becoming, except that this river is constantly overcoming resistance. But thirdly and most importantly, Nietzsche as a genealogist is a physician of culture. In keeping with the medical terminology he often employs in *The Genealogy*, it is more accurate to describe the soul's formation as a "cyst."[9] Cysts emerge when fluid fails to drain from the body. Cysts have distinct membranes and thus are abnormal tissue growth. Whether benign, cancerous, or ganglion, cysts may be symptomatic of a severe health problem. This interpretation is strongly supported in the same section. In fact, Nietzsche characterizes the soul as "*dünn wie zwischen zwei Häute*" (as thin as between two skins).

Adding these comments to the epistemic interpretation of drives above, it is more accurate to say that drives are much like designated channels. They are physically established cognitive dispositions with predetermined outlets much in the same manner that specific ducts (e.g. the Pancreatic, Cystic, Lactiferous etc.) carry various fluids away from the body. When these outlets are blocked, they backflow, overrun these selfsame conduits, and cause the liquids to pool. The container of these pools of different fluids from varied channels is elastic and expands, forming the soul.

The above description of how the soul forms is far too metaphorical, however. How can we clarify Nietzsche's point? How can we justify it? One way to think about the 'soul' operationally is to think about the object of the self's concern. What Nietzsche is suggesting is that our instincts, now understood as reliable, epistemic dispositions used to navigate our environment, are unreliable indeed, they are false because acting on them will get one killed in the terrifying backdrop of any empire where one is enslaved. What happens now is that the enslaved person

[9] See especially Note 2 of the Genealogy.

must employ other cognitive skills and layout choices, decision trees if you will, which calculate where the branches of these trees might lead. In doing so, which–might be done quickly or which might be done over a substantial period (leading to brooding)–one takes *oneself as an object*: one views the different paths one might take, contemplates the consequences associated with these paths, and weighs the pros and cons of each. Again, the metric for said weighing, it should be stressed, is not in tribal codes of honor and norms that well-served the enslaved person before his capture but in the meager terms of mere survivability. This reading emphasizes the concept I mentioned in Chap. 4: selective cognition. The environment of an empire like Rome induces the slave to focus on oneself as the object of awareness, thereby significantly augmenting a plastic evolutionary pathway that becomes crucial in terms of survival value. On the other hand, when selective cognition is applied to oneself, it platforms and channels tendencies for brooding and self-analysis that make one susceptible to priestly "medicine." I will examine this connection in more detail when I turn to the affective dimension.

In keeping with the cognitive dimension of the internalization of drives I am discussing here, I now want to tackle the final and perhaps most challenging line of the passage: "the soul takes sides against itself." In thinking about this line, it should be noted that Nietzsche employs the term (*gegen sich selbst Partei nehmende*n). This point further extends the analysis above. Once more, I think Kaufmann's translative choice is incorrect. His interpretation of "Parteti" is not robust enough: *Partei* in this sense is used to denote a political entity or, more accurately and in keeping to the naturalized method I adopted above, a channel not just with a specific function but with a plan. As noted in Chap. 3, it is not just that drives need to find an outlet for their expression, but that drives compete with other drives to be the only drive expressed. As previously documented in Chap. 3, many passages in Nietzsche's *oeuvre* substantiate this position. This is a natural reading of the above sentence: vested parties dominate others. As I noted, this aspect of drive theory, which I called the agonic element, is perhaps the most difficult to naturalize. In arguing that drives have agendas, we are but a stone's throw away from claiming that drives are like little agents.

But there is another significant aspect to this idea that the drives take sides against one another that has gone unnoticed in the secondary literature; it remains unclear why the drive to dominate suffuses every human instinct, at least according to Nietzsche. Instead, Nietzsche contends that the meta-urge of domination imbues every drive: a drive wants to express itself and master other drives. This dual-drive expression claim is found in many of Nietzsche's works. Below, I repeat two passages from Nietzsche's *oeuvre* to substantiate my thesis.

The first is from *Beyond Good and Evil*, section 7:

> But anyone who considers the basic drives of man ... will find that all of them have done philosophy at some time-and that every single one of them would like only too well to represent just itself as the ultimate purpose of existence and the legitimate master of all of the other drives. For every drive wants to be master-and it attempts to philosophize in that spirit.

The second is from Nietzsche's unpublished works, his Nachlass, section 481 of *The Will to Power:* "It is our needs that interpret the world: our drives and their For and Against. Every drive is a kind of lust to rule; each one has its perspective that it would like to compel all the other drives to accept as a norm."

Once more, we can answer this question by thinking of drives as implexes with cognitive and affective components. Here I provide an answer from the mental side. The enslaved person finds himself furrowed in a new setting where violence, humiliation, and coercion abound. On the one hand there are the dispositional attitudes of how one may act in one's tribe, which might entail striking back against those who attack you (in this case, one's master). Another alternative would entail fleeing from the tribe altogether into the wilderness and taking one's chances there–a common tactic in early political states it turns out.[10] But, on the other hand, the knowledge, informed now by cause and effect thinking, says that these actions will bring about more suffering for the slave himself and those he cares about. In that sense, the subject takes sides against itself: if understood functionally, all this statement means is that the new

[10] See Daniel Graeber, (*Debt the First 5000 Years*, New York Melville House Publishing), 2014.

captive of the empire is unsure which path to pursue (e.g. flee, strike out against one's master, or accept one's newly found position) and there are opportunity costs for whatever choice is made.

If that broad schematic interpretation is correct, then how justified is it? I now turn to put historical flesh on this skeletal framework above.

Section II: The Treatment of Slaves in Roman Society

My purpose in this section is not to provide a detailed account describing how Roman slaves were treated–doing so would require much more than a section of a book chapter. Nor is it to explain the obvious: the treatment of slaves was a brutal enterprise. Instead, my task is to support Nietzsche's perspectival description in GM II 16. My interpretative work-around suggests that Nietzsche's description is not an objective one *per se*; it is perspectival through and through. Therefore, it is metaphorical because the descriptions are skewed per the emotional and cognitive states of those perceiving and describing. Nietzsche employs a perspectival method (mentioned in III 12) in order to provide a multitude of perspectives on the event he is depicting. But this point is crucial to bear in mind: the account is warranted. There is a great deal of evidence to support Nietzsche's narrative. From the standpoint of tribal captives taken to faraway markets, the description of the state as a violent machine, with beasts of prey operating its levers, is accurate. From the perspective of slave-owners, enslaved people are viewed as mere things (*res*). This perspective is, in fact, codified in Roman slave law. In his *Domus*, the male head of the household (*Paterfamilias*) regularly beat his slaves. Moreover, *slaves* are considered instruments and, in the words of the writer Varro, little more than "talking tools." They are treated much like farm animals, especially those employed in *Latifundia* (large agricultural estates), and managed accordingly. I am explaining, then, the coeval development of subjectivity from the slave perspective in this section. In keeping with implexic genealogy, I illuminate slave subjectivity, which involves a cognitive aspect and affective part.

I now flesh out these two perspectives, the slave point of view on the one hand and the warrior artists on the other, by delving more deeply into the history of this peculiar relationship.

In turning to the history of slavery in Rome, noted ancient historian W.W. Buckland's description is striking. He evinces, "The distinguishing mark of slavery in Rome is something else, and modern writers have found it in rightlessness. A slave is a man without rights, i.e. without the power of setting the law in motion for his own protection."[11] The slave in Roman society was viewed as a thing (*res*) and was subjected to brutal indignities and violence. But how did this development come about? This firm distinction between the rights of freemen and the lack thereof of enslaved people in the late Roman Republic and Early Roman Empire is just one of the many problems scholars will grapple with when coming to terms with Roman slavery.[12] The problem comes to light because, on the surface, at least, the distinction seems to reveal a blatant contradiction inherent in the general Roman legal principle of *Jus Naturale*. The *Jus Naturale* was a way of conceiving the rights of individuals independently of communal norms and laws in which that individual found himself. It has its roots in Western legal thinking in Plato's *Laws* and it was later reinterpreted by Stoic thinkers.[13] In commenting on the Stoic conception of *Jus Naturale*, Cicero declared that it was the domain of right reason applied to command and prohibition.[14] Under *Jus Naturale*, all men were free according to nature.

However, as Graeber and Wegner explain, the growth of slavery as an institution in the late Republic (by some estimates, slaves represented anywhere from 35 to as much as 40% of the population of the Italian Peninsula) led to a radical reinterpretation and scope of *Jus Naturale*. It was a reinterpretation that was prompted because of the material interests of the very Roman jurists (many of whom owned hundreds of slaves)

[11] W.W. Buckland, *The Roman Law of Slavery: The Condition of the Slave in Private Law from Augustus to Justinian*, Cambridge University Press, 1908, 2.

[12] David Graeber and David Wengrow, *The Dawn of Everything* New York: Penguin 2021, 508.

[13] Michael Zuckert, "Bringing Philosophy Down From the Heavens," *The Review of Politics* Vol. 51, No. 1 (Winter, 1989), pp. 70–85 p. 71.

[14] Cicero, *Laws* I. 2.

who were responsible for creating and interpreting Roman laws.[15] According to Michael Zuckert, *Jus Naturale*, was gradually reinterpreted to reflect a more "natural" understanding. Zuckert writes, "It is thus natural in a sense which even modern readers can readily recognize: it is natural as *effective* and as shared by men and other animal beings. As natural in this sense it is not, whatever the scholars may say, the best and highest." (My Italics)[16]

With such a reinterpretation of the *Jus Naturale* in hand, slaves were then placed in another legal category altogether: the *Jus Gentium*. This legal category covered non-citizens of Rome. Slaves were categorized as captives–foreigners who had been conquered in battle and had forfeited all their rights as a result.[17] But what is perhaps most interesting is that the reclassification of slaves led to a new conception of property. The jurists, driven by their material interests, sought to solve this problem in the legal sphere, namely, how can one own a human person who has rights accorded to it in virtue of being a person. According to Orlando Patterson, the jurists came up with the legal fiction of *dominium* (absolute ownership) to see themselves out of it.[18] Dominium ossifies two categories *persona* (owner) on the one side and *res* (thing) on the other. It was this notion of *Dominium* which defined the relationship between these two. It was predicated on the earlier, uncodified tripartite relationship of the master, slave, and enslavement.[19] As Patterson remarks, "*Dominium* marked not just absolute power defined as the capability to derive the full economic value of a thing to use and enjoy its fruits as well as to use it up to alienate it but perhaps most significantly it has a psychological meaning of inner power over a thing beyond mere control. … It becomes impossible to understand why they would want inner psychic power over

[15] Graeber and Wengrow, *The Dawn of Everything*, 509.

[16] Michael Zuckert, "Bringing Philosophy Down from the Heavens," *The Review of Politics* Vol. 51, No. 1 (Winter, 1989), pp. 70–85 p. 76.

[17] Buckland, 3.

[18] Orlando Paterson, *Slavery and Social Death*: A Comparative Study, Harvard University Press, 1982, 31.

[19] Graeber and Wengrow, 510.

it unless we understand that, for most purposes, the thing on their minds was a slave."[20]

Now that property was redefined as ownership that had no connection to the community, the master's complete authority over his household where the slave lived was ultimately justified by brute power. The head of the household was free to rape, torture, or kill any of his slaves at any time. Moreover, whatever action the master took would be considered nothing more than a private affair.

To understand the full consequences of this strange, horrifying, yet intimate relationship between an enslaved person and his master, consider the standpoint of the enslaved. Thus, the slave in the Roman household was part of the *familias* but yet was, legally, a thing. His master beat him, and yet he trimmed his master's hair. Female slaves were raped and yet expected to fetch towels for the wife of the *Paterfamilias*. Slave tutors were responsible for teaching the children of the master one day and being savagely flogged the next. In the words of Patterson, slaves are "socially dead": they are stripped of their social standing, their dignity indeed in Roman law, and their very humanity.

The above description provides a viewpoint into the domestic violence slaves faced. What of the slaves who worked on the large agricultural estates? To get a sense of how slaves were treated in that context, we need only turn to Varro's account: "Some divide these into two parts: men, and those aids to men without which they cannot cultivate; others into three: the class of instruments which is articulate, the inarticulate, and the mute; the articulate comprising the slaves, the inarticulate comprising the cattle, and the mute comprising the vehicles."[21] When it comes to buying slaves, Varro's advice is reminiscent of how a farmer might breed animals. He observes, "Avoid having too many slaves of the same nation, for this is a fertile source of domestic quarrels. The foremen are to be made more zealous by rewards, and care must be taken that they have a bit of property of their own, and mates from among their fellow-slaves to

[20] Patterson, *Slavery and Social Death*, 31.

[21] Varro, *On Agriculture (De Rustica)*, Trans. W.D. Hooper, and H.B. Ash Loeb Classical Library, 1934, 17.1.

bear them children; for by this means they are made more steady and more attached to the place."[22]

From this evidence, it is clear that slaves, from the perspective of Roman jurists and the slave-owners themselves, is such that they were treated as mere talking tools at best and things at worst. What is clear is that they were deprived of their humanity and dignity. Moreover, slaves were kept in line by brutal beatings, horrific tortures; a master could pluck out a slave's eyes, and in extreme cases, the knowledge that if a slave should murder his master, all the slaves within the household could be subsequently executed.[23] Perhaps even more shocking is that these practices were legal and backed up through state enforcement.

Using this evidence to flesh out the Internalization Hypothesis, it is now clear why the drive to seek vengeance against one's master, the instinct to strike back against one who assaults the slave, was seldom initiated. This reading stands in stark contrast to the traditional view. That interpretation holds these same instincts were primed and energized, and because an instinct is dammed up energy, it has to find new ways of expression. They, therefore, turned inward.

Under my reading, however, we can understand why enslaved people who find themselves in the household of a brutal, seemingly nearly all-powerful master would develop a bad conscience (or simply the inability to retaliate). The enslaved individuals in modern parlance are suffering from post-traumatic stress syndrome.[24] Slaves had their tribal identities

---

[22] Varro, *On Agriculture*, 17.1.

[23] Lucius Pedanius Secundus was murdered by one of his slaves so Tacitus explains "either because he had been refused emancipation after Pedanius had agreed to the price, or because he had contracted a passion for a catamite, and declined to tolerate the rivalry of his owner." (*Tacitus Annals* Vol. 5 Book XIV. 42Loeb Classical Library, 5 volumes, Latin texts and facing English translation: Harvard University Press, 1925 thru 1937. Translation by C. H. Moore (Histories) and J. Jackson (Annals).

[24] Compare the above descriptions of slave treatment to the definition of trauma in the DSM V: The Exposure to actual or threatened death, serious injury, or sexual violence in one (or more) of the following ways:

1. Directly experiencing the traumatic event(s).
2. Witnessing, in person, the event(s) as it occurred to others.
3. Learning that the traumatic event(s) occurred to a close family member or close friend. In cases of actual or threatened death of a family member or friend, the event(s) must have been violent or accidental.

stripped, their social network demolished in short, their meanings are taken from them. Such brutality reflects what the sociologist Orlando Patterson calls "social death"—the slave's loss of ethnicity, family, and membership in a tribe or a state. However, this furrowedness of self promotes self-investigation, which leads to impotence precisely because there is no clear-cut direction to resolve the dilemma or trilemma the slave finds herself in (flee, strike back against one's master or accept one's new standing). In finding oneself in this grim Hamletian condition, the enslaved person desperately seeks new narratives, especially of the religious variety, that will help solve the problem, telling the enslaved person what to do.

If my cognitive account is remotely accurate, then it is understandable why the slave appears to have internalized their drives, even though such a diagnosis is inaccurate. The true story is that the slave's choices are all sub-optimal, assuming that the slave lacks the constitution to take their own lives–a final alternative it seems that many slaves ended up choosing.[25]

The other side of the equation now needs to be investigated. What were these "semi-animals" like before being captured and shuttled to Rome? Nietzsche provides us with minimum details in this regard. He notes that the instincts of these semi-animals included a longing for adventure, the wild, and to prowl (GM II 16). Suppose my interpretation is correct, namely, that these "semi-animals" denote tribal people living in communities organized by kinship in general and Germanic tribes in particular. In that case, we need to put further historical flesh on Nietzsche's minimal description to determine if my interpretation is warranted.

Yet there is another crucial reason for examining the collective psyche of these early tribal communities. It takes us back to Morrison's helpful interpretative framework. Morrison, if we recall, argued that the events described in section 19 occur, chronologically speaking before section 16 and that such an interpretation lines up with the view of the anthropologists of Nietzsche's day. The one problem with Morrison's explanation is that it does not seem to jibe with the standard interpretation of section 16.

---

[25] Josephus, *The Works of Josephus Trans. William Whiston, The War of the Jews* (Grand Rapids MI: Bakersfield Books, 1981) Book 7, Chapter 9.

The section describes the injection of bad conscience in human history. If we recall from Chap. 4, I argued that Morrison's interpretation is correct, yet there was a significant unresolved issue. I take up that issue now.

Nietzsche's depiction of humans before the advent of the first state in section 19 is soaked in blood and violence. Early tribal communities use animal and human sacrifices to appease the gods. Thus, if the Internalization Hypothesis claims subjectivity is nothing more than the stymieing of hostile drives, why didn't slave morality develop in tribal communities? Why didn't the seedbed of bad conscience exist there? I argue that Nietzsche's psychological account of early tribal society, at least in Northern Europe before the emergence of the Roman Empire, is justified. I explain why violence in these societies did not become internalized for such individuals, given Nietzsche's account.

The first step of my argument is that if these semi-animals to which Nietzsche refers are in fact captured tribal people, then Nietzsche's description of internalization must at best only be hyperbolic. I supplied a solution to this problem by demonstrating that the Internalization Hypothesis may be interpreted along the lines of the Separation Thesis. If that is right, then drives themselves are an implex of cognitive and affective threads. I demonstrated that enslaved peoples do not internalize their drives but rather discover that their tribal dispositions are false. They now have to rely on a stripped-down impoverished capacity of inference, reckoning, and conjecturing in order to survive their new-found accommodations.

The second part of my solution will be to examine what life was like for early Germanic tribes. To help me with this endeavor I turn to the Roman historian Tacitus's work *Germania*. Tacitus's ethnographic picture tells us many things about early Germanic tribes. The first is that neither their kings nor high-ranking warriors (generals) have much authority over their tribespeople. Tacitus notes: "In the election of kings they have regard to birth; in that of generals, to valor."[26] And furthermore that, "Their kings have not an absolute or unlimited power."[27] In describing the generals of these same Germanic tribes, Tacitus again remarks, "their

[26] Tacitus *A Treatise on the Situation, Inhabitants and manners of Germany* (Germania and Agricola) Trans. John Aiken, Cambridge University Press, 1823, Chapter 7 line 50.

[27] Ibid., Chapter 7 line 51.

generals command less through the force of authority, than of example. If they are daring, adventurous, and conspicuous in action, they procure obedience from the admiration they inspire."[28]

In addition, women, too it seemed, were allowed to give counsel. Indeed Tacitus mentions that "armies are rallied by the females through the earnestness of their supplications, the interposition of their bodies, and (this point is particularly important to stress) the pictures they have drawn of impending slavery, a calamity which these people bear with more impatience for their women than themselves."[29] Furthermore, the chiefs of a tribe were expected to consult with the entire tribe on any matter of great importance.[30]

The contrast between a tribal member in the Germanic tribes and an enslaved person could not be any starker. Power and authority within this tribal life is predicated on deeds. Insofar as one can develop warrior virtues: courage, battle prowess, wise counsel etc. one can command. Such dispositions are rewarded. Compare this fact with Ancient Rome where authority was conferred through mere relationships and where this relationship was strictly enforced via the state. The striking difference between these two environments would not have been lost on enslaved individuals in the Roman state.

Although Germanic peoples did have slaves, there is a sharp difference between their form of enslavement compared to those of slaves in the Roman society. Tacitus writes in this regard, "The rest of their slaves have not, like ours, particular employments in the family allotted them. Each is the master of a habitation and household of his own. The lord requires from him a certain quantity of grain, cattle, or cloth, as from a tenant"[31] While a master could kill his slave, this action, Tacitus remarks, was often committed in "the heat of passion."[32] The enslaved person in early Germanic societies is, operationally speaking, more of a serf than what we find in ancient Rome. In fact, many freedmen were enslaved as a result of

[28] Chapter 7, line 50.

[29] Tacitus, Chapter 7 lines 54–55.

[30] Ibid., Chapter 7 line 71.

[31] Tacitus, Chapter 25.

[32] Tacitus, Chapter 25.

gambling debts and freely went into servitude because their honor demanded nothing less.[33]

What are we to make of these facts? It now becomes clear why the bad conscience was incapable of taking root in the Germanic tribal society. In addition to having means of cleansing ill feelings toward others in the form, as Nietzsche mentions in GM II 19, animal and human sacrifices, the domination by the chiefs of the tribe of such peoples was not what we find in Rome. There is far more freedom and social opportunity, in general, to be found in these ancient communities than in the enwalled cities of the Roman Empire.

If my interpretation is correct, we must turn to the last piece of the puzzle. If slaves constituted some 35–40% of the population of Roman society at its peak (first century A.D), why were there not more organized, large-scale attacks on Roman overlords by slaves? Although Rome had slave uprisings from time to time, one would think that these revolts would only amplify as Rome's slave population grew in the first century A.D. However, this was not the case. The last major slave uprising, led by Spartacus, was the third servile war (74-72 BCE).[34] Why did large-scale rebellions fizzle out at exactly the same time as slave demographics grew?

It is here that Christianity, according to Nietzsche, comes into play. Suppose Nietzsche's account is accurate. Namely, that bad conscience intensified in the Roman Empire due to the material and social conditions in which enslaved peoples found themselves. In that case, some force must have prevented a collective, organized resistance to Roman authority. In keeping to the cognitive dimension, Christianity preaches an appealing narrative that speaks to the post-facto rationalization that the enslaved person might tell themselves to become numb to the suffering they would surely experience in their new predicament. According to Nietzsche, the priestly class preaches this narrative, saving the enslaved people from mounting a full-scale and suicidal war against the nobles. In broad brushstrokes, the priests teach the following. First, they acknowledge that nobles should pay for their crimes. They preach a religion of revenge (which they will come to weaponize later). However, they next

---

[33] Tacitus, Chapter 24.

[34] For a clear introduction to Spartacus's war, see Barry Strauss *The Spartacus War* New York Simon and Schuster, 2009.

claim that the nobles are evil-doers and will be punished for their transgressions in the afterlife. The consequence of this apocalyptic preaching has a calming, hypnotic effect on the slave psyche: the slaves conclude it is not up to them to retaliate against their noble overlords in the Here and Now—God will exact His revenge on them on the slave's behalf. A clear direction with ritual practices is offered to the slave, relieving him of his paralysis and the terror of having to bear the burden of a wrong decision. The Hamletian problem the slave faced is resolved: the answer to his natural predicament is provided in a celestial voice.[35]

In returning to what prompted this discussion, namely the genesis of promise-making, I submit that Nietzsche's analysis is too narrow. Nietzsche's true aim in GM II should not be to explain the genealogy of promise-making *per se* but rather how rigid moral codes come to be viewed, cognitively speaking as valuable in an absolute and necessary sense. This is not to deny the unconscious support that attends all actions deemed binding duties; this aspect is well-supported. No, that aspect, as shown in Chap. 4, supports Nietzsche's analysis on the mechanical side. However, what is lost in Nietzsche's critique is that moral principles, like the Ten Commandments, have a practical value along the cognitive axis. They are effortlessly rememberable and undemanding to follow, leaving no room for interpretation. Most importantly, following them offers significant survival protection. They are highly functional in many different empires and can help keep a person on the lower rungs of the social order out of trouble.

[35] This is a brief summary of the main lesson of GM : III 16–20. There has been renewed interest in Nietzsche's priestly type especially in regard to the question of value creation. Two thinkers in particular have done trailblazing work in demonstrating flaws with the traditional account regarding the creation of slave values. See Bernard Reginster, "Nietzsche on Ressentiment and Valuation," *Philosophy and Phenomenological Research* 57.2 (1997): 281–305. and R. Anderson in "On the Nobility of Nietzsche's Priests," in *Nietzsche's On the Genealogy of Morality: A Critical Guide,* ed. Simon May [Cambridge: Cambridge University Press, 2011], 24–55. According to Reginster, the quintessential attitude of slave morality is resignation; resignation that he cannot aspire to the life to create his own values–the quintessential attitude of nobility. Reginster explains: "Thus the slave accepts his masters' high estimation of the noble life and their low estimation of himself, and therefore never even forms the expectation to live the life his masters value. The attitude characteristic of the slave is his resignation to a worthless way of life." 287. In my view, Iain Morrisson's "Ascetic Slaves: Rereading Nietzsche's On the Genealogy of Morals" *(Journal of Nietzsche Studies,* Vol. 45, No. 3 (Autumn 2014), pp. 230–257 advances and clarifies the work of Reginster and Anderson in new ways. He offers the best explanation of how slave values eventually overtook noble ideals. My thesis provides a naturalistic underpinning to Morrison's work.

Moreover, slave morality is marked by an unconscious feeling of impotence; one is resentful that one cannot be like the nobles one despises. For the slave, however, good and evil values are subtended by the illusion of a unified free subject: the slaves argue that they are agents and therefore responsible for their actions. They unknowingly project their reactive, impotent values onto the nobles (GM I 11). The slaves judge that the nobles, too, are free, and therefore, they also are subject to evaluation. Again, it follows that the nobles should be held accountable and subsequently punished for their crimes, just as the slave is.

Why would slaves come to the idea that they are agents able to make choices independently of any social, material, or even bodily context? As we saw from Chap. 4, the answer is their reliance on instrumental rationality, a meager processing of cause and effect, and the hedonistic calculus that informs it. The slaves who survive in their newfound domiciles are stripped of their natural dispositions. They have to utilize their most fallible organ—their consciousness in order to make sense of their lives. As we discovered, slaves were beaten daily and subject to excruciating tortures in extreme circumstances. These tortures form a causal relationship between actions and consequences. Those slaves who were more adept at anticipating the patterns of their master's violent tendencies did better than those who did not. Dwell once more on the close relationship slaves had with their masters.

On the one hand, they were part of the master's domicile: they attended to the most intimate tasks required. They were given specific designations corresponding to the work they did (e.g. the *aquarioli* [female bath fillers], *Archiater* [physicians], *Anteambulones* [retinue]). And yet these personal relationships were fraught with impending violence and terror.

With one side of the implex explained, I now turned to the other side: the affective.

Section III: The Affective Thread: A Neoplastic Concern

Most scholars agree that both drives and emotions play significant roles in Nietzsche's philosophical psychology. However, elucidating each component's distinct roles is more difficult to capture. As discussed in Chap. 3, some scholars like Peter Poellner argue that any attempt to divine the difference is insignificant. Consider for a moment his rather capacious view of affects. Affects for Poellner are so broad that they cover mental territory assigned to drives, as noted in Chap. 3. Poellner writes, "It will be convenient to retain Nietzsche's broad usage of 'affect' for *any* mental episode which constitutively involves a *pro- or con-attitude* (or as I shall say, a favouring or disfavouring) with a distinctive phenomenology—some experience of attraction or repulsion."[36]

Notice that affects involve a phenomenology of attraction or repulsion. This statement closely resembles the urge aspect of drives I noted earlier. If this were not enough to think that affects can replace the work of drives, the next passage from Poellner surely does:" 'Affects' in this sense may include, for example, a feeling of shame, an occurrent desire for something absent, as well as a bodily sensation experienced unqualifiedly as painful or pleasant."[37] Notice now that conscious desires for some object that is not present cede to affects yet two additional aspects attributed to drives from Chap. 3: (1) that affects are evaluative. In having a desire for some object, I judge it as significant insofar as it is wanted. (2) A more substantial interpretation of Poellner's line above suggests that emotions can mark out, as distinct, some objects from the environment as opposed to others. In other words, emotions make things and events salient, in the terms of Katsafanas.

Moreover, it may be plausibly argued that aspect 1 of drives, namely their biological rootedness, is better covered by employing the concept of affect rather than drive. There is ample support in the secondary literature to suggest that humans and mammals share comparable neural pathways that track aversions or attractions to similar stimuli. If emotions can do the same work as drives then the latter are redundant.[38]

Poellner is not alone in voicing this interpretation. Christopher Janaway also acknowledges that affects for Nietzsche are "aversions and inclinations." In addition, he also argues that employing a wide variety of

---

[36] Peter Poellner, "Affect Value and Objectivity" in *Nietzsche and Morality* Edited by Brian Leiter and Neil Sinhababu Oxford University Press, 2007 227–261, 229.

[37] Peter Poellner, "Affect Value and Objectivity", 227–261, 229.

[38] We will examine this point in more detail below where I flesh out Impure Somatic Theory.

said affects regarding contemplating the origin of some value, in a genealogical vein, activates a more profound understanding regarding the nature of the value under investigation.[39] The question then is this: are drives and affects the same? If not, what sense can they be viewed as independent modules of mental capacity? If they are separate modules, do they operate independently of each other, and if they do not, what are their points of convergence?

In a recent paper, Christopher Fowles makes substantial progress in answering the above questions. Fowles is the first author to provide a framework that clarifies what affects are in Nietzsche's philosophical psychology and how affective generation gets started. According to Fowles, the critical move concerning understanding Nietzsche's theory of emotions is distinguishing between two types of affect theory: somatic and non-somatic. Given the importance that Nietzsche places on the body and, more specifically, physiology in the later writings, it is clear that Nietzsche's view of affects belongs to a somatic type of emotive theory.[40] The question that must be answered is just what is a somatic theory of affects and what kind of somatic theory does Nietzsche profess?

To answer this second question, Fowles uses Barlassina and Newen's impure somatic theory (hereafter IST) as a template to frame key passages in Nietzsche's *oeuvre* where affect (*Affekt*), emotions, feelings (*Gefuhle*), and other cognate concepts are discussed at length.[41] According to these authors, the aim of developing this theory is to address several unresolved difficulties in traditional somatic approaches of emotion–what I shall call the pure variety–like those put forward by Jesse Prinz and Antonio Damasio. Unfortunately, these particular advantages of IST are not highlighted by Fowles. I will redress this failure by underscoring the aspects of IST that track well with Nietzsche's theory of affects.

Where to start? I begin by working through Fowles's reconstruction of Nietzsche's theory of affects. Fowles identifies two critical components in

[39] Christopher Janaway, *Beyond Selflessness*, 160–164.

[40] "Indeed, every table of values, every thou shalt known to history or ethnology, requires first a physiological investigation and interpretation, rather than a psychological one; and every one of them needs a critique on the part of medical science." (GM II: 17 Note 2).

[41] Barlassina, L and Newen, A. "The Role of Bodily Perception in Emotion: In Defense of an Impure Somatic Theory" *Philosophy and Phenomenological Research* 1–42, 2013.

this regard: (1) the causal extraction mechanism and (2) the practical need to identify a particular emotion by subsuming it under the appropriate affect word. Such affect words will also be involved in a complex web of linguistic etiologies which further and somewhat subtly modulate (or so it is intimated by Fowles) the raw "feel" or "feeling seizure" of the emotion, as Dewey once put it. According to Dewey, when we experience an emotion, the feeling part or the raw *quale* is fixed; the raw feel of anger, for example, is very easy to distinguish from fear.[42] In what follows, I will put forward my own schema for understanding emotions. I will then apply this framework to Nietzsche's peculiar view of emotions.

I return to the original IST to extract additional critical features that help put further flesh on Nietzsche's theory when viewed from the standpoint of implexic genealogy. It is this part that remains significantly underdetermined in Fowles's presentation. Fowles focuses on external input, which is understandable. "Nietzsche's picture starts with an occasioning object, perceived qua stimulus owing to one's psychophysiology" he notes. But if that is true, then Fowles's account is not as fulsome as we think; his Nietzschean affects model is reactive and passive. For Fowles, exteroception triggers a cascade of physical processes in a subject, exciting the causal extraction mechanism. The causal extraction mechanism leads the subject to find the right affect word under which the feeling can be subsumed. This subsumption is a falsification yet further informed and colored by the subject's unique enculturation.

It is understandable why Fowles focuses on an external stimulus, as affects, when they become conscious reflections, typically are appraisals of one's physical environment, a vital aspect of the IST, at least with respect to more complex affective states like guilt. Unfortunately, this component of affect, namely its appraisal, which Barlassina and Newen borrow from Richard Lazarus, is significantly undertheorized in Fowles's

[42] John Dewey, "The Theory of Emotion. (2) The Significance of Emotions", *Psychological Review* 2, (1895): 13–32, 15–16. This raw feel cannot be explained via James's somatic account Dewey clarifies: "By this I understand him (James) to mean that he is not dealing with emotion as a concrete whole of experience, but with an abstraction from the actual emotion of that element which gives it its differentia—its feeling quale, its 'feel.' As I understand it, he did not conceive himself as dealing with that state which we term 'being angry,' but rather with the peculiar 'feel' which any one has when he is angry, an element which may be intellectually abstracted, but certainly has no existence by itself, of as full-fledged emotion-experience."

rendering of Nietzschean emotions.[43] This is yet another issue I have with Fowles's otherwise insightful analysis—the role of appraisal, on the cognitive side, like its physiological antithesis, its feeling seizure, is not mentioned by Fowles. Yet, both perform significant work in Nietzsche's theory. In what follows I put forward a six-fold view of affect that tracks well with Nietzsche's genealogical account.

After providing a new framework for understanding Nietzsche's theory of emotions, my next task is to explain, genealogically, how the causal extraction mechanism became entwined with the practical need of linguistic subsumption. This account is in keeping with the spirit of Implexic genealogy. Implexic genealogy demonstrates how the biological and conceptual intersect yet remain separate. Both are necessary in order to provide a genealogical account for the emergence of a phenomenon. Neither is reducible to the other. In Chap. 6, I provide a vignette of Augustine's conversion experience as expressed in the saint's *Confessions* as a test-case of sorts for this claim.

Section IV: Somatic and Non-Somatic Theories of Emotion

Before turning to Nietzsche's theory of affects, we must distinguish between the somatic and non-somatic approaches to emotion. The somatic theory of emotion is often associated with William James. James argued that, "during an emotion the brain causes the body to change, and that feeling of emotion is the result of perceiving the body's change."[44] The standard somatic model reverses the order of the non-somatic interpretation of affect. In order to better understand the somatic theory of which there are two main distinctions, pure and impure, we would do well to examine the non-somatic model first.

[43] Lazarus, Richard. "From Appraisal: The Minimal Cognitive Prerequisites of Emotion." In *What Is an Emotion?* 2nd edition, edited by Robert C. Solomon, 125–131. Oxford: Oxford University Press: 2003.

[44] Antonio Damasio, *The Feeling of What happens,* (New York: Harvest Court, 1999), 28.

A traditional model of affect theory, at least the one advanced in the early to middle of the twentieth century, examines emotion from within a conceptual philosophy of language framework. These theories broadly argued that there is the perception of a stimulus, the stimulus then causes one to experience a mental state, and then there is a corresponding physiological response. For example, suppose Johnny visits his local zoo and sees a lion break out of its enclosure. The traditional model says there is an exteroception of a lion; this perception causes Johnny to feel afraid, and this perception triggers a physiological reaction: for example shaking, trembling, rapid heartbeat, and so on. At this stage, the affect may merely be a feeling that is not consciously brought to mind until later. In other words, Johnny has a flight, fight, faint, or freeze response.

One advantage of this theory is that it can readily explain the seeming intentionality of emotional states. If Johnny were asked what made him afraid, he could point to the escaped lion. This seemingly self-evident truth, namely that emotions have an intentional component, "an aboutness" is one that many somatic approaches have difficulty explaining.[45] Later, we will see how IST handles this problem.

In now looking at the somatic framework, this approach takes the three components above: Perception→Affect→State (PAS) and alters the order of the last two parts. Looking at the above example again, a somatic approach would explain the end product, Johnny's state of fear, as follows: Johnny sees a lion, the mere perception of this animal causes a series of bodily sensations (e.g. rapid heart beating, faster, shallower breathing, trembling etc.) which then produces the mental affective state fear.[46] The proper order of these states then is Perception →State→Affect (PSA). The claim made by all somatic accounts is that it is the body's physiological response that plays a causal role in creating the affect. For the purist,

---

[45] See Barlassina and Newen, Impure Somatic Theory, 5.

[46] As Fowles clarifies, "The claim characteristic of the somatic approach is that bodily perturbation makes "a causal contribution" to the generation of affective mental states (Barlassina and Newen, "Impure Somatic Theory," 640). Instead of S, A, P, somatic theories claim the correct order to be S, P, A: my perception of the bear, S, causes a series of bodily changes, P, which are then causally related to the affective mental state, A. This is what we find in Nietzsche's writings." (Fowles, "The Heart of the Flesh" 119). I quoted this passage because it is clear that Fowles borrows his account of Nietzschean affects from Barlassina and Newen and yet, strangely, excises vital components from their model.

the affect is nothing other than that specific physiological processing of the exteroception; fear, for example, produces a different cascade of physiological responses than anger. Affects are reducible to their peculiar interoception. For the impurist, the affect is a mixture of cognitive and interoceptive elements. The recognition of the aboutness of the emotion is integrated with the interoception for IST. Barlassina and Newen comment: "In any case, according to our theory, emotions are constituted by the integration of interoceptive states with representations of external objects."[47] The impurist remains a somatic theorist because interoception is a necessary component for the production of emotions, but it is not sufficient for said production. With this distinction between somatic and non-somatic models explained, I now turn to Fowles.

Section V: Fowles's Interpretation of Nietzsche

In the conclusion to his article, Fowles provides a helpful summary of the affective position he ascribes to Nietzsche. In what follows, I will quote the concluding passage marking out the claims Fowles makes first before clarifying each. Fowles will then add these two components to a stripped-down and ultimately, ineffective IST framework. In contrast, I take Fowles's insights and add them to a richer, more robust IST model that makes room for Deweyan "feeling seizures."

Keeping with the Separation Thesis, we may divide Fowles's interpretation of Nietzschean affect theory into two components: a physiological feature and a narrational feature. I should clarify this separation is not something Fowles explicitly does. I now quote Fowles's physiological summation:

> Bodily sensations alter features of one's psychology, modulating exteroceptive interpretation and exciting the cause-extracting mechanism. Affective interpreting makes a causal connection between one's state and surroundings, valences these surroundings, and makes salient certain features and affordances. This process occurs partly under the pressure of practical-

[47] Barlassina and Newen, 27.

> psychological necessity, so as to provide an object in relation to which one's affects can be discharged."[48]

This passage focuses on the physiological feature of emotions. After clarifying the contribution that unconscious, biological systems provide to the generation of emotions, I turn to the cognitive contribution and involvement in generating emotions. Fowles makes three central claims in the above passage.

The first I call the Exteroceptive Trigger Claim (ETC). Fowles argues that bodily perturbances that manifest interoceptions responsible for producing emotional states begin with an exteroception sufficiently potent enough to enact a physical response. The bodily perturbance or interoception is necessary, though not sufficient, for manufacturing the emotional state. However, one of the problems with pure somatic theories is the quandary of connecting these non-cognitive perturbances to emotions, for there may be other bodily disturbances that produce interoceptions, yet such interoceptions are clearly not affects. Barlassina and Newen provide two examples: fatigue and inner ear pressure.[49] Internal ear pressure is an interoception related to changes in one's environment but is not, on its own, an emotional state. Thus, more must be said about the particular perturbance that brings about an affective state. Unfortunately, this is a problem that Fowles does not adequately address. The IST defuses this problem by noting that an appropriate cognitive judgment must accompany an emotional state. Physical disturbances must be accompanied by a narrational understanding to count as emotions. Indeed, one might claim that the causal extraction mechanism creates this very distinction.

Following Fowles, the second claim I call the Causal Extraction Mechanism (CEM). This thesis argues that the interoception of bodily states activates a physical module of the body responsible for obtaining an exogenic origin of the perceived disturbance. This part will require much further elucidation, which I provide below.

[48] Fowles, "The Heart of the Flesh" 137.

[49] Barlassina, and Newen, "The Role of Bodily Perception in Emotion" 18.

The third claim is the Homeostasis Claim (HC). The claim made here is that when one experiences a powerful emotion, the body naturally seeks to discharge it. The purpose of said release is for the body to return to balance or non-disturbance. It might be helpful to compare such a state to a non-emotional perturbance like extreme fatigue due to exercise. According to some exercise physiologists, fatigue is a way of signaling that the usual steady-state internal environment of the body is undergoing severe stress. Physical stress produced by heavy exercise signals to the subject that said exercising needs to be halted in order to redirect resources from muscles to more vital systems and to ensure that the body, as a whole, does not become overheated. Ament and Verke explain:

> During exercise the contracting muscles generate force or power and heat … This generated energy will deplete the energy stocks within the body. During exercise, metabolites and heat are generated, which affect the steady state of the internal environment. Depending on the form of exercise, sooner or later sensations of fatigue and exhaustion will occur. The physiological role of these sensations is protection of the exercising subject from the deleterious effects of exercise."[50]

Analogously, a stimulus that promotes a powerful psycho-physiological disturbance that becomes registered as an emotion drains precious mental resources from the subject's cognitive economy. One way to concretize this might be to suggest that when one is under the influence of a powerful emotion that the brain is prevented from doing its primary job of pursuing objects like food that guarantee the survival of the body and conversely assess and predict risks in one's environment. The intense focus and obsession with an affect where there is both a fierce feeling seizure and a significant drain on intellectual resources, inhibit these two main functions of cognitive activity.

There is something else to notice about this claim. Consider that affect is doing the work of aspect two of drives mentioned in Chap. 3, namely the aim claim but also takes on the role of aspect three: the urge feature. Let me explain. In thinking that the affect is veridical, the subject seeks

---

[50] Ament and Verke, Sports Med. 2009;39(5):389–422. *Exercise and Fatigue.*

out some object or event in one's surroundings as the cause for one's emotional perturbance. Although Fowles isn't clear on why the mechanism does this, he indicates that it is a physiological response and that the physiological conditioning of the person determines, in part, the degree of falsification that the extraction mechanism will allow the emotion to be vented. The feeling creates saliences within its environment to either quell through satisfaction, or dissipate through aversion, the raw feel of the emotion. What is essential to bear in mind about this last claim is that Nietzsche's view is a somatic theory, impure though it may be. Thus, the body ultimately conditioned both the emotion, including its feel, and valence (avoidance/attraction properties). But the affordances created by the extraction of the affect mechanism fail to satisfy because, as Fowles claims, the affect is falsifying full stop. We will look at this in more detail below.

Turning to the narrational side, we need to investigate two additional claims. Quoting again from Fowles's helpful summation, he writes,

> This process (psychological modulation of the affect identified through the causal mechanism) is linguistic interpretation, through which one's state is subsumed under an affect-word. One might also bring the putative relationship of one's condition to a cause-object extracted by affective interpretation to a point of reflection, in the form of (often intricate) linguistically articulated etiologies."[51]

There are two related ideas here: (1) Once the causal extraction mechanism identifies the feeling, it is further subsumed under an affect word. The linguistic formatting of the affect allows for further nuanced interpretations of the emotional state. In addition, there is an attempt to understand the cause of the feeling further and how the emotional state might be satisfied if the valence is attractive or how it might be quelled if the valence is aversive. This need to discharge the emotion is once more due to the homeostasis disposition of the body. I will call this claim the Linguistic Modulation Claim (LMC)

[51] Fowles, "The Heart of the Flesh", 137.

(2) The LMC is always embedded and further supported by complex narrations mainly of the religious variety. These narratives augment the refinement of the affect state and provide distinctive pathways in order for a more finely calibrated homeostasis to be satisfied. For example, if one is Catholic and feels guilty because of some sin committed, then one can alleviate one's guilt by going to confessions, saying Hail Mary's and so on. I call this claim the Narrational Satisfaction Claim. (NSC).

In what follows, we have five claims:

(1) ETC: Exteroceptive Trigger claim
(2) CEM: Causal Extraction Mechanism
(3) H.C.: Homeostasis Claim
(4) LMC: Linguistic Modulation Claim
(5) NSC Narrational Satisfaction Claim

Overall, I think Fowles's framework is correct, but I have some quibbles with it. One issue pertains to ETC: an external stimulus is often not needed to produce the affect in question. Consider Nietzsche's explanation for the emergence of guilt from bad conscience. Bad conscience is a kind of brooding that becomes intensified as a result of a cycle of appraisal, which generates a more intense feeling of the raw *qualia* or feeling seizure aspect of the emotion, which, in turn, causes a new assessment producing an even more intense feeling and so on. The feature of our affective system just described, I call it the Internal trigger claim (ITC). Under my framework, ITC will replace ETC. I demonstrate a more comprehensive, accurate, and pertinent explanation of Nietzsche's affect theory by incorporating this claim into my analysis.

There is a second and related problem with Fowles's approach. Fowles's interpretation cleaves to an overly rigid biological determinism similar–though not explicitly stated–to Leiter's type-fact reading of Nietzsche I discussed in Chap. 3. For Fowles, the causal mechanism *is conditioned* by the subject's physiological state. This interpretation is supported by utilizing passages from Nietzsche's *Twilight* where Nietzsche, as I demonstrated, is at his most deterministic. Moreover, the affect is *inherently falsifying*. The subject is led to believe, via CEM, that the emotion generated by the interoception can assist with the discharge of the raw feel whether positive or negative. But if the mechanism is inherently deceiving, then it is not functional. Two problems emerge from this fact: (1) How did this non-functional mechanism come to be? Why would the body have such a mechanism? and (2) If the mechanism is inherently deceptive then why is it so successful? For it is clear—both from Nietzsche's genealogical investigation and from phenomenological introspection that the causal extraction mechanism does assist at least to some degree with the discharging of an emotion. Indeed, the entire thesis of GM III is to argue that the ascetic ideal, though rooted in ressentiment, is a survival mechanism—it helps the herd release their pent-up frustrations and abuse suffered at the hands of the nobles. The result of this slow-drip release of pleasure is to prevent the masses from launching a full-scale yet suicidal war against their overlords. Thus, there must be some epistemic virtue to the mechanism itself. However, what that is, precisely, is undetermined by Fowles's theory. A solution to this puzzle requires us to understand, if not the genealogical origin of the causal extraction mechanism, at the very least its amplification and why it is successful, albeit incompletely, in assisting the body to reach homeostasis. I provide the solution below.

Perhaps the most critical passage that Fowles quotes to support his interpretation is the following from Nietzsche. I will state this passage in full as it is essential to highlight that Nietzsche's simple and incomplete view of affect, given below holds that an emotion is a construction of the intellect, a fabrication, and confabulation of causes that do not exist.

> All bodily general feelings that we do not understand are interpreted intellectually, i.e. a reason is sought for feeling one way or another, in people, experiences, etc., so something adverse, dangerous, alien, is set as the cause of our malaise [Verstimmung]: in fact, it is sought in addition to the malaise, for the sake of the conceivability [Denkbarkeit] of our state.—Frequent blood-flows to the brain, with the feeling of suffocation, are interpreted as anger: the persons and things that rouse us to anger are releases for the physiological state.—Subsequently, after a long habituation [Gewöhnung], certain occurrences and general feelings are themselves so regularly connected that the sight of certain occurrences produces the state of general feeling, specifically any congestion of the blood or excitation of the semen etc. it brings with it through close association: we then say, "the affect is aroused." (NF 1883: 24 [20]) Nachgelassene Fragmente

Fowles parses this quotation by employing a rigid psycho-physiology. His interpretation is not so much false but narrow: a genealogical interpretation examining the full scope of the claims made therein would significantly soften such a reading. In any case, for Fowles it is this type-fact of the individual that explains, causally speaking, that person's affective reaction to a given stimulus. More specifically, the causal extraction mechanism is excited due to the body's physical response to the stimulus presented. This mechanism seeks a "cause" for one's condition.[52] However, it is the physiological state and not the cognitive module or, so holds Fowles, that extracts one aspect of the subject's environment as a cause rather than some other. Moreover, the subject's physiological state selects the affective response to the body's internal state.[53]

One of the critical passages Fowles uses to support his position is drawn from the section on Cornaro's diet in *Twilight of the Idols*. In that section, Nietzsche declares that Cornaro mistakes the cause for the effect: Cornaro believes that his meager diet is causally responsible for his long life. But this inference, Nietzsche claims is a mistake. It is the opposite; it is Cornaro's constitution that causes him to restrict his caloric intake. (T.I. The Four Great Errors) Thus, just as Cornaro is mistaken about the true causes behind his food regimen, we are mistaken in thinking that affects accurately represent the cause responsible for our feelings. It is instead the opposite; the affect is generated not from the external stimuli but the body's response to it.[54]

Fowles concretizes his reading by turning to how the resentful individual falsely represents reality. The causal extracting mechanism picks out a cause that explains the affect in the person of resentment. One's bodily state triggers this process. Such moral evaluation is "an interpretation, a kind of interpreting" undertaken by affects. Nietzsche describes the interpretation itself as a "symptom of certain physiological states, as well as of a certain spiritual level of dominant judgments" (NF 1885: 2 [190]; cf. 1880: 6 [445]).[55] This is the part of the causal sequence that the

[52] Fowles, The Heart of the Flesh, 120.

[53] Fowles, The Heart of the Flesh, 124.

[54] Fowles, "The Heart of the Flesh", 125–126.

[55] Fowles, "The Heart of the Flesh", 126.

person does not understand; the person believes that affect, (which comprises both the word and the feeling) reflects the exteroception. It does not. The affective explanation of one's emotional state is false. Moreover, the affect becomes imbricated with "the stock of etiologies stored in memory, which have been forged through experience."[56] These etiologies become habituated, leading the individual to redeploy these explanations in new scenarios, thus providing additional justification for the initial interpretation.

In establishing my solution, it is vital to keep the point I made about Stern earlier, for it is salutary here. It is impossible to present a theory of affects that accurately captures all of Nietzsche's claims regarding emotions and feelings in his *oeuvre*. Some passages will need to take interpretative priority over others. For Fowles, it is clearly those passages that are decidedly more physiologically inflected. In contrast, I emphasize those that are fluid, which is to say, genealogical.

Now that the affect has been identified and further justified according to the subject's repository of memories where a similar interoception was encountered, the individual in question now seeks out the underlying cause of the affect. In conjunction with this process, specific features of the person's living conditions are made salient, which will then be conducive to discharging one's state. This saliency is perspectival in that it provides an evaluation homing in on those surroundings which are valenced first in either positive or negative terms.[57] However, what precipitates this process is the particular physical state of the individual.

In broad brushstrokes, the above account is Fowles' analysis regarding the physiological aspect of Nietzschean affects. I agree with the

[56] Fowles, "The Heart of the Flesh", 126.

[57] Fowles fleshes out this point in the following: "Social restrictions and their corresponding punishments produce a range of complex psychological responses, including (perhaps most importantly) bad conscience. Nietzsche writes of drives being accompanied by "either a good or a bad conscience." These complex, compound affective episodes involve the drives co-occurring with an "attendant sensation of pleasure or displeasure," acquired as "second nature" in relation to drives "already baptized good or evil," or noted as "a characteristic of beings already morally determined and evaluated" (D 38). 129 On multiple occasions, he contrasts the "right class" of causes, to be identified by the "anatomically educated," with the causes sought by those less well-versed. The latter group, we are told, seek "a moral explanation" for their state." (NF 1884: 26 [92]; cf. 1885: 38 [1]; GM III.17 128 The Heart of the Flesh, 130.

mechanisms of Fowles's theory. My disagreement stems from Fowles's deterministically inflected reductionism.

Turning now to the narrational facet of Fowles's position, the elucidation itself is insightful and tracks well with my understanding of Nietzsche's *Genealogy*. Once the causal extraction mechanism is excited and the affect produced, there is an attempt to understand it. Fowles notes: "In order to feel [x]," and so on, linguistic interpretation must occur. As we have seen, subsuming one's state under an existing affect-word involves more than simply attending to one's state of feeling: it involves the positing of a cause for one's state."[58] This desire to discover the reason for one's affect is first triggered by the body's response to dispel the charged interoception and then secondly by the cognitive-practical need to bring one's state to a point of A.R. or affective reflection.[59] Fowles suggests that it is only by transporting this unconscious desire to conscious thought that the subject can judge those affordances which have the best chance of draining the energetic needs of the emotion. But here again, there is a tension in Fowles's interpretation. For consider that if AR is initiated to direct the subject to those affordances that may best drain the emotion, which is the "feeling seizure" of Dewey, then the causal mechanism is not as falsifying as it initially appears.

Furthermore, affect words are rooted in more complex and extensive psychological and ethical frameworks. On this point, Fowles is spot on. He notes that the concept of sin is embedded in a web of broader metaphysical, moral, and psychological views, involving notions such as *causa sui* free will, claims about the nature of moral norms, and so on. Within such a framework, habituation to this interpretation facilitates the identification of fine-grained affective states.[60] These well-calibrated affective states lead one to modulate their emotional state (recognize the differences between bad conscience and guilt, e.g.) and then correspondingly comport one's embodiment to alleviate these feelings. However, suppose the action leads to a quelling of the feeling in relation to guilt, for example. In that case, Fowles is also wrong in asserting that, "In such

[58] Fowles, "The Heart of the Flesh", 134.

[59] Fowles, "The Heart of the Flesh", 135.

[60] Fowles, The Heart of the Flesh", 133.

circumstances, almost any putative etiology will do to facilitate the relieving of one's state."[61] Some religious practices are *undoubtedly better* at discharging emotion than others. Indeed, it is precisely for this reason that Christianity won out against other mystery cults, or so Nietzsche demonstrates. Thus, Fowles' falsification thesis leads him to take up another indefensible claim. I propose to sort out what Fowles got right and what needs to be corrected.

I now employ a modified version of Fowles's framework. Fowles's theory is predicated on Barlassina and Newen's IST, but critical components of the latter's theory are missing. However, these components are essential in explaining the function of the causal extraction mechanism and how the apparatus intersects with cognition. I then demonstrate how the three most critical pieces of Fowles's analysis, namely the causal extraction mechanism (CEM) and the LMC Linguistic Modulation Claim and (NSC) Narrational Satisfaction Claim, can be better understood and incorporated into my model.

First, instead of focusing on the exteroceptive cause, as Fowles does, I turn to the internal, dynamic, psychical movement of the subject. Here I am referring to the captured tribal person living in an empire. As such, he is always and already interpreting affects, reliving traumatic experiences, and predicting the peculiar and very often violent behavioral dispositions of his *Paterfamilias*. As discovered from the above section, what Nietzsche calls base cognitive abilities (e.g. cause and effect thinking, inferring etc.) of the slave are always in a state of high alert because these and only these tools will help him survive in his new environment. As a consequence, this vibrant mental economy of the enslaved person is potent enough to trigger a bodily response all by itself. Continual renewal of external stimuli is not necessary.

My argument, drawing now from Chap. 4 and the first section of this chapter, is that this triggering process is not caused by a raw drive or physiological response to external stimuli *per se*, but is rather initiated by the perseveration of traumatic events which give rise to cognitive strategies of bodily self-preservation. I called this the Internal Triggering Condition. I now use my conclusions in the section above and from

[61] Fowles, The Heart of the Flesh", 130–131.

Chap. 4 to support my framework below. To distill my argument, I demonstrated that, in the beginning, when slaves faced the first undignified strike by their master, that exteroception (physical hurt) triggered an affective episode, anger. The disposition to strike back is halted because the enslaved person understands that any counter-action will have severe consequences. Although the action is terminated, the anger that drove the initial reflex is not quelled—it leads to trauma. The slave's cognitive system is put on notice as it were. It is now trained to notice behavioral patterns of a few select individuals (the *Paterfamilias* being one) and make predictions (what Nietzsche refers to as "thinking," "reckoning," "inferring" in GM II 16 etc.) to prevent further physical trauma and dishonor.

Barlassina and Newens support this point. They demonstrate that current empirical research shows that a mere thought (e.g. I need to study for my anatomy test) can, all by itself, trigger a somatic response. This physiological reaction to a "mere" idea then engenders an interoceptive response resulting in an affect. The feeling is now perceived by, and linguistically reconstructed for, consciousness, as "I am feeling anxious." They write in this regard: "Take this case. John thinks about tomorrow's exam; this cognitive state triggers a set of bodily changes in John; when the interoception of such bodily changes integrates with the cognitive state that triggered them, John undergoes fear. Thus in contrast to Prinz an affect is not just its interoception of a bodily process rather it is an integration of understanding and the feedback data from the body."[62] Emotions as the authors put it are "multi-modal phenomena." They continue: "Thus, we depart from Prinz's pure somatic theory in that we deny that emotions are constituted by interoceptive states alone. This is why our theory counts as an impure somatic theory of emotion: because it maintains that bodily changes causally contribute to emotions, but denies that the perception of such bodily changes is all that there is to the constitution of emotions."[63] How the integration of these two, cognitive evaluation on the one hand and interoception on the other occurs, they do not say. My position argues that this integration is represented, at first, symbolically speaking, namely, as a hostile drive. I then apply the

[62] Barlassina and Newen, 27–28.

[63] Barlassina and Newen, 27.

Separation Thesis to the idea of drive and argue that it is better to view drives as implexes: they are intersections of cognitive and affective components. It is the integration of what Nietzsche calls "consciousness" the "weakest and most fallible organ" construed here as instrumental rationality alongside an affective component that explains how we internalize feelings and the corresponding values that they subtend. (GM II 16). Let me explain.

A feeling that eventuates in hostility is aroused when an enslaved person feels degraded when forced to perform a task for his master. It is vital to notice that degradation as the most likely affective response, is valenced at first as something negative. In reply to enforced servitude and the physical abuse endured by the enslaved person, they desire to retaliate against their master. However, a hostile reaction (e.g. striking or perhaps even killing his master) dare not be invoked; the enslaved person knows what might happen to him should he take any retaliatory compensation, (see the above section on cognition). The memory of the beatings received by the slave is stained with impotence and humiliation. It is because of this imprinting that they are remembered in precise detail. Recall what Nietzsche writes about the power of forgetting and how memory was burnt into the slave. "Now this animal which needs to be forgetful, in which forgetting represents a force, a form of robust health, has bred in itself an opposing faculty a memory, with the aid of which forgetfulness is abrogated in certain cases –namely in those cases were certain promises were made". (GM II I) In addition, the subject as we know has been traumatized, which has also reflexively curtailed any physical action. All of the slave's survival systems are put on notice.

To continue, for the enslaved person, the perseveration of negative thoughts, the repeated playback as it were of physical beatings and other tortures at the hands of the slave-master, form a traumatic memory. This memory sets off a cascade of physical processes which cannot be effectively discharged because *there is no adequate affect word that satisfies the discharging of this powerful feeling seizure*, namely, traumatic pain. Following Fowles, the causal extraction mechanism already present before the formation of the first state becomes intensified. It goes into overdrive because there is no affect word in the slave's linguistic repertoire to explain what the slave is feeling. The slaves think: Who is responsible for our ill feelings? Who is to blame? However, no answer is forthcoming. They lack the sophistication and causal etiology to subsume what they feel.

There is a consequence for this lack of linguistic subsumption. Notice that underwriting the Causal Extraction Mechanism is HC, the Homeostasis Claim. The Homeostasis Claim says that one's psychic economy is such that it prefers a steady-state system. The purpose of CEM is to find the right affect word in order to alleviate the burden on one's emotional resources. If the CEM is successful, the extra psychical energy is safely offloaded. But in the slave's case, the CEM fails, and thus he must find a new outlet to vent his intense feeling seizure in order to reach homeostasis, a natural condition of the body. Where does he find the space to discharge this negative feeling? He finds it within himself: "The entire inner world, originally as thin as if it were stretched between two membranes, expanded and extended itself, acquired depth, breadth and height, in the same measure as outward discharge was inhibited." (GM II 16).

While it is true that slights, abuses, and physical attacks were not new to the members of early German tribal communities, these offenses pale in comparison to those found in the domestic habitat the new slave finds himself in. Customs and other tribal norms helped to assuage and discharge and otherwise dampen negative feelings within the tribe. The German *Vergeld* or blood debt was one of these ways; ritual sacrifices would be another. However, in the new environment of the Roman *Domus*, the slave is not only stripped of these opportunities of discharge but is subjected to violence and indignities hitherto undreamt. The intersection of these three axes: the intensification of violence on the one hand, the lack of freedom in general, and the lack of coping mechanisms or so argues Nietzsche in GM II 16, necessitate the need for the slave to find new conduits for the proper offloading of negative emotions.

New affect words and the etiologies that support them are introduced with the advent of Christianity. They build on and modulate the old *quale* of more primitive emotions. However, given that the IST is an integrative theory, these very words and the narration embedding them modulate the valence itself. What was once deemed negatively is turned into its opposite. For example, physical and emotional trauma inflicted on a slave by his master turns into brooding and following Eric Berne "after burn."[64] The unresolved *quale*, along with the judgment the master is "evil" supplied by Christian etiologies, morphs this negative valenced brooding into revenge fantasies against the master in the slave's psyche. The slave alters this valence by taking pleasure in living out these fantasies and judging himself to be morally superior to the *Paterfamilias*. And voila, the slave revolt in morality takes hold. Significantly, the memories no longer need an exteroceptive trigger-they can be set off independently of any cause.

I show that these primitive *quales* are appraised and either endorsed or sanctioned. Newen and Barlassina also point out this aspect of IST. Moreover, they explicitly borrow from Richard Lazarus's appraisal theory of emotions. The role cognitive appraisal plays in the formation and intensification of emotions is absent from Fowles's account, yet it is a crucial component of IST. I will now explain how these "feeling seizures" become intensified when they are embedded in Christian rhetoric. Together they become mutually conditioning. I will analyze this component in detail in the next chapter.

Turning to NSC, eventually, one cult, one narrational etiology wins out, Christianity. But why? Nietzsche hints at a reason, but it is not fully fleshed out. Here is my answer. The solution to this puzzle may be divined by examining the causal interrelation of three components: traumatic memory, the causal extraction mechanism, and the role of homeostasis. My argument in brief, is that the feeling seizure of traumatic memory is so concentrated and augmented that it is only attenuated in those slaves who believe in a final explosive point, the Day of Judgment. Such an idea appeals to the physiological side of affect theory because it portends a total release of negatively valenced feelings in one overwhelming ecstatic catharsis. The causal mechanism is not entirely useless or false; it is able to hit upon the correct narration, albeit for the wrong reason.

What's more, there is evidence to support my interpretation. First, as Orlando Patterson notes, Rome was rather peculiar compared to other empires and slave-holding communities. He writes: "Rome was different and the slaves' religious life a great deal better; not that Roman masters were any less cruel they may have been even more brutal rather Rome had a culture that was far more inclusive with institutions that were

[64] Eric Berne, *What Do You Say After You Say Hello*? New York: Grove Press Inc. 1977, 442.

incomparably more flexible and in no area more so than religion."[65] Patterson goes on to argue that it was because of this religious openness to all strata of society that "Christianity found many of its earliest converts among the slave populations of the Roman Empire although the fact is surprisingly difficult to authenticate. What is certain, however, is that the slave experience was a major source of the metaphors that informed the symbolic structure of Christianity."[66]

In the next chapter, I intend to explore how one may understand the internalization of Christian practices by examining how Christianizing practices operate from the inside. To help me with this endeavor, I demonstrate how emotions lead to self-formatting. I intend to use the critical method of genealogy (separating the drama of punishment from its procedures) and apply it to a new target. In keeping with IST, I hold that affects comprise minimally five elements and very often, in the case of intense feeling seizures a sixth. On the physiological side, we have four: (1) a somatic reaction that elicits a perturbance capable of exciting the Causal Extraction Mechanism (in the case of an enslaved person a triggering cause i.e. The Triggering Claim); (2) in extreme circumstances, a behavioral paralinguistic piece (weeping, groaning, yelling, shaking); (3) the feeling of the emotion itself, its *quale and* (4) The Homeostasis Claim which instinctually seeks a return to a steady-state of non-perturbance.

On the cognitive side, I integrate the following with the physiological/behavioral: (5) The phenomenological object I take to be responsible for my feeling (e.g. I am afraid of this lion before me, I feel ashamed before God etc.). Regarding the phenomenological object that I am principally interested in, it should be noted that it will very often be embedded in complex, religious narratives; Finally, (6) An appraisal or judging component concomitant with the object in question. Here I am closely following the letter of Barlassina and Newens' IST by highlighting a critical aspect that Fowles neglects to mention, namely, Lazarus's appraisal theory of emotions. I add to this model Fowles's contribution which is the Causal Extraction Mechanism and the etiological component. Finally, I borrow form John Dewey's *Theory of Emotions* by stressing the

[65] Orlando Patterson, *Slavery and Social Death a Comparative Study*, 68.

[66] Ibid., 70.

importance of this *quale* in fomenting new emotions and new etiologies. I contend that both the behavior associated with the emotion and the *quale* or "feel" (to borrow Dewey's term) are older than the individual phenomenological object part and appraisal dimension of one's emotional experiences. I further contend that when the behavior associated with this *quale* is exaggerated, the feeling becomes intensified and refined over time. These behaviors and feelings initiate further refinements of the causal extraction mechanism and the etiologies that subtend them. These feelings are then appraised and tethered to new relations of meaning (phenomenological objects with their corresponding religious etiologies).

The above framework, skeletal as it is, requires some fleshing out. The next chapter demonstrates how my position tracks with concrete Christian forms of subjectivization. I examine two kinds of subjectivization in that chapter: Augustine's internalized furrowed model and Tertullian's externalist framework of subjectivization.

References

Ament and Verke, *Sports Medicine.* 2009; 39(5):389–422. Exercise and Fatigue.

Anderson, Lanier R. "On the Nobility of Nietzsche's Priests," in *Nietzsche's On the Genealogy of Morality: A Critical Guide*, ed. Simon May Cambridge: Cambridge University Press, 2011.

Barlassina and Newen, "The Role of Bodily Perception in Emotion: In Defense of an Impure Somatic Theory" *Philosophy and Phenomenological Research* 1–42, 2013.

Berne, Eric. *What Do You Say After You Say Hello?* New York: Grove Press Inc. 1977.

Buckland, W.W. *The Roman Law of Slavery: The Condition of the Slave in Private Law from Augustus to Justinian*, Cambridge University Press, 1908.

Cicero, Marcus Tullus. *Treatise on the Commonwealth and The Treatise On the Laws* in Two volumes Francis Barham Trans Edmund Spettigue, 1842.

Deem, Michael J. "A Flaw in the Stich–Plantinga challenge to Evolutionary Reliabilism", *Analysis* Vol 78, Number 2, April 2018, 216–225.

Fowles, Christopher. "The Heart of Flesh: Nietzsche on Affects and the Interpretation of the Body". *Journal of the History of Philosophy*, Volume 58, Number 1, January 2020, 113–139.

Graeber, Graeber and Wengrow, David. *The Dawn of Everything.* New York: Penguin 2021.

Graeber, Daniel. *Debt the First 5000 Years,* New York Melville House Publishing, 2014.

Hatab, Lawrence. *Nietzsche's On the Genealogy of Morals an Introduction* (Cambridge Introductions to Key philosophical Texts, Cambridge, Cambridge University Press, 2008.

Janaway, Christopher. *Beyond Selflessness: Reading Nietzsche's Genealogy* (Oxford: Oxford University Press, 2007.

Leiter, Brian. 2002. *Nietzsche on Morality.* New York: Routledge.

Morrisson, Iain. "Ascetic Slaves: Rereading Nietzsche's On the Genealogy of Morals". *Journal of Nietzsche Studies,* Vol. 45, No. 3 (Autumn 2014), pp. 230–257.

Nozick, Robert. *Philosophical Explanations* Harvard University Press, 1984.

Nagel, Jennifer. *Epistemology a Very Short Introduction* (Oxford University Press, 2014).

Paterson, Orlando. *Slavery and Social Death: A Comparative Study* Harvard University Press, 1982.

Plantinga, Alvin. *Warranted Christian Belief* (Oxford: Oxford University Press, 2000).

Poellner, Peter. "Affect Value and Objectivity" in *Nietzsche and Morality* Edited by Brian Leiter and Neil Sinhababu Oxford University Press, 2007, 227–261.

Reginster, "Nietzsche on Ressentiment and Valuation," *Philosophy and Phenomenological Research* 57.2 (1997): 281–305.

Strauss, Barry. *The Spartacus War* New York Simon and Schuster, 2009.

Tacitus *A Treatise on the Situation, Inhabitants and Manners of Germany* (Germania and Agricola) Trans. John Aiken, Cambridge University Press, 1823.

Tacitus *Annals* Vol. 5 Book XIV. 42Loeb Classical Library, 5 volumes, Latin texts and facing English translation: Harvard University Press, 1925–1937. Translation by C. H. Moore (Histories) and J. Jackson (Annals).

Varro *On Agriculture (De Rustica),* Trans. W.D. Hooper, and H.B. Ash Loeb Classical Library, 1934.

Zuckert, Michael. "Bringing Philosophy Down from the Heavens", *The Review of Politics* Vol. 51, No. 1 (Winter, 1989), pp. 70–85.

6

A Test Case: Comparing Augustinian to Tertullian Christian Subjectivity

This chapter takes the six-fold framework of emotions worked out in Chap. 5 and applies it to Christian subjectivizing practices. I then combine this framework with two essential genealogical methods: the Separation Thesis and the rule of conceptual transformation. Finally, I superimpose these methods and use them as a prism of sorts to explain a test case, for my new interpretation of the Internalization Hypothesis, namely, Augustine's conversion as depicted in the Saint's *Confessions*.

After demonstrating the success of the above methods, I turn my attention to resolving the final problem of the work: the homunculus issue. In contrast to other authors, I do not offer a reduction of agency to more primeval "adders and subtractors" to borrow Dennett's phrasing. Instead, I demonstrate how one can continue to use my framework of emotion to explain how the internalization of values a la the Christian came from a more primitive and clearly more externalized understanding of the self. Next, I demonstrate the evolution of Christian subjectivization by turning to Tertullian's *De Spectaculus*. I then compare and contrast Augustine's subjectivization to that of Tertullian's in order to show how the internalization hypothesis helps to offer a new way to resolve the homunculus issue.

B. Lightbody, *A Genealogical Analysis of Nietzschean Drive Theory*,
https://doi.org/10.1007/978-3-031-27148-9_6

Subjectivization:

The notion of subjectivization I develop here is borrowed from the work of Michel Foucault. In the Frenchman's later works, such as the *Hermeneutics of the Subject*, Foucault adds a new dimension to his genealogy of power of the 1970s.[1] He articulates the process of what one might call self-organization (subjectivization) in one of his last interviews: "I will call the process of subjectivization the procedure by which one obtains the constitution of a subject or more precisely of a subjectivity which of course is only one of the given possibilities of organization of self-consciousness."[2] This dimension argues that in order to account for the production of specific historical forms of subjectivity one must also turn to what subjects say, think, and do to themselves. Concretizing this insight in genealogical terms, we could say that when religious discourses, rituals, and psychoanalytic technologies of the self become coupled to corporeal strategies of our own historical dispositif (i.e. the carceral regime) like surveillance and discipline, they forge a powerful tandem capable of explaining how the heartland of subjectivity is carved out.[3] But, as Foucault duly notes, the tragic element of this process is that we become a tool of our own self-management such that we become co-opted by bio-power. "Just as power relations can be affirmed, only by being carried out [Deleuze declares in his wonderful exegesis of Foucault] … so the relation to oneself, which bends these power relations can be established only by being carried out."[4]

---

[1] Michel Foucault, *The Hermeneutics of the Subject: Lectures at the College de France 1981–1982*. Edited by Frederic Gros. Translated by Graham Burchell. (New York: Palgrave Macmillan), 2005.

[2] Foucault, "The Return of Morality," 242–254, 253.

[3] The question of how one may think of ethics as aesthetics is posed by Foucault in one of his last interviews. He says: "What strikes me is the fact that in our society, art has become something which is related only to objects and not to individuals and life…. But couldn't everyone's life become a work of art?" Michel Foucault, "On the Genealogy of Ethics: An Overview of a Work in Progress," In *The Foucault Reader*, edited by Paul Rabinow, (New York: Pantheon Books), 1984, 340–372, 350. Although not fully worked out by Foucault, due to his untimely death in 1984, an important aspect of this aesthetics of existence is the "will to experiment" with our limit-attitudes with the purpose of "going beyond them." Foucault, "What Is Enlightenment?" *The Foucault Reader*, 50.

[4] Gilles Deleuze, *Foucault*, Translated by Sean Hand. (Minneapolis: University of Minnesota Press, 1988), 102.

In what follows, I demonstrate how my framework and Nietzsche's methods can account for the formation of what appears to be a radical *sui generis* shape of subjectivization, namely, the Christian convert. I open my argument by demonstrating how my impure somatic theory (IST) can explain what appears to be a novel form of self-organization, namely Augustine's conversion experience as expressed in the Saint's *Confessions.* My argument, in brief, holds that Augustine's conversion episode can be explained, genealogically, by my IST framework, which also comprises insights from Dewey and Fowles. The purpose of this explanation is to serve as a test case for the two central claims of the Internalization Hypothesis. The next step is to continue using I.H., now reimagined, to explain what Nietzsche calls simpler forms of subjectivization.

Section I: Augustine's Conversion

In Book VIII Chapter 12, passages 28–29, we find the paragraphs where Augustine converts to Christianity and takes up a vow of chastity. The depth of Augustine's anguish is profoundly moving. I now quote the passage in full:

> 28. And, not indeed in these words, yet to this effect, spoke I much unto You —But You, O Lord, how long? How long, Lord? Will You be angry for ever? Oh, remember not against us former iniquities; for I felt that I was enthralled by them. I sent up these sorrowful cries —How long, how long? Tomorrow, and tomorrow? Why not now? Why is there not this hour an end to my uncleanness?
> 29. I was saying these things and weeping in the most bitter contrition of my heart, when, lo, I heard the voice as of a boy or girl, I know not which, coming from a neighbouring house, chanting, and oft repeating, Take up and
> read; take up and read.... So, restraining the torrent of my tears, I rose up, interpreting it no other way than as a command to me from Heaven to open the book, and to read the first chapter I should light upon. For I had heard of Antony, that, accidentally coming in while the gospel was being read, he received the admonition as if what was read were addressed to him, Go and

> sell that you have, and give to the poor, and you shall have treasure in heaven;
> and come and follow me.... No further would I read, nor did I need; for instantly, as the sentence ended — by a light, as it were, of security infused into my heart — all the gloom of doubt vanished away.[5]

It is difficult to find a corresponding extract in either Greek or Roman sources (at least of the pagan kind). The closest work might be that of Marcus Aurelius's *Meditations* (*Ta eis heauton*). Although the motivation behind the *Meditations* is clearly transformative, we would not call it spiritual. The Roman Emperor's work does not have the emotional indicators and motivating sources that would mark a typical journey of "the spirit" such as anguish, longing, and torment. Augustine's *Confessions* marks a clear break with earlier forms of subjectivizing practices of the Pagan type or some would hold. If that's true, then a genealogical attempt to account for these subjectivizing shapes stalls.

In order to explain Augustine's seemingly *sui generis* spiritual form of subjectivization, I intend to use the critical method of genealogy (separating the drama of punishment from its procedures, the Separation Thesis) and apply it to a new target. Here is how it works. In keeping with the IST view of feelings I developed in Chap. 5, I hold that affects comprise six elements which may be divided into two parts: a physiological side and a cognitive side. On the physiological side, we have four: (1) a somatic reaction that elicits a perturbance capable of exciting the causal extraction mechanism (in the case of an enslaved person a triggering cause i.e. The Triggering Claim); (2) in extreme circumstances, a behavioral paralinguistic piece (weeping, groaning, yelling, shaking); (3) the feeling of the emotion itself, its *quale and* (4) The Homeostasis Claim which instinctually seeks a return to a steady-state of non-perturbance.

On the cognitive side, I integrate the following with the physiological/behavioral: (5) The phenomenological object I take to be responsible for my feeling (e.g. I am afraid of this lion before me, I feel ashamed before God etc.). Regarding the phenomenological object that I am principally interested in, it should be noted that it will very often be embedded in

[5] Augustine, *The Confessions* of St. Augustine, Book VIII, Chapter 12, 28–29.

complex religious narratives; Finally, (6) An appraisal or judging component concomitant with the object in question. The judging component will entail understanding the affect according to the appropriate affect word *a la* Fowles and then, of course, attempting to understand the cause or causes producing the emotion and the affordances that quell or even enhance the feeling seizure (*quale*). As indicated in Chap. 5, I borrow the term and concept of *quale* from John Dewey, which he uses as shorthand for "feeling seizures" or "raw feel." I then append Richard Lazarus's appraisal theory–which, it should also be noted, plays a pivotal role in Barlassina and Newen's IST but is absent from Fowles's retreading of their theory–to Dewey's raw feel aspect of emotion.[6] The search for the right affordance, in terms of its "appraisal" side and "feel" side, it is vital to note, is under considerable pressure from claim four, the Homeostasis Claim.

In now demonstrating how these components work in concert, I contend that both the behavior associated with the emotion and the *quale* or "feel" are older, more ancestral than the respective phenomenological object part–embedded, as it is, within a newer, relatively speaking, religious narrative–which then influences the appraisal dimension of one's emotional experiences. My argument is that when the behavior associated with this *quale* is exaggerated, the feeling becomes intensified and refined over time. Overseeing this process is the Homeostasis Claim which stipulates that the body of a subject is under pressure to reach a state of emotional equilibrium much as bodies are driven to seek states of rest when undergoing extreme physical exercise. When the *quale* of a subject's feelings is suddenly and greatly intensified, there is a corresponding amplification of paralinguistic behaviors associated with these acute emotions.

However, the old customs and rituals that were successful in the past for both venting and giving meaning to these feelings and behaviors, fail. The subject begins seeking new etiologies to make sense of her predicament due to the causal extraction mechanism. When a new, successful

[6] Richard Lazarus, "From Appraisal: The Minimal Cognitive Prerequisites of Emotion." In *What Is an Emotion*, 2nd edition, edited by Robert C. Solomon, (Oxford: Oxford University Press: 2003, 125–131.

narrative is found, it appraises and tethers these feelings and behaviors to the suitable causal etiology which comes to assist the subject in reaching a state of homeostasis.

Let me concretize the above explanation by now drawing on my interpretation of GM II. Captured tribal peoples, who now find themselves enslaved, have their negative, Deweyean "feeling seizures" amplified; any prior form of suffering these individuals experienced prior to their enslavement pales compared to what they are currently feeling. These feelings, which we might call "trauma," using our own narrational codices, necessitate entirely new etiologies to help enslaved people arrive at homeostasis. At the same time as newly enslaved people are adjusting to their horrific treatment by their masters, they are exposed to novel religious narratives (especially of the Christian kind). These fresh belief systems begin to replace the old tribal practices and rituals subjects used to reach homeostasis (see GM II 19–20) prior to enslavement because either (1) the old methods are no longer available or (2) they simply prove ineffective when it comes to venting these 'unique' adverse emotions. The causal extraction mechanism is triggered and goes into overdrive in order to identify new affect words that would allow the feeling seizure to be appropriately interpreted and, therefore, vented.

The causal extraction mechanism and the religious etiologies that support the so-called causes responsible for the feeling, help explain the subjectivization problem noted above because emotions, as appraisals, assign both sanctions and endorsements to affective expressions and behaviors such as in the case of Augustine, weeping, groaning, and wailing. These paralinguistic activities not only go unchecked in *The Confessions* but indeed are also encouraged and therefore amplified, leading to a new form of subjectivization–the Christian convert.

The very content of these so-called spiritual practices, such as the Christian's relationship to her faith, Scripture, and God, are responsible for internalizing the subject. My affective genealogical approach helps to elucidate how Christian subjectivization takes place.[7] I now turn to the

[7] I develop what I call "affective genealogy in an earlier article. Brian Lightbody "The Relations of Affect and the Spiritual: Towards a Foucauldian Genealogy of Spirituality", *Philosophy Today* Vol. 65 Issue 1 Winter 2021, 161–183.

fundamental methods of genealogical analysis to put further flesh on my investigation.

I return to GM I 4's point about the etymological tracing of words and how, when this method is coupled with the Rule of Conceptual Transformation found in GM I 6, it produces a potent tandem. I draw the reader's attention to GM I 4 once more: "The signpost to the right [Rechten] road was for me the question: what was the real etymological significance of the designations for 'good' coined in the various languages?" (Nietzsche's emphasis). Nietzsche's turn to employing etymological evidence to assist with his genealogical analysis he calls a fundamental insight. As noted in Chap. 2, this insight may be construed in one of two ways. However, what is common to both is the following: Nietzsche wants us to understand that we use vestigial remnants of concepts that once closely orbited the body. When we combine this method with Nietzsche's rule of conceptual transformation, we will find that they make an incisive, powerful team.

Turning now to GM I 6, Nietzsche notes: "A concept denoting political superiority always resolves itself into a concept denoting superiority of soul." He demonstrates this hypothesis by tracing the etymological roots of the Latin *bonus* (good). He elucidates that contemporary notions of goodness are tainted: goodness was initially used as a descriptor to mark out high status, political station, or tracing the term even further back, to the powerful physicality of male bodies. It was only later, Nietzsche proclaims, that goodness described character. Nietzsche writes: "I believe I may venture to interpret the Latin *bonus* as the warrior provided I am right in tracing bonus back to an earlier *duonus* (compare *bellum=duellum=deun-lum*, which seems to me to contain *duonus*). Therefore, *bonus* as the man of strife, of dissension (duo) as the man of war." (GM I 6) As noted in Chap. 2, Nietzsche's insight was to trace the roots of words that denoted practices that revolved around specific bodies, (especially warrior and priestly). I will use this same insight but apply it to emotions. Therefore, I will bring together Nietzsche's etymological tool noted above with the method of separating the meaning of punishment from the act of punishment itself. I will superimpose these two lenses and apply them to the affective realm.

Returning to the *Confessions*, I draw the reader's attention to Augustine's striking depiction of his agitated "spiritual" crisis state. Augustine is neither ashamed of weeping (*Fletus*) nor groaning (*gemitus*) before the object of his consciousness, God, or, more accurately stated, Augustine's conception of how God views him. Indeed, one notices that Augustine's state of misery, illustrated by his paralinguistic emotional behavior, reaches a climax as one moves through the *Confessions*. For example, in the opening of Book VI, Augustine states that he is not yet whimpering in prayer, but this all changes when the reader reaches Book VII, when his moaning finally commences.[8] Finally, in Book VIII, we arrive at the nadir of Augustine's agony, where he declares that he is "pregnant with weeping" (*Fletus gravidus*).

But as Philip Burton notes, Augustine's shameless uninhibited lamentation and moaning is inconsistent with the widespread ancient Greek and Roman observance of self-control, especially for men.[9] What's more, it is clear that Augustine himself embraced these observances. Burton writes:

> In purely human matters, Augustine does espouse a version of μετριοπάθεια [Metrio (medium) Patheia (state)], proportional passion; this he fails to realize after the death of his anonymous friend in Book 4 but after the death of his mother in Book 9 he is able to hold in check the tears at his funeral, then consciously release these tears he was holding in check.... Alongside this espousal of μετριοπάθεια in human affairs is a quite different attitude towards God; there can be no question of proportionality where one of the terms is infinite.[10]

Augustine promotes the curbing of emotional states in response to human matters but exhibits and endorses unchecked, grief-stricken behavior concerning his relationship to the divine. How are we to make sense of this paradox?

---

[8] Philip Burton, *Language in the Confessions of Augustine*, Oxford: Oxford University Press, 2007, 162.

[9] Burton, 151.

[10] Burton, 163–164.

Here is what I propose. In contemplating his sinful ways, an incredibly powerful somatic perturbance is induced within the saint. This feeling seizure or *quale* is not new; it is similar to the raw feeling one might experience when one loses a child, mother, or close friend. The causal extraction mechanism is excited and identifies the affect as "anguish" or some other cognate affect. Working in conjunction with the causal extraction mechanism is Augustine's belief system, namely Christian etiology, which also informs and colors the cause for the feeling. In other words, the affect word becomes integrated, following Barlassina and Newen, along the cognitive dimension where it becomes further modulated: "I feel ashamed or guilty before God." (the new abstract phenomenological object to be investigated genealogically). This appraisal of the feel causes the *quale* to become further augmented as the feeling is endorsed: Augustine's shame before God is well-warranted, at least according to Augustine's own lights. A flashpoint is reached where the feeling *demands* to be vented under pressure from the body's need for homeostasis. However, there is a problem: the venting of such a powerful *quale* was initially expressed and condoned (following Nietzsche) in socially accepted behaviors (e.g. grieving and weeping for the loss of a child, mother, or close friend). There were constraints to these expelled expressions of sorrow—what Greek and Latin authors called moderation (μετριοπάθεια, *moderatio*). The behaviors linked with these feelings (weeping, groaning, and in some cases, ululation [*Eiulatus*]), as viewed in the case of Augustine, are then exaggerated, causing the *quale* itself to become further magnified. Augustine's para-linguistic behaviors (e.g. groaning, "wherein the sound of my voice appeared choked with weeping") are evaluated and authorized; indeed, they are praiseworthy and defensible because the phenomenological object of anguish for Augustine is himself. He feels abject disgrace before the all-judging gaze of God. It is his complete self (*tota sui*), that is on trial after all. Given Augustine's openness at this critical juncture to see his experience through a Christian framework, he understands that his past actions (along with his intentions motivating those very actions) are observed and judged by an almighty Creator who is deemed perfect in every conceivable way. Augustine's emotional reaction to what he perceives as the rebellious, insolent, sinful nature of his youth bears witness and endorses his "feeling" of conversion.

Given Augustine's narrative, (along with the cathartic ecstasy of the Bishop's affective response to his guilt precipitated as it is by the homeostasis requirement), there is only one adequate reaction to Augustine's full recognition regarding his insubordinate and depraved ways. "I shall go into my bedroom," Augustine reveals, "and sing love songs to you groaning with groans beyond telling."[11] As Augustine swings back and forth from reprimanding himself before God the Hangman and rejoicing before God the Redeemer, these clashing, powerful emotions serve to excavate Augustine's sense of, and attachment to, the deep self. Based on his experience, Augustine views this movement as a crucible of sorts—he has undergone a conversion experience.

Augustine's transformation is not a metamorphosis (μεταμόρφωσις) but a *conversio*, a turn of direction toward God Himself. It is an about-face accomplished only through spiritual anguish but where 'spirituality,' genealogically understood, is the product of a prior narrational/*quale* analysis. A genealogical tracing of this kind of spiritual, Christian subjectivization is possible. I demonstrated that the skeins that makeup Christian spiritual subjectivity can be explained, genealogically, by employing my model of affects. Following IST, Fowles, and Dewey, I take up a six-fold analysis in this regard. Next, I repurposed Nietzsche's technique of tracing words denoting emotions. I analyzed *the Confessions* looking for language that referred to the practice of grieving. I then fused this technique with the critical methodological principle of genealogy, namely, to separate the act of punishment from its interpretation. Through my affective theory of analytics, I demonstrate how Augustine's conversion story remains grounded in older behavioral practices of expressing grief that were intensified and re-interpreted to new ends, namely oneself.

The above example explains Augustine's subjectivization, his conversion experience, where he becomes a full-throated Christian. In brief, Augustine's spiritual transformation is explicable, genealogically speaking, by analyzing how interoceptive *quales* are augmented through a

[11] Augustine, *The Confessions of St. Augustine*, Book XII Chapter 16, 23.

combination of intensified behavior and the etiologies that make sense of them. These intensified *quales* must now be vented following the homeostasis condition. The result is a cathartic ectasis that Augustine appraises and uses to confirm his experience as a conversion.

This explanation partly demonstrates the truth of the Internalization Hypothesis: the inability to vent drives, according to some established social practices, forces the self to exhaust these powerful feeling seizures in new ways. These new practices become reinforced because they are successful in reestablishing emotional balance. In recalibrating an emotional state, the subject appraises the cause behind the very affective episode as justified where the process continues unabated.

There is a second part to the Internalization Hypothesis, however. The Internalization Hypothesis also claims that the process of drive incorporation is gradual: the soul, at first Nietzsche claims, was as thin as a cell membrane. The new self takes sides against itself; its battle is no longer one with the challenges of the wild, as it were, but is against itself. I explained this idea of where the self is furrowed and at war with itself not by thinking that drives are suffused with evaluative qualities but by showing that drives are implexes denoting cognitive and affective components.

In fleshing this second aspect of the Internalization Hypothesis, I will turn first to the cognitive component. How might we operationalize taking "sides against itself"? My answer is this: a self takes sides against itself insofar as it lacks harmony. Plato is perhaps the first philosopher to describe this condition with any precision. As he demonstrates, in *Phaedo*, we experience ourselves as deeply furrowed entities: we are torn between two very different kinds of desires namely those of the soul on the one hand and that of the body on the other. But more than this, he reveals a deep-seated longing in the philosopher-type: a desire to return home, to be reunited with *Nous* (mind).[12] In retreading Plato's answer, we might say that we thirst for knowledge, self-improvement, and for leading good lives, but we are also entities that are lazy, ignorant, and subject to vice. My argument is that enslaved tribal people would have been furrowed along the cognitive axis: they wished to flee or retaliate against their master but knew the potentially painful consequences they might experience

[12] See Brian Lightbody, *Dispersing the Clouds of Temptation* (Eugene OR: Pickwick Press, 2015), 7.

if they were to do so. They are, therefore, agentially stuck as it were, making them ripe for a particular religious narrative (e.g. Christianity) to swoop in that would make sense of their condition and therefore provide them with both meaning and guidance.

Along the emotional axis, I demonstrate that taking sides against oneself entails a clash of affective orientations. Returning to Plato, when we are furrowed, cognitively speaking, we also feel torn emotionally. We feel conflicted and divided. Cognitive indecision is often accompanied with a sense of negative affectation—in such states, especially if prolonged, we feel depressed, inauthentic, alienated, and weak-willed.

In now putting further flesh on my analysis, if my judgment is correct, then my model should also explain how Augustine's conversion–an experience that surely would resonate with many contemporary individuals–is simply a further development and refinement of an earlier, more externalized shape of subjectivity. After all, there is unquestionably a deep sense of furrowedness in Augustine's writings; it is clear that Augustine's self is divided and that his spiritual battle is with some other part of himself.

This explanation, if we recall, is in keeping with Nietzsche's hypothesis in GM I. One of the primary goals of GM I is to show how the battle between Rome and Judea played out within the history of the Roman empire, between noble classes and slave classes has been internalized; the clash between these two groups is no longer interpersonal but intrapersonal. Individuals are furrowed, divided between their active instincts like egoism and selfishness, and their reactive, enculturated opposites: altruism and selflessness. Suppose that's true. Then, by superimposing the rule of conceptual transformation onto the internalization hypothesis, I should be able to reveal how the ongoing process of this internalization of drives, as implexes, took shape.

In order to flesh out my thesis, the following question needs to be answered: Can one find an earlier Christian model of subjectivization that is fomented based on a perception that one belongs to a persecuted group? In other words, the strife and turmoil one feels within this earlier model of Christian subjectivity is predicated not on an internal struggle with another part of the self but rather because the individual *really is* tyrannized by some other faction in society. If a proto-model of Christian subjectivization can be explained using my framework, we have found the solution to the *homunculi* problem that eluded Riccardi because simpler interpretations of subjectivity with less reflexivity, and therefore less self-tumult, are possible. I argue that Nietzsche himself provides a clue in solving this problem when he quotes at length from Tertullian's *De Spectaculus.* My argument is not to reduce a drive component to a mere adder or subtractor physiologically understood as Riccardi envisions. Instead, I undertake to solve the problem genealogically. Let me now explain my procedure.

Section II: Tertullian's "Cruder" Christianity

Tertullian's *De Spectaculus* is an emotionally charged invective against pagan forms of entertainment. In general, Tertullian's message is an advisory to Christians, warning them that engaging in pagan spectacles like the theater, blood sports such as gladiatorial games, or even competitive athletic events like boxing and wrestling is sinful and may lead to their very damnation. In fact, in one part of *Spectacles*, Tertullian notes that demons attend such events and have been known to possess an audience member or two![13] Thus, Tertullian's screed points to an otherworldly dimension and preaches that just as we humans observe such spectacles on earth, God is the ultimate spectator watching every moment of our lives. By analogy just as there are winners and losers in many of these events, there will be winners and losers on Judgment Day—and one does not wish to be a loser in this cosmic game for one's soul.

Despite the text's rhetorically inflected and emotionally colored substance, the topic of *Spectacles*, which I will turn to below, is underpinned by arguments. One such suggests that if Christians seek entertainment, it is better to refrain from sin because there will be more glorious spectacles in Heaven awaiting the righteous. In a way, the argument is not dissimilar to Pascal's wager where it is in our rational best interest to follow Christian virtues because doing so will allow us to lead more productive lives on earth *and* reap eternal salvation and blessedness. Over 1000 years

[13] Tertullian, *De Spectaculus*, XII.

earlier, Tertullian argued in much the same way: "Moreover, what a spectacle is already at hand—the second coming of the Lord, now no object of doubt, now exalted, now triumphant! What exultation will that be of the angels, what glory of the saints as they rise again! What a kingdom, the kingdom of the just thereafter! What a city, the new Jerusalem!"[14]

Moreover, Tertullian also counsels that Christian literature, rituals, and practices avail one of countless opportunities to test their mettle against temptation. This argument suggests that our admiration of physical contests, like wrestling, boxing, and so on, are poor reflections of a spiritual battle where we win our glory if we are courageous enough. As Tertullian recounts: "Do you want contests in boxing and wrestling? Here they are --contests of no slight account, and plenty of them. Behold impurity overthrown by chastity, faithlessness slain by faith, cruelty crushed by mercy, impudence put in the shade by modesty. Such are the contests among us, and in these we win our crowns. Do you have desire for blood, too? You have the blood of Christ."[15] Notice that the 'spiritual' battle, for Tertullian, is mainly drawn in terms of keeping to the Christian path in the face of a hostile, recalcitrant society that mocked, disparaged and in more extreme cases, sometimes outright persecuted them, especially in times of crisis (drought, famine) etc.

Such we might say is the propositional content of the piece. However, what is most striking about *De Spectaculus* is the emotionally charged rhetoric that colors and informs Tertullian's argument. Tertullian's style is similar to Augustine because there is a clear-cut emotional crescendo as the reader moves through each chapter, just as there is in the *Confessions.* Also, both texts end in emotional catharses. However, the target of the invective, vitriolic language of each text is very different in the two works. For where Augustine directs his shame and anger against himself, Tertullian's rebukes are directed against the powerful, high-ranking Roman officials who preside over the spectacles Tertullian rails against. Consider the passage Nietzsche quotes from *Spectacles:*

[14]Tertullian, *De Spectaculus*, With an English translation by T.R. Glover, (Harvard University Press), 1931, XXX.

[15] *De Spectaculus* XXIX.

> What a panorama of spectacle on that day! Which sight shall excite my wonder? Which, my laughter? Where shall I rejoice, where exult--as I see so many and so mighty kings, whose ascent to heaven used to be made known by public announcement, now along with Jupiter himself, along with the very witnesses of their ascent, groaning in the depths of darkness? Governors of provinces, too, who persecuted the name of the Lord, melting in flames fiercer than those they themselves kindled in their rage against the Christians braving them with contempt? But there are yet other spectacles to come--that day of the Last Judgment with its everlasting issues, unlooked for by the heathen, the object of their derision, when the hoary age of the world and all its generations will be consumed in one file.[16]

The substantive interpretations of the passage in the secondary literature are mainly in agreement. The standard reading claims that Nietzsche marshals Tertullian as an expert witness to testify that the German's philosopher's diagnosis of Christianity, namely that it is a religion founded on ressentiment, is correct. The upshot of Nietzsche's characterization of Christianity is that the cruel hostile animal instincts depicted in GM II 16 have not been so much transcended but internalized and co-opted. Christians are impotent because they cannot direct their violence against their enemies in this world and must construct another to unleash their hatred.

Turning now to the secondary literature we can find the above analysis confirmed in a at least three commentaries on the *Genealogy*. According to Conway, Tertullian confirms, in rabid rancorous detail "that the arrival of the Kingdom of God will permit the weak and bedraggled to take delight in the suffering of their erstwhile *oppressors*."[17] Leiter agrees with this assessment noting:

> His most striking actual example of a man of a man of ressentiment, The Church Father Tertullian, is offered as an example of the "eternal hate" that informs Christianity. Ressentiment, then, is Nietzsche's term of art for a special kind of festering hatred and vengefulness, one motivated by impotence in the face of unpleasant *external stimuli*, and that leads (at least

[16] Tertullian, *De Spectaculus*, XXX.

[17] Daniel Conway, *Nietzsche's On the Genealogy of Morals*, 48.

among the impotent) to the creation of values that devalue or at least make sense of those unpleasant stimuli.[18]

To close out this reading, I turn to Lawrence Hatab:

> Why would he talk of an "insatiable gaze" upon torments that go on for eternity?… Why is retribution necessary and why did it take on a form of (total and eternal) victory? Part of Nietzsche's answer is that a worldly *lack of overt power* not only redirects power to the inward imagination (confirmed by Tertullian's "imagining spirit"), but the lack of any worldly satisfaction and its effects also prompts an escalation of power beyond its natural (agonistic) structure of overcoming something toward the unnatural vision of a total disarmament and degradation of opponents.[19]

In the above quotations, I italicized descriptions of external conditions that were either oppressive or repressive for early Christians. What we see in Tertullian is a proto-Christian subjectivization where the enemy is without rather than within. According to this reading, the explanation for Tertullian's subjectivization, in keeping with the original view of the I.H. supposes that drives that cannot be expressed outwardly turn inward. What I criticize is the all too symbolic explanation of this process. In contrast, I now apply my six-fold analysis of emotion to Tertullian's work to reveal a more lucid exposition and accurate analysis of how so-called internalization takes place.

Tertullian's text begins with arguments that attempt to steer the Christian away from Pagan spectacles, especially of the gladiatorial variety. His argument can be distilled into two categories: (1) It is inconsistent for self-avowed Christians to go to these games because it arouses base emotions and base emotions give rise to temptation and, therefore, sin. Tertullian's opprobrium is mainly directed against tragic plays because these plays would often use scantily clad prostitutes in various roles. "The very prostitutes, the victims of public lust, are produced on the stage, more unhappy in the presence of other women - the only class in the

[18] Brian Leiter, *Nietzsche on Morality*, 204.

[19] Lawrence Hatab, *Nietzsche's On the Genealogy of Morals An Introduction*, 66. Also see David Owen's analysis in *Nietzsche's Genealogy of Morality*, 88.

community whose notice they escape; they are paraded before the faces of every rank and age."[20] Indeed his vitriol for the performances of tragic plays is expressed well by one scholar who writes: "Tertullian positively drools over the prospect of seeing tragic actors trembling, suffering, 'more vocal in their own tragedy,' and incidentally (though it is not relevant here to our purpose) charioteers 'red all over in the wheel of flame.'"[21]

(2) As the name of the title of the work suggests the events Tertullian decries are spectacles and, therefore, idolatrous. Christians are forbidden to engage in the worship of idols. "Even if the images are but few in its procession, one image is idolatry; if but one chariot is drawn, it is yet Jove's car; any idolatry in any form, meanly equipped, moderately rich, splendid, is still reckoned idolatry in its guilt."[22] These two arguments draw out the doctrinal implications and, therefore, normative expectations for Christians from their very own religious discourses and practices.

So far, so good, we might think. Tertullian is advancing a cogent, well-supported argument against attending various spectacles from a Christian standpoint. Finally, however, in section 19, we see a turn where Tertullian asks the question:

> It is a good thing, when the guilty are punished. Who will deny that, unless he is one of the guilty? But who will pledge himself that it is always the guilty who are condemned to the beasts, or whatever punishment, and that it never inflicted on the innocent too, through the vindictiveness of the judge it may be, the weakness of the advocate, the severity of torture?[23]

Tertullian switches from working on the Christian's intellect to his sentiments. He asks the Christian to ponder: How can one take pleasure in the torture of another human being if that person is innocent? Of course, such an action marks a contradiction for the Christian, but interestingly, Tertullian goes on to say something else:

[20] Tertullian *De Spectaculus*, XVII, 275.

[21] Victor Power "Clerical animosity Towards the Theatre" *Educational Theatre journal* Mar., 1971, Vol. 23, No. 1 (Mar., 1971), pp. 36–50, 42.

[22] Tertullian, *De Spectaculus*, VII, 251.

[23] Tertullian *Spectaculus*, XIX. 279.

> Certain it is that innocent men are sold as gladiators for the show, to be victims of public pleasure. Even in the case of those condemned to the games, what can you say to the fact that punishment for the smaller offence should carry them on to murder? And yet the innocent cannot take pleasure in the punishment of another, when it better befits the innocent to lament that a man like himself has become so guilty that a punishment so cruel must be awarded him.[24]

On the surface, it appears that we have an incoherency in the text. There seems to be a tension between the Christian's avowed, "love thine enemies" and Tertullian's call for the evil to be punished in a most gruesome, cruel manner for all eternity. This conflict is arrived at because of how Tertullian's emotions have been engaged. Using my six-fold analysis, I make sense of the tension.

Here is what I propose. Tertullian is at pains to demonstrate the performative contradictions inherent in attending spectacles to the Christian.[25] He argues that although, technically, there is nothing in the Gospels against attending Pagan events, they nonetheless embroil the faithful Christian in sinful ways. However, in thinking about each event, before he then writes about them, varied somatic perturbances are produced in Tertullian. That is to look at the matter from the physical side. On the mental side, these perturbances give rise to distinct *quales*. For example, in thinking about the lewd behavior of tragic play-actors, Tertullian's sexual feeling is excited. In turning to vividly describe the torture, murder, and dismemberment of participants in gladiatorial

[24] Tertullian, *Spectaculus*, XIX.

[25] See Emily Cain "Tertullian's Precarious Pan-opticon: A Performance of Visual Piety", *The Journal of Early Christian Studies* Vol. 27 Issue 4 2019, 611–633. "This brings an interesting parallel to Tertullian's rhetoric of a visible and visual performance of spirituality. Tertullian had analogized God as the sun to demonstrate that God remained pure in the face of the impurity of earth. The sun, however, also serves as the visible watchtower of the panopticon that gazes upon the ring of the earth. The divine watchtower is unverifiable: humans may never know if or when they are seen, but they may assume that they are always seen by the divine gaze. Both men and women must perform visibly before the divine gaze by avoiding harmful sights. This panopticon is not the disciplinarian panopticon of the prison, but mimics more closely the power dynamics of the hospital or the school. This rhetoric helps Tertullian to describe the shared Christian performance of difference. Christians are different than others by performing their visible purity before the watchtower of the divine gaze." 629.

combat, a very different *quale* bubbles up to consciousness. But there is also something else that happens.

In seeking to use the most effective and colorful language to dress his point to the Christians, the language intensifies the *quale* itself. Consider how Tertullian describes the tragic theater: "Its supreme charm is above all things contrived by its filth - filth in the gestures of the actor of the farce - filth acted by the buffoon playing the woman, banishing all sense of sex and shame, so that they blush more readily at home than on the stage, filth that the pantomime undergoes, in his own person, from boyhood, to make him an artist."[26] In thinking about the contradiction implied in the Christian who "who shudders at the body of a man who died by nature's law the common death of all, will, in the Amphitheatre, gaze down with most tolerant eyes on the bodies of men mangled, torn to pieces, defiled with their own blood; yes, and that he who comes to the spectacle to signify his approval of murder being punished, will have a reluctant gladiator hounded on with lash and rod to do murder."[27] Again, a distinct feeling is not just stirred but amplified.

When contemplating his powerful and intense emotional states, Tertullian's causal extraction mechanism seeks to understand them. The causal extraction mechanism is a function of a more basic physiological state, namely the need for homeostasis. At this late stage of *Spectacles*, Tertullian's agitated mind seeks nothing less than repose. But notice in an ironic twist that Tertullian judges that the true enemy of the Christian is not the Christian's own weakness, his impotence but rather the Pagan overlords themselves: the governors, the playwrights, emperors, philosophers, and the ringmasters of the circus are to blame for the Christian's lack of resolve and weakness of will. They are the ones who create spectacles that addict good people. The judgment produces a new feeling of what we might call self-righteousness. It is appraised and endorsed, and a new evaluation is made manifest from that endorsement. It is they, the Pagans themselves, that need to be punished. They are responsible for Christians becoming wicked. It is the Pagan that made me do it! This judgment is then placed within the already existing, albeit causal Christian

[26] Tertullian, *Spectacles*, XVII, 275.

[27] Tertullian, *Spectacles*, XXI, 283.

etiologies containing elements, among others, of *causa sui* freewill (justifying the punishment of the Pagans, which is ironic given Tertullian's judgment) and the idea of a Redeemer/Punisher God.

Comparing Augustine and Tertullian, it is clear why Nietzsche quotes the penultimate violent *ekstasis* passage from *Spectacles*. The traditional interpretation suggests that Nietzsche wants to show the impotence baked into slave morality. The same violent instincts rule slaves in the end as their masters; the difference is that these instincts cannot be vented naturally. Instead, a fantasy world must be created to discharge negative states. Hostile instincts are internalized.

In contrast, my argument is that the true motivation behind these negative emotions is a product of alien and external forms. The logic of Christianity, whether this includes the incarnation, the notion of heaven, or *causa sui* free will, is a conceptual development meant to decipher and utilize ancient affective neural pathways. Such concepts are not *sui generis* but emerge, genealogically speaking, due to prior material conditions and practices. I now cash this out in the currency of the narrative I develop in Chaps. 4 and 5. I contend that the continued focus on traumatic events combined with the need to create survival strategies by enslaved people themselves in early states like Rome became docked to various religious etiologies (Roman mystery cults). One such spiritual etiology, namely Christianity, proves more successful than all others because it allows the slave to release the trauma he has experienced at the hands of his *Paterfamilias*. The cathartic release of emotion attached to physical, and mental trauma allows the enslaved person to return to some semblance of emotional balance, keeping with the homeostasis claim. The most successful way of achieving this affective equilibrium is to construct a fantastical apocalyptic transcendent world predicated on a final day of judgment. This revenge fantasy that is the essence of Christianity, or so Nietzsche contends, is one that is built up over many generations taking what it finds useful in other traditions and reworking them.

As proof for my diagnosis consider, for example what Nietzsche writes in the *AntiChrist*:

> With every extension of Christianity over ever broader, even ruder masses in whom the preconditions out of which it was born were more and more

> lacking, it became increasingly necessary to *vulgarize*, to *barbarize*, Christianity–it absorbed the doctrines and rites of every subterranean cult of the *Imperium Romanum*, it absorbed the absurdities of every sort of morbid reason. (AC 37)

Christianity, fundamentally for Nietzsche, both doctrinally and in practice, is a theology of revenge against these evil ones. Again, consider yet another passage from the *Antichrist* in support of my interpretation:

> From now on there enters into the type of the Redeemer, step by step; the doctrine of judgement and return, the doctrine of death as a sacrificial death, the doctrine of the resurrection with which the whole concept of "blessedness," the whole and only actuality of the evangel, is conjured away--in favor of a state after death! (AC 41)

In providing a more accurate reflection of the material and social conditions of Roman life cognitively speaking and being able to connect and release primeval emotional pathways than other religious cults, Christianity, as a value system, flourishes.

Section III: Returning to the Homunculus Problem

I turn to the final concern with my explanation in hand: the homunculus problem. You will recall that the problem, as identified by Riccardi, poses a significant issue for drive theory. I outlined the three issues I had with Nietzsche's drive psychology as they connected with homunculism in Chap. 2. These three problems were evaluative, ontological, and agonic. Briefly stated here, drives seem like little minds in that they can evaluate the features of some object to pursue independently of the subject. Second, drives are responsible for the constitution of subjectivity itself and have all the properties and features we would normally ascribe to intentional agents. Thirdly, the agonic claim states that drives can read what other drives find valuable and can then co-opt the intentional directionality of said drive. My solution to dissolving the problems Nietzsche's theory of psychology, which drives engender, is in line with Riccardi's general strategy, which is to maintain Dennett's intentional theoretic defense in that one may continue to ascribe psychological properties to the sub-components of drives to arrive at what Dennett calls bare adders and subtractors. As Riccardi puts it: "Recall that Dennett's understanding of the personal/subpersonal distinction allows for the use of personal predicates to describe sub personal states and processes."[28]

Here is where I depart from Riccardi. Where Riccardi continues to work with drives as a fundamental component of our psychology that works hand in glove with affective states, I treat drives as symbolic vehicles of will to power.[29] If the reader recalls, will to power is marked by its dehiscence. As Heidegger rightly claims, will to power is a distillation of life itself; it can only be understood operationally. Nevertheless, in describing will to power as a kind of distillation of becoming, Heidegger arrests the overflowing, dynamism of life itself.

For this reason, thinking of will to power as a dehiscent is preferable– we only come to know the manifestations of will to power in terms of Aydin's ground forms. Will to power is 'comprehended' only by way of recognizing the new phenomenon that emerges from a constantly ongoing transformation in the same way one only recognizes the new butterfly emerging from its pupae. In other words, the complete causal process threading through the almost infinite stages from caterpillar to lepidopteran remains unknown.

I then showed how the Separation Thesis, the Internalization Hypothesis, and the rule of conceptual transformation are each means of operationalizing this insight on will to power. To take this last example, consider Nietzsche's second iteration of the rule of conceptual transformation once again. Migotti's helpful interpretation of this specific rendering of this method suggests that one cannot provide a singular etymological tracing for the roots of some concept, value, or practice. Instead, the guiding thread for one's tracing the respective genealogical forks of some phenomenon reveals several equally viable paths. The way

---

[28] Riccardi, *Nietzsche's Philosophical Psychology*, 65.

[29] Notice what Riccardi writes on p. 67 "This suggests that affective states mediate between one's drives and the environment. The drives prime our very experience of the external world: they make us look for objects that can satisfy their goal."

forward then means that we must examine how seemingly incommensurable threads, from a conceptual standpoint, became one as a result of some alien force. In contrast, to explore the abstract elements that tie the threads together in a Socratic fashion leads to *aporias*. Fleshing this idea of alien forces out a bit more, the investigation, in other words, must analyze the factors that took what were once motley threads and created a skein from them. Concretizing this insight in Chap. 2, I showed how "nobility" came to mean many things; there is no obvious reason why the word has come to take on such disparate meanings. Only by investigating the term genealogically, as Migotti, does is there a chance of making sense of how these very incongruent meanings came together

However, there is another difficulty here: these forces, as manifestations of will to power, cannot be understood in themselves but necessitate further symbolization and interpretation. I contend that the Separation Thesis, the Internalization Hypothesis, and the rule of conceptual transformation offer ways to explain what I call the mechanical or stable forces of operation that brought said threads together. They operationalize Nietzsche's refutation of form/function thesis, as advanced in GM II 12.

With this recap in mind, my answer to the homunculus problem is to reinterpret the Internalization Hypothesis. The Internalization Hypothesis is a way of operationalizing the formation of agency itself. If my analysis is right then we need to dig deeper into the fundamental claim made by I.H. namely that, "all instincts that do not discharge themselves outwardly turn inward– this is what I call the internalization of man: thus it was that man first developed what was later called his soul,"(GM II 16). I suggest there is another and far superior way of construing the Internalization Hypothesis than simply appealing to the mysterious process known as the ingestion of drives. There were two critical components in this equation. First regarding instinct which I take as a neo-plasm for a drive, a drive is an implex. I define implex zoologically "as the point where muscles are attached to the integument of an arthropod."[30] Drives, then, are symbolic interpretations of two intersecting threads: cognition and affect. Impure Somatic theory helps make sense of how these two may be integrated. This theory helps to solve the homunculus issue's first

[30] Collins Dictionary https://www.collinsdictionary.com/dictionary/english/implex.

aspect, namely that drives are evaluative. For suppose a drive denotes the intersection of cognition and affect. In that case, the object a drive pursues *qua* the cognitive vector will, insofar as it is a mental state, be representational and thus responsive to considerations and judgments as to why it should be pursued.

The second component of the Internalization Hypothesis is its attempt to explain the emergence of the soul. As noted, the soul for Nietzsche is a collection of drives, but if drives are evaluating entities, then Nietzsche's attempt to naturalize the soul reinforces the homunculus fallacy. For consider that if drives are agential, then we are no closer to explaining what agency is in using drives as the *explanans*. The *explanans and explanandum* are the same. My model provides a solution to this problem by using Augustine's conversion experience as a test case for the emergence of his specific kind of Christian subjectivization.

Augustine's conversion experience is a battle of sorts between two sides of the self, with each part taking up an assessment of the other. This explanation refers to Nietzsche's assertion that the novelty of the emergence of "an animal soul turned against itself, taking sides against itself" (GM II 16). What's more, different affective valences are marshaled in support of these antithetical, cognitive assessments. Such contrasting affects are evaluated according to other affect words and various etiologies. Augustine's tortuous, travail is, in truth or so Nietzsche's analysis holds, an intrapersonal battle between Rome vs Judea taking place between two psychical factions within Augustine. Once more, the agonic and ontological aspect of drives has been explained by demonstrating how parts of the soul simply refer to different interests and where interest comprises cognitive and affective elements. My six-fold affective analysis explains the various components involved in this battle between two separate selves. Finally, I explain how Augustine's conversion experience may be explained genealogically by examining the more primeval and ancient threads that became interwoven to create a new phenomenon: the conversion experience.

There then remains one final issue to resolve: the implicit claim of the Internalization Hypothesis, which suggests that the development of the soul was the result of the "inpsychation" of instincts that were once directed to the outside world and that when these instincts fail to find their appropriate external targets turn inward. If the claim is treated following the standard model, it borders on a tautology that explains nothing. My model, in contrast, illuminates how to think about this contention. My argument is threefold.

First, GM II 16 does not refer to a state of the Pleistocene era where proto-human beings lived at the mercy of their animal drives. That is the claim made by the standard reading, as demonstrated in Chap. 4. Nietzsche's language, or so I suggest, is hyperbolic, metaphorical, and perspectival. The semi-animals to which he refers are tribal peoples. The passage then describes what happened when these peoples, principally of Germanic origin, were captured and enslaved by "blonde beasts of prey" or Roman overlords.

Second, I demonstrated how the new conditions in which tribal peoples found themselves led them to become furrowed, both cognitively and emotionally speaking. Two factors caused this lack of direction: (1) their forcible capture by Roman soldiers, where they were then placed in a new hostile environment. They soon discovered that their new predicament meant that their old tribal dispositions were false; (2) They suffered trauma at the hands of their respective *Paterfamilias*. These factors and the unique social condition of Rome that allowed enslaved people to participate in religious rituals made them receptive to just one of many spiritual traditions in Rome of the early century A.D, namely, Christianity.

Third, I then jumped a hundred or so years and examined one crystallized form of this new kind of subjectivization: namely, that of Tertullian's as depicted in his *De Spectaculus*. I demonstrated that Tertullian's spiritual struggle is not so much against internally emergent sides within himself a la Augustine but is external: his fight is with the world, the values of the Roman empire. He rails against the pagan spectacles presided over by the Roman overlords of his day. Some of these forms of entertainment posed real hazards to Christians (e.g. *Dominatio ad bestias*).[31] Concomitant with the object of his opprobrium, his emotions are directed outwardly as well: where Augustine's negatively valenced emotions are directed at

[31] Tacitus, *Annals*, Loeb Classical Library, 5 volumes, Latin texts and facing English translation: Harvard University Press, 1925 thru 1937. Translation by C. H. Moore (Histories) and J. Jackson (Annals), XV.

himself, Tertullian's, instead, target his very real and very dangerous pagan oppressors. In demonstrating how my six-fold affective Impure Somatic Theory explains both Augustine's more sophisticated and nuanced Christian subjectivization as well as Tertullian's more primitive less reflective form, I thereby demonstrate, genealogically, how the ongoing development of the soul "expanded and extended itself, acquir[ing] depth, breadth and height in the same measure as outward discharge was inhibited." (GM II 16) For the discharge here may be understood as the feeling seizure of one's emotions. As these emotions became further attended to, they were transformed by the very Christian etiologies which made sense of them. They then became redirected, inwardly, carving out deeper, ever more reflexive molds of Christian subjectivity.

To conclude this chapter, I should reiterate that my diagnosis of "drive" as the symbolic intersection of older cognitive and affective systems (with these systems themselves having older hard-wired and soft-wired components) is not a reduction in the ontological sense of that term. Implex should be understood functionally. By thinking about a drive, as an implex, we can make sense of how particular drives came to be by retracing each "muscle" of the particular drive in question to an earlier source. Thus, my project is to replace one picture of human agency, namely as a container for internalized drives, with another that proves more fruitful, explanatorily speaking. I hope I was successful in this endeavor.

References

Augustine. *The Confessions of St. Augustine*. Translated by J. G. Pilkington. From Nicene and Post-Nicene Fathers, First Series, Vol. 1. Edited by Philip Schaff. Buffalo, NY: Christian Literature Publishing Co., 1887.

Burton, Philip. *Language in the Confessions of Augustine*. Oxford: Oxford University Press, 2007.

Cain, Emily. "Tertullian's Precarious Pan-opticon: A Performance of Visual Piety" *The Journal of Early Christian Studies* Vol. 27 Issue 4 2019, 611–633.

Conway, Daniel. *Nietzsche's On the Genealogy of Morals: A Reader's Guide.* Lanham, MD: Rowman and Littlefield, 2008.

Deleuze, Gilles. *Foucault*. Translated by Sean Hand. Minneapolis: University of Minnesota Press, 1988.

Dewey, John. "The Theory of Emotion." *Psychological Review* 1 (1894): 553–569. https://doi.org/10.1037/h0069054.

Foucault, Michel. *Discipline and Punish: The Birth of the Prison*. Translated by Alan Sheridan. New York: Vintage Books, 1977.

Foucault, Michel. "On the Genealogy of Ethics: An Overview of a Work in Progress." In *The Foucault Reader*, edited by Paul Rabinow. New York: Pantheon Books, 1984a.

Foucault, Michel. "The Return of Morality." In *Politics, Philosophy, Culture: Interviews and Other Writings*, 1977–1984. Translated by Alan Sheridan, 242–254. New York: Routledge, 1988.

Foucault, Michel. "What Is Enlightenment?" In *The Foucault Reader*, edited by Paul Rabinow. New York: Pantheon Books, 1984b.

Hatab, Lawrence. *Nietzsche's On the Genealogy of Morals An Introduction.* Cambridge University Press, 2008.

Lazarus, Richard. "From Appraisal: The Minimal Cognitive Prerequisites of Emotion." *In What Is an Emotion*, 2nd edition, edited by Robert C. Solomon, 125–131. Oxford: Oxford University Press: 2003.

Leiter, Brian. *Nietzsche on Morality* London: Routledge, 2002.

Lightbody, Brian. *Dispersing the Clouds of Temptation* Eugene OR: Pickwick Press, 2015.

Lightbody, Brian. "The Relations of Affect and the Spiritual: Towards a Foucauldian Genealogy of Spirituality", *Philosophy Today* Vol. 65 Issue 1 Winter 2021, 161–183.

Power, Victor. "Clerical animosity Towards the Theatre" *Educational Theatre Journal* Mar., 1971, Vol. 23, No. 1 (Mar., 1971), pp. 36–50.

Riccardi, Mattia, *Nietzsche's Philosophical Psychology* Oxford: Oxford University Press, 2021.

Tacitus *Annals* Vol. 5 Book XIV. 42Loeb Classical Library, 5 volumes, Latin texts and facing English translation: Harvard University Press, 1925–1937. Translation by C. H. Moore (Histories) and J. Jackson (Annals).

Tertullian, De Spectaculus, With an English translation by T.R. Glover, Harvard University Press, 1931.

7

Conclusion

My mother once showed me our genealogical family tree. She indicated how the horizontal lines symbolized the union of what were once two distinct families while the vertical lines denoted their offspring. As she traced these lines, she would tell a story about each person and each tree branch. For example, this one was a police officer. Another was a farmer, and over there was a nurse who worked at an asylum. Finally, she would tell me stories about the stems who failed to make their own lines. One was killed in the Great War, and the other died in infancy.

In thinking about my direct ancestors, my imagination would run wild: I would think not only about the stories I heard about my forebears, but my mind raced with questions about my own future. I now realize that my questions could be grouped into two categories: questions about identity and questions about what others would say about me when I died. Questions about my identity would take the form of: What would I be like if grandfather didn't marry grandmother? How would I have been different? Or what if my grandfather were killed in WW1 instead of his brother, my Great Uncle Charlie? Would I have been born to another family in another country? Would I have a doppelganger?

B. Lightbody, *A Genealogical Analysis of Nietzschean Drive Theory*,
https://doi.org/10.1007/978-3-031-27148-9_7

Questions about my own future would materialize as: In the future, will I tell the same stories to my own children? Would their children talk about me when I died, and what would they say? Indeed, I often wondered if I would be one of those twigs whose vertical line ended.

Of course, the questions pertaining to identity strike me, many years later, as non-sensical; I could not be Brian Lightbody if my parents married other spouses or if my great-grandmother, twice removed, died of cholera. This sense of identity as being platformed on "necessary continuity" is a special kind of relationship that only biological entities have. It is different from other relations denoting causality like composition or constitution. It is named D-Continuity by Colin McGinn.[1] It denotes the radical *de re* notion that if any part of my etiology were somehow different—if anything about the chain of causal links giving rise to the zygote from which I sprang (e.g. the specific pairing of gametes from my parents and their parents and their parents, parents etc.)—were altered, I would not be me. Although my personal identity, the sense of who I am, is conceptually distinguishable from the chain of causal links that gave rise to my biological origin, the latter, ontologically speaking, is necessary to communicate with any sense about the former.

This brings me to the future directed questions I would ask. In telling a child about one's great-grandparents one is hard-pressed not to explain who those grandparents were and what they did. It is not difficult for children at that point to zoom out and project a future relative asking those very same questions to their mother or grandmother about themselves who is now deceased. It seems to me that the reason why these two, namely, the lines of descent and the stories about those forming the horizontal lines of intersection that become the family network, are intermingled is apparent; no one wants to picture themselves as just another face on the family tree. No one wishes to recognize themselves as an ancestor. The stories we are told about our ancestors, while truthful, hide a more profound truth: we are attempting to find meaning in our own lives while looking at life's very erasure.

[1] Colin Mcginn, Chapter Four: "On the Necessity of Origin" in *Knowledge and Reality* (Oxford Clarendon Press, 1999 57–64), 62–64.

In connecting this vignette to philosophical genealogy, it was shown there are also two lines: a diagnostic tracing of the ills of society and its cure. The diagnostic component, so I contend, corresponds to the mechanics of drive inheritance. The curative feature is tantamount to the story that is told about how these drives were transmitted. The story's purpose allows us to make sense of our history and our value system. In this way, Bernard Williams and Michel Foucault are both correct regarding their respective descriptions of genealogy. As Williams notes "A genealogy is a narrative that tries to explain a cultural phenomenon by describing a way in which it came about, or could have come about, or might have come about."[2] Some of the narrative will consist of real history, which to some extent must aim to be, as Foucault put it, "gray, meticulous, and patiently documentary."[3]

However, what Williams fails to identify is precisely what requires explanation. Does a genealogy illuminate the vertical lines or their horizontal intersection? More precisely put, he has run the two together. These should be kept distinct, or so the Separation Thesis tells us. Foucault does not make that mistake. Foucault is very clear when describing what genealogy is and what the genealogist does. Genealogy is a historical practice that must stick to the *Herkunft* of history and recognize that the stories founded on such a tracing are undetermined. Genealogy is not just a species of conceptual engineering, whether that engineering is one that is speculative, quasi-speculative, or documentarian *of the pudena origo*. As I have called it, implexic genealogy is critical of how the narrative of these concepts and practices came about. Indeed, more forcefully and clearly stated, genealogy holds that concepts are symbolic interpretations of concrete disceptations. The genealogical story that supposes to account for these accounts is suspect too.

But if the stories are unwarranted, then why believe a genealogy? The answer is that the both the lines of descent and those that run horizontal are accurate. One might question Nietzsche's interpretation of the 12

---

[2] Bernard Williams, *Truth and Truthfulness An Essay in Genealogy*, Princeton University Press, 2002, 20.

[3] Michel Foucault, "Nietzsche, Genealogy, History" *Language, Counter-Memory, Practice Selected Essays and Interviews by Michel Foucault*, Ed. Donald Bouchard, 1977, 139.

tables of Rome or the reasons given for the tortures he describes in GM II: 3 for examples, but there is no doubt that bodies were subjected to these brutal practices.

Yet, as Macintyre states, we are "story-telling animals" and need to make sense of these practices.[4] At this point, the lines of inheritance intersect with the nodes: no tracing can occur without finding hubs of connection. These hubs are analogous to the stories we tell about the lines. In terms of what can be said about the lines themselves, they represent battle lines: they are only indications of the discernible punctuations of the expansive, form-giving current of life itself, which is will to power.

The notion of will to power I articulate in this work is the refusal of any pretense of symbolic form. All that can be said about will to power is that it is dehiscent—it is a bursting forth of some new power-discourse constellation whose meaning cannot be reduced to the biological, affective, or economic scaffolding that gave rise to its very being. Returning to the family genealogy analogy, the lines and the nodes, the etiological and the conceptual, sit side by side but in no way is the latter reduced to the former. As I call it, implexic genealogy runs on two tracks: the vertical and the horizontal. The vertical is analogous to the vertical pedigree of a family tree: the line that traces what has been done to somatic systems from regime to regime, from dispositif to dispositif. The horizontal corresponds to the narratives that reshaped our subjectivization from the inside. These two intersect but do not meet: there remains an interstice in between.

In thinking about implexic genealogy, the concept of D-Continuity is critical to keep in mind: while the butterfly emerging from a chrysalis is continuous with the caterpillar that came before, it cannot be reduced to its earlier lepidopteran form. Will to power is neither an Aristotelian substance nor a pure plenum of becoming. As Heidegger calls it, it is a hybrid of the two; a distillation of being itself. It is *dunamis* without *entelechia*. *Energia* whose *ergon* cannot be crystalized.

Although will to power might then be construed as the causal explanation for the emergence of new practices, values, and more robustly construed life-forms, such an explanation in the final analysis, so my reading

[4] Alasdair MacIntyre, *After Virtue* (University of Notre Dame Press, 1981), 216.

holds, cannot be rendered. For using the concept of "causal" as opposed to "conceptual" for understanding the actual genealogical process for some phenomenon is just another symbolic interpretation of will to power. Thus, the robust claim made in this work is that genealogical interpretations of historical phenomena remain on the formative side of will to power; they are attempts we employ to render what is inherently without meaning, meaningful. It is for this reason that Foucault, who I believe to be the most astute interpreter of *On the Genealogy of Morals* to date, calls what I've been labeling the mechanical side of genealogy (e.g. the examination of bodily practices) as, at best, a tracing; it is a *Herkunft* and a *Geborgen*.[5] Nietzsche provides the proof for this assertion in many different ways. Therefore, my conclusion is a distillation of the upshot of these many different kinds of proof.

References Used in this Chapter

Foucault, Michel. "Nietzsche, Genealogy, History" *Language, Counter-Memory, Practice Selected Essays and interviews by Michel Foucault*, Ed. Donald Bouchard, 1977.

MacIntyre, Alasdair, *After Virtue*. Indiana, University of Notre Dame Press, 1981.

Mcginn, Colin. "On the Necessity of Origin" in *Knowledge and Reality* Oxford Clarendon Press, 1999, 57–64.

Williams, Bernard. *Truth and Truthfulness An Essay in Genealogy*, Princeton University Press, 2002.

[5] Foucault, "Nietzsche, Genealogy, History", 140.

Index[1]

[1] Note: Page numbers followed by 'n' refer to notes.

B. Lightbody, *A Genealogical Analysis of Nietzschean Drive Theory*,
https://doi.org/10.1007/978-3-031-27148-9

CPSIA information can be obtained
at www.ICGtesting.com
Printed in the USA
LVHW051526300423
745679LV00003B/455